Elizabeth Coffey

AND THE LITTLE ONE SAID

THEY ALL ROLLED OVER AND EIGHT FELL OUT

mereo

This book reflects the author's present recollections of experiences over time. Some names and characteristics have been changed, some events have been compressed, and some dialogue has been recreated.

Mereo Books

2nd Floor, 6-8 Dyer Street, Cirencester, Gloucestershire, GL7 2PF
An imprint of Memoirs Books. www.mereobooks.com
and www.memoirsbooks.co.uk

Title of Book: And the little one said
ISBN: 978-1-86151-690-9

First published in Great Britain in 2021
by Mereo Books, an imprint of Memoirs Books.

Copyright ©2021

The address for Memoirs Books can be found at www.mereobooks.com

Mereo Books Ltd. Reg. No. 12157152

Typeset in 11/15pt Century Schoolbook by Wiltshire Associates.
Printed and bound in Great Britain

*There were ten in the bed and the little one said roll over,
roll over, so they all rolled over, and eight fell out...*

For Dylan, Amy and Lucy

Contents

Foreword
Acknowledgments
Introduction

Foreword

By **Tony Jordan**, award-winning screenwriter
of *EastEnders, Life on Mars, Death in Paradise*
and many more

———◁◆▷———

I met Liz some years ago, when my wife Tracy discovered
the joy of Facebook, reaching out to old school friends and
in doing so, rekindling her once close friendship with Liz.

It wasn't long before we met up and I discovered that she
shared my passion for writing. One night as we talked long
into the night about telling stories, she asked me if I would
read something she had written. Now this may seem like a
small thing, but you have to remember that this was one of
my wife's closest friends, re-discovered after two decades.
What if I'd hated what she'd written?

You can probably guess that as I'm writing this foreword
to her book, I didn't hate it. What she asked me to read
was extraordinary. In fact, everything she's asked me to read
since has also been extraordinary. It seemed that as Tracy
found an old friend, I'd found a new writer with real talent.

We talked a lot over the months that followed as
I encouraged her to pursue her love of writing, trying to
convince her that she had the talent to turn writing into

a career. I helped her to recognise what she was already doing so brilliantly, her amazing characterisations, narrative structure and hooks that left you on the edge of your seat. Fortunately, you don't have to take my word for it: you can now read her published 'bottom-drawer' stories on Amazon and you'll see for yourself that her characters are layered and three-dimensional, her narrative is beautifully crafted and does what only the best writers can do; she makes you feel that she's telling her story not to a faceless, anonymous reader, but to a friend.

The more I got to know Liz and the more I heard about her own personal story, the more I encouraged her to write about herself, telling her that her own story was far more of a roller coaster ride than anything she could make up.

The end result of those conversations is this book about the insane number of cruel blows Liz and her family have been forced to deal with. These revelations of life-changing accidents, awful deaths, addiction, mental health issues and suicide will shock you and live in your memory forever, yet they are tempered with an unforgettable warmth. They will teach us all the true meaning of family.

As the youngest survivor of this remarkable story and the only family member to walk away unscathed, it's left to Liz to share her journey with us, something she does with heart-rending honesty. It's such a compelling story, full of charm and real wit. It is both heartbreaking and laugh-out-loud funny, and it reveals a spirit and an unfaltering courage that will leave you speechless. It reminds us how powerful family bonds can strengthen our resilience to overcome even the darkest times and enable us to somehow survive adversity.

Above all, this book is about the healing power of grief. Liz's story conveys a message of hope, that there is more to life than we know, and death is not the end, because we are connected by a greater power: love. And love can never die...

A pleasure to read, beautifully written. Well done Liz, gold star.

Tony Jordan

Acknowledgements

I have to start by mentioning my better half, the Clyde to my Bonnie, my partner in crime, my therapist, my rock, and above all, my best friend, the one and only Oliver Martin. Where would I be without you?

I am eternally grateful to my Boom-Boom brother, David 'I don't do sick' Ball, who has been on this journey with me and almost got off the bus but didn't. Dave, you are an inspiration to me. Big kiss, little sis, X.

My three reasons to smile through the darkest of dark times. My brave, funny, trio, Dean, Teri and Joe. Thank you for being strong and encouraging me to share this story. I love you guys to infinity and beyond.

Big love to my 'Balls', my courageous niece and nephews Jo-Jo, Fraser, David Jnr and Freddie for being mini-me towers of strength to your dad and also me throughout the painful years.

Thank you so much to Ellen and all the staff at Hafod-y-Green for making my sister Di's last few years the best they could be.

Huge appreciation to my brilliant editor Chris Newton for answering all my questions since day dot and for his superb command of the English language, guidance, wisdom and most of all his eternal patience.

My publisher Mereo Books, for everything from formatting, design, to cover creation.

Heaps of gratitude go to my readers Martina Healy and Marina Sawyer for helping me dot the I's and cross the T's. You two are the best missing word detectives ever.

Recognition for my publicist Elly Donovan PR, first and foremost for her compassion and secondly, for believing in me and pushing to get my story out there.

A very special mention to my favourite human 'beans', the lovely Tracy and Tony Jordan, for supporting me every step of the way and generally making my world a happier place, but above all thank you for being the sole reason I put pen to paper.

Extra special thanks with squirty cream, chocolate sprinkles and a cherry on top to my cheeky bubba, granddaughter, Ella, for bringing light into the darkness in a way that no one else could.

Introduction

The man of steel and the London lady

I was born under a gooseberry bush, my dad told me, He also told me he was a Canadian Mountie and he had broken his permanently disfigured elbow as a WWII fighter pilot, not falling off his pushbike, like Mum said. They were in their mid-forties when they had me, the last of the line, so I never knew them as young adults. Dad said Mum looked like Hedy Lamarr – she did, she was beautiful. Mum said Dad looked like Inspector Clouseau – he didn't, apart from his diddy moustache. Mum's wit – so droll.

By the time I'd reached seventeen they were ready to retire from parenting. I felt abandoned back in the day, but now I'm older and wiser, I get it. After eight children, one of whom, my twin brother, was stillborn, they deserved some peace. In her usual sensitive fashion Mum told me my twin had been pickled for medical science, and I grew up with a natural acceptance somewhere out there that I had a twin who looked like a jar of onions.

Mum was in two minds about moving to Wales, but Dad, being a Welshman, couldn't wait to return to his roots, so she agreed to give it a go. Moving to Anglesey was the best decision she ever made, putting an end to her long-suffering manic-depressive episodes. It turned out to be great fun having parents living by the sea.

But after ten blissful years of fulfilling his prize vegetable-growing passion, my lovely, gentle dad was struck down with lung cancer. *Nessun Dorma* was top of the charts at the time and there wasn't a dry eye in the room when it came on the radio; poignant to us as a family. Dad used to sing it as a young tenor in the Treorchy Male Voice Choir and in later life, the bath. He sounded like Pavarotti too. I was devastated when he died. He was my man of steel and I was the apple of his eye. My daughter Teri was only three, but my son Dean was five and old enough to ask, "Mummy, why did Grandad shake my hand and say goodbye?'

Two years to the day after Dad died I gave birth to my third child, Joe. The doctors gave him a thirty percent chance of survival, but he flew out like superman and proved them wrong. The miracle of Joe overtook the pain of losing Dad, not just for me but for the whole family. From that moment on every grim anniversary of Dad's passing was spent eating cake and singing happy birthday to Joe.

Mum finally let go of Dad's stuff, apart from his signature flat cap. Sally inherited his tools. Steven was given his gold watch. Diana got his piano. Lesley had his car. David didn't want anything, and nor did I, apart from his photo ID card from work. It lived in my bag, and on the way to playgroup

Joe would kiss the man he grew up knowing as 'Grandad in the purse'. After Dad's death we naturally assumed my city-bred mother would want to move back to the smoke, but she didn't. The beauty and tranquillity of Wales had worked its way into her blood and I for one couldn't blame her, not wanting anything to do with a past plagued with mental health issues. So she moved into a smaller bungalow and came to be fondly known by her Welsh neighbours as 'the London lady'.

Generous to a fault, Mum dedicated her life to her children and grandchildren, always giving us money, forever buying presents. If I was ill, she would pack her bags, come and stay and do all the shopping, cooking and cleaning. She wasn't afraid of hard work – in fact she wasn't afraid of anything, my battle-weary mother. After the hardship she had been through and survived, it wasn't blood she had running through her veins, it was more like liquid iron. There was nothing half-hearted about my Islington born one quarter Spanish mum, she either loved you or couldn't stand you, and woe betide you if it was the latter. It makes me smile when I recall her comment to one of my brother's wives-to-be on their special day: 'You look like you're going to a bleeding funeral'. When Catherine Tate created *Nan* I figured she must have met Mum. Rena Ball, the brave London lady who made us all. A proper, real, say-it-as-it-is, bulletproof Cockney with a heart of pure gold.

My friends would often try to solve the Rubik's Cube conundrum of my brothers and sisters. They'd say things like: 'Sally's the oldest, then John, or is it David? God, your family is confusing.' To save you trying, I'll set the record straight. Boss baby Sally was born first, in 1945, with fair curly locks and strikingly different one-green one-brown eyes. Next came Action Man John, aka John-boy, two years younger than Sally and the polar opposite with straight black hair and dark skin. A year later out popped chubby cheeks David, a male carbon-copy of Sally. After a four-year gap (my parents needed to come up for air) Steven was born. Another boy, and another darky, with afro locks this time. Poor Mum, she only wanted four girls so, sucker for punishment, she kept going.

Four years later, boom, two for the price of one, twins Mimi and Fifi appeared. Really, Mum? Dad put his foot down and they were renamed. Diana popped out first, one of the fair clan, followed nine minutes later by Lesley, a new addition to the dark side. The one light, one dark zebra stripe theme had continued.

Almost a decade later, in 1963, I 'accidentally' slipped into existence. Be careful what you wish for, Mum. She had indeed got her four girls, with three boys thrown in. Mum got her own back on Dad's Mimi-Fifi ban by ignoring his wish to call me Sian (Welsh for Jane) and had me christened Elizabeth. And did I keep up the theme? I did. Sally, David, Diana and I were pink-faced and fair like Dad, chalk to the cheese of John, Steven and Lesley, who inherited Mum's Spanish genes but, sadly they were a team player down. We all knew my twin brother would have kept up our family's zebra tradition and been dark – well, that's how we chose to picture him, naturally.

After eighteen years of childbearing, the family was complete, and distinctly split. A close-knit bunch, people called us. So close, I don't know how our family of nine fitted into our three-bed terraced council house in Borehamwood. Although that was pretty average for our street. There were twelve in the O'Keefe household, ten in the Smith's, and as rough neighbourhoods go ours was up there. Being stalked by the paedophile six doors down was a regular occurrence. The O'Keefe's dog (or was it a wolf?) savagely attacked and killed my sister Lesley's Cockapoo, Boopie, and Mrs Marshall was bludgeoned to death with an axe by her young lover while she slept.

But it wasn't all bad. Daring each other to pinch lollies from Mr Buck's ice cream van was a thrill, as was jumping onto the back of the milk float and getting yelled at and chased by the angry milkman. The big field at the end of our street lent itself to rock concerts in the summer and football matches every weekend, so there was always something going on.

When I was very young, I slept on a camp bed in Mum and Dad's room. John was on a put-you-up in the dining room when he wasn't away with the army. Sally, Diana and Lesley had the biggest bedroom. David and Steven shared a bunk in the box room. There were lots of to-ings and fro-ings; people moved out, then moved back in. Lesley came home with her tail between her legs after a disastrous flat share with a lesbian in Willesden, much to her evil twin's delight. I was demoted to sharing the double bed with Diana to minimise their bickering. She used to wake me by climbing into bed after a night on the tiles and wrapping her freezing limbs round me like an octopus. I was her human hot water bottle, she said, loads of fun – for her.

There were eight years and five months between me and the twins. How special it was, being the youngest by far. My kinfolk were a supercool bunch who loved, protected and spoilt me rotten in their individual ways. Sally, my second mum, was *always* buying me clothes and wicked stuff from abroad: my yellow clogs from Amsterdam, my purple tie-dye kaftan from India. John bought me boxing gloves, and taught me how to punch like a man and defend myself. David took me for white knuckle rides in his Mini Cooper S, or whatever sporty racing machine he was driving. Steven would take me to the park and push me on the swings so high I almost looped the top, and afterwards we'd nip to Hanson's in the village and devour a scrumptious cheese pasty. Diana would do my hair and makeup, then doll me up in her dresses and platforms to make me feminine and pretty. Lesley showed me how to make mud pies on the same day she taught me how to smoke. I puked my guts up, but it wasn't the cigarette's fault, it was the sickly pack of raw jelly cubes she'd stolen from the kitchen cupboard.

Middle child Steven drew the short straw. Being a year apart John and David were bosom buddies, getting into scraps and coming home smothered in cuts and bruises, but the four-year gap was way too big for Steven to fit in. Diana and Lesley were four years his junior, plus they were girls. They played spiteful pranks on him, so Steven was left to find his own friend – Tommy Daniels, three doors down.

One by one they left home, and by the time I was a teenager I had the box room to myself. Not the big bedroom – it was kept as a shrine to facilitate the family boomerang. I loved having my own space but I missed the chaos of my crazy, funny siblings. Silence can be deafening when you're not used to it.

Then it struck me that being the 'little one' of the family, there was a high probability that my dearly loved much older brothers and sisters were all going to die before me. I didn't expect it would happen quite so soon – and each one in spectacularly tragic and different circumstances.

CHAPTER ONE

Please god, not both of us

⸺◦◦⸺

Coronary Obstructive Pulmonary Disease. Life is cruel. My sister Lesley (Lel) was fifty-two, no age to be diagnosed with such a decrepit-sounding disease. As a family we'd already suffered the pain of losing Dad and my brother John-boy, so I couldn't face the thought of saying goodbye to another sibling. I cried on and off most of the way home.

Olly, my better half, the Clyde to my Bonnie, my partner in crime, tried to make me see the bright side.

"You're right, there's no cure Liz, but it is treatable, they can halt its progression, Lel said, so long as she stops smoking, and she has. And your mum's given up too, so that's good."

"Whatever," I sulked. "Why did she have to get it in the first place?"

"She did smoke around forty a day Liz, since forever."

"So?" I defended her. "Loads of people do."

"I know love, sorry, I'm only saying."

"I get it, it's self-inflicted," I begrudgingly admitted. "I'm just angry Olly, it's horrible, like a bloody death sentence."

"She's not going to die Liz. It's manageable, and she's going to manage it."

What would I do without Olly and his simplistic black and white way of seeing life, his pearls of wisdom, his unbendable, dependable never-ending support? They say the best relationships grow out of friendship, and although we had been in a relationship for five years prior to that we were best friends for seven years. He saved me and my children when their father left me facing repossession. He put food on the table, helped with my bills *and* gave me a car. He was my rock throughout the demanding times of single motherhood. Although we hung out together I never saw him as anything more than a friend until my brother David arranged a family barbecue and casually said to me one day, "Bring Oll if you like?"

I was befuddled by this. "Dave, we're mates, we're not joined at the hip."

"Yeah you are," he laughed.

I thought about that. I thought about it much, during the course of my ridiculed charcoaled-Halloumi burger weekend in Cardiff. In truth, I thought of nothing else...

Olly and I met at playgroup. His mum Pam owned a Montessori school and was the only one brave enough to take on my youngest, my lively little Superman, Joe. Olly was there one day, and Pam introduced us and told him I was a singer/songwriter. Cringeworthy. I only told her I loved singing in the bath and I'd written some lyrics to my brother Steve's guitar riffs, hardly Bob Dylan, but it just so happened that he was a producer of music. Bingo! A match made in musical heaven – which amounted to nothing, because we had too much in common and never got past the talking stage. Olly: a British brown-haired Dalai Lama. I'd get lost in those green eyes, listening to such wise beyond-his-years wisdom about anything and everything. He had a healthy outlook on life which was refreshingly different. I didn't realise then how much I was going to rely on that one day. We'd chat for hours until one of us blurted out, 'Oh my, look at the time,' because that's what best friends do. Now, thanks to my stupid brother, why did he have to sow the seed? I found myself pondering whether we were more than 'best friends'. Perhaps, possibly, who knew? One way to find out. I didn't know how or when, I was so nervous thinking about it, but I was determined to broach the subject.

That's when I hatched my genius plan: birthdays. We always bought each other a daft gift. Actually, I always bought him one, so he had no choice but to reciprocate as my birthday was the day after his. I practised my speech over and over so much, not saying it was not an option. The challenge was set. I gave him his present – anti-sarcasm breath spray – and waited patiently for him to pop the question: "What do you want for your birthday then?"

The words rolled off my tongue. "A hug."

He responded by laughing out loud, in my face. The beast. But, come my birthday he did it. He gave me a hug for the first time ever in our seven-year friendship, and the strangest thing happened. We got stuck. My ~~stupid cupid~~ clever brother Dave was right, we were joined at the hip.

Olly passed my family's stringent testing measures and was accepted into the clique with flying colours – eventually. Upon meeting Lel she concluded he was nice, but he did look a bit like an axe murderer. I also warned him about the taboo subject of her neon-white new dentures, but he foolishly asked what was wrong with them when she brought them up – literally. No, she did. She spat them out and launched them at his head. Honestly, such a naughty forty-eight year-old-child who took everything to the next level of wrong. Olly took Steve's drunken aggressive punch on the arm – and threat to kill him if he ever hurt me – in good faith too.

At least Sal saw that Olly was a genuine and caring human, although she agreed with Lel about the axe murderer likeness. According to Di, he didn't have shifty eyes – a good sign – but now the axe murderer likeness had been mentioned... Jeez, my weird, overthinking, overprotective, singleton siblings. Steve was twice divorced. How those poor women put up with his binge-drinking long enough to marry him was a wonder of the world.

Spinster Lel wasted her life in a long-term relationship with an unhappily married man who always promised to leave his wife but never did. Widows Sal and Di never found lasting love again. Those four were disasters in the game of love, throwing rocks whilst living in glasshouses, but it was because they wanted the best for me, the baby of the family. I knew that, deep down. The only family member who didn't cast a stone who was also in a relationship was Dave. I was pleased about that. It made me feel less abnormal.

COPD aside, a dose of Mum-medicine had been just the ticket. I dried my eyes with my jumper sleeve as we pulled into the petrol station. Olly squeezed my leg.

"Cheer up, my love, Lel wouldn't want you to be upset, she seemed on top of it all."

She did. I couldn't deny it. My sister had taken her bad news better than I had. It was a shock to my system, but she was hardly at death's door, and still doing an admirable job as Mum's live-in carer/comedienne.

We were cruising home along the motorway engrossed in conversation about Lel's emphysema, which seamlessly led on to the subject life after death, when it happened. A gigantic orange light filled the passenger window, followed by an almighty bang. I heard myself scream as I watched the juggernaut snaking uncontrollably next to us. Olly's hands were frantically spinning the steering wheel this way, then that, as we pirouetted across the motorway.

It was surreal, as though sound had been muted, everything seemed to be happening in slow motion. As the ground became the sky, a strange calm descended upon me.

I remember thinking, *Please God, not both of us, it's not fair on my children.*

After that, blackness.

FOUR HOURS EARLIER

I needed a dose of Mum-medicine, the ingredients being snooker or Wimbledon, depending on the season, and Mum's favourite *Pobol-y-cym*, the long-running Welsh soap. Not forgetting *Loose Women, Eggheads, Weakest Link,* jam tarts, lemon slices and cup of tea after tea. Moreover, I needed to see Lel, and satisfy myself she wasn't going to die. I gazed out of Mum's lounge window, absorbing the breathtaking view of rolling fields and the mountains beyond; Snowdonia National Park, giant peaks resembling over-risen cakes dusted with icing sugar. In the background I could faintly hear Di, the family chatterbox, yelling into the phone like Steve Wright's Mr Angry character. Mum put the receiver down, did that big long sigh thing she always did, rolled her eyes, and scrunched her face like Steptoe's Wilfred Brambell.

"What's she rabbiting on about now?" I asked.

"Lucy put a brick through her car window."

"Lucy did what? Di must have driven her nuts."

"Amy upset her as well, told her to stop interfering."

"Amy's had a baby Mum. I don't get why Di is so angry all the time?"

Princess Diana

Di was always angry. Or maybe that's me being harsh. Fierce, perhaps, was a better description. Fierce, vain and a proper socialite. We called her Princess Diana because she behaved like a princess, the only dress-wearing female in the family. Any excuse to tart herself up and flaunt it Di would be there, especially during the Tramp era. Sally and her husband Mike hung out with the rich, famous and even royalty at that exclusive Mayfair nightclub. Starry-eyed teenager Di would often tag along. She was spotted by photographer David Bailey one night. He told her she could be a top model because she was 'beautifully different' and gave her his number, but she lost it. Kind of summed up her life in a nutshell.

At twenty-one she got engaged to the love of her life, and the next day he was tragically killed in a car accident. When she did marry, the divorce they decided not to get (and forgot to cancel) arrived in the post the day her husband died of cancer, so she had no inheritance to help raise Amy and Lucy. Poor Di. Bad luck haunted her.

She was 'beautifully different' from the rest of us, the only member of the family with blue eyes. John used to say she was the milkman's, ridiculously funny, seeing as she was a twin. He also joked that she got Lel's share of the brains, and I have to agree Di was a superbrain. She could add up any amount of numbers like lightning, without a calculator. The downside of her super constantly calculating mind was forgetfulness. Lel consistently got her a special birthday card, but Di didn't bother: she'd say "I forgot". Priceless. How can you forget your twin sister's birthday? When they bickered, which was frequent, Di could be heard shouting at Lel, "I'm nine minutes older than you don't forget". Like that made her superior. Funnily enough, she was. Di did not suffer fools. Di was the mature one. Di was the leader and Lel the underdog. Di was the first one to walk, and she milked it, by walking all over her wriggling twin. Something she continued to do into adulthood, and it wasn't just Lel who suffered, she drove me nuts at times.

'You always want the last word, don't you?' she would say. I fell into her trap every time, and so began the "yes you do, no I don't" squabble. It would go on until I ended up pulling my curly hair out in frustration, because only then would she be satisfied. Couldn't play games with her either, she won, of course, and would chant-sing 'winner, loser,' pointing from herself to me with that smarmy smirk until I cried and wanted to smash her gold hexagon glasses.

To the rest of the world Di was a kind soul, a people lover, a selfless person who put the needs of others before her own. In fact beautiful Di was nigh on perfect. A straight 'A' student superbrain, a super-talented princess. She sang like Dad, played piano like Dad and fluttered her eyelashes at Dad. Di was 'Dad's one'. Di was clever. Di was the smart one who got herself (and Lel) a job at the Medical Research Institute in Mill Hill. They used to sneak me in at weekends, and I bore witness to some horrific sights. Cats with nuts and bolts in their heads like Frankenstein, blind mice with lumps and bumps all over them. Massive animal lover Di risked her job by smuggling a crate of chicks home to save them from the chop, and we fed them milk with little droppers until she found them a home at a local farm. Lel tried to do the same, but she got caught and sacked. Di was better at everything, apart from dancing – she danced like a plank, Lel said. She couldn't cook like Lel either. The best Di could do was tin-open a mean Fray Bentos chicken pie.

But when she wasn't teasing me, she was awesome. I loved and admired her. Super trendy Di in her six-inch platforms and Levis flares, cruising around in her white convertible Triumph Vitesse with her bleached blonde hair and gold hexagon glasses. As a sister, she would defend me to the end. She once almost throttled a nurse who dared to inject antiseptic into a deep cut in my leg without numbing it first. God help anyone who dared pick on me. Princess Diana, fierce, vain and loyal...

Mum did her big sigh thing again. "Di's terribly upset about Lel. It's not easy for her bringing up those two girls on her own, you of all people should understand."

"I get that Mum, but the way those three are behaving, there's going to be a tragedy in that little triangle if they carry on like this." A wash of doom came over me.

"What did you say? I can't bloody hear you, where's my hearing aid Lizbeth?" She started faffing around. Same old story, Mum accusing everyone of misplacing her junk.

"It was here, in the office." Mum's office being the seat next to her on the sofa where nobody was permitted to sit, comprising tissues, books, her makeup bag, newspapers, pens, a magnifying glass, you name it, and – the elusive hearing aid.

"Here it is." I pulled it out from under a pile of magazines.

Lel walked in carrying a tray. "She accused me of nicking her Fairy soap earlier."

"What did you say Lesley?" Mum frowned and fiddled with her aid. "I can't hear you, there's no batteries in this stupid thing, what have you done with them?"

"They're with that horrible old green soap I stole in a secret box labelled 'Rene's Junk' because I've always wanted hearing aid batteries haven't I, you old duffer!" she shouted.

Duffer was Lel's adaptation of 'fucker', because she found it hard not to swear.

"There you go lovey." My sister smiled bravely and handed me a cup of tea. She was trying to make *me* feel better about *her* condition. It didn't work.

"I don't want you to die, promise me you won't start smoking again?"

"I won't. I don't want me to die either lovey."

Lelly-Bertus

Lovey was our joint nickname, derived from my short-lived film industry makeup artist career and her shorter-lived artist chauffeuring career. I quit, but she got the sack because she upset supermodel Twiggy. Not that I had a favourite, they were all my favourite, in different ways, but Lel was a bit special. Everyone had a soft spot for her. She treated me like a grown-up. I told her everything; I always regretted it, but I still told her everything.

She stuck up for me when Di was being evil, and we'd join forces and seek revenge. I have fond memories of the time we snuck a worm into her bed, then ran for our lives. Hearing Di screaming blue murder from the bottom of our 100ft garden was a joy. Cheeky tomboy Lel with her dark curly locks, mischievous brown eyes and scruffy dungarees; no match for her fair haired, blue-eyed, dress-wearing twin. There was a pitiful innocence about Lel, a real what-you-see-is-what-you-get vulnerability. All she wanted to do was make people laugh and have fun, to sweeten the underdog pot which always turned sour and got her into trouble. Thus, Di earned the honorary title of 'perfect' and Lel was labelled the naughty one.

She did tell lies though, pointless lies. She'd ring me and say, 'Lovey, call me at six and say you're half an hour away so I can get rid of Sheila.' I would state the obvious: 'Lovey, just tell Sheila to go home at six.' She'd hit back with, 'shut up and ring me.' Meaning there'd be another pointless lie to follow, which would involve me having to speak to Sheila, who I didn't know, or want to speak to, and worse, lie to her. It was Lel who blurted out to my friend that she'd seen his dad getting off with another woman outside our local, the Suffolk Punch. Everyone had, including me, but it's not what you do is it? Chuck a bowling ball into someone's family and watch them fall down like skittles. Lel did that. Okay, it wasn't a pointless lie, it was a harmful truth. Another endearing little quality she possessed, which leads seamlessly onto the next one: back-stabbing. Why did she snitch to Dad and say I'd been staying at my boyfriend's every Friday night, not Tracy Tyler's? Because Dad took her down a peg and called her unladylike when she fell off *my* bike pissed and broke her collarbone. I wouldn't have minded, but the whole pointless 'staying at Tracy's' lie was her idea.

Fate was cruel to her in the motherhood department, and consequently she loved her nieces and nephews like her own and they reciprocated. Being a big kid herself she understood them and played with them, what's not to love? Lelly-Bertus, the immature half of the twins, by a less important whole nine minutes. My Dean, who made up funny names for people like his Auntie Lel, added the Bertus bit, and it stuck.

When I was sixteen she had her own flat, and it was so cool. I'd be there all the time, drinking cider, scoffing chocolate, smoking mixed herbs, pretending it was weed, singing, dancing, listening to music. She loved music. Lel was the life and soul of the party. Talking of parties reminds me of her love-hate relationship with her loud northern neighbour Hilda. She kept banging on the door one night, shouting through the letterbox. Lel begged me to answer and say she was out, but I refused. I hated lying, she knew that, but she begged so much that in the end I succumbed and opened the door – about an inch. Hilda ranted on about how Lel had promised to go to her Pomagne party blah-blah-blah. Like a stuck record I kept repeating 'She's not here Hilda, honest,' until a voice in the background shouted over the top of me, 'Oh all right I am here.' Hilda's eyes nearly fell out of her head, and she totally flipped. Life and soul Lel went off to the Pomagne party and I, 'the fucking little liar', wasn't invited. Classic Lel. Completely untrustworthy, especially where alcohol was concerned, but when she wasn't stabbing you in the back or telling pointless lies she was the most caring human ever.

After she got sacked from the research and the film industry job she got a job at Stanmore Orthopaedic as a carer. She loved chatting with patients and cracking inappropriate gags about their missing limbs, and they adored her. The cheeky tomboy had found her vocation. Underdog Lel grew up with the chip-on-shoulder belief she was 'Mum's one', because Di was 'Dad's one'. Yet Lel was the angel who nursed Dad on his death bed, not Di. Lel was the one who quit her hospital job to be with Dad. She slept by his side on a camp bed and got up in the night every hour and rubbed his back when he coughed and coughed until he was sick. I don't know how she did it.

After Dad died she took the role of nanny to Sally's son Dylan, and when he flew the nest she moved in with Mum to be her full-time carer. It was peace of mind for the family knowing she was there and qualified for the role. Lelly Bertus, the chain-smoking, farting, swearing, caring angel who nurtured people by day, and by evening needed a glass of wine, or four...

"Ready, Beak?" Olly appeared in the doorway. "We need to hit the road before dark."

I hated driving at night, especially the four-hour jaunt home.

"Beak?" quizzed Mum.

"He calls me Beak because I'm a bird, not in the chauvinistic sense, but because I have wings." I held up an arm, displaying my baggy jumper sleeve. "That's the reason my nose is always cold, apparently it's not a nose, it's a beak."

I loved it when my mum laughed. The corners of her eyes crinkled up, the corners of her mouth downturned, and no sound came out – just a long wheeze. She turned to Lel, her wheeze mutating into a rolling-eyed Steptoe scrunch. "Did you make those bloody sandwiches?"

"What do you think, you old duffer?" Lel shook the sandwiches in Mum's face.

"Sod off, Lesley." Mum pushed her away. The banter between those two was hilarious.

"Ring me when you get home please Lovey." Lel poked a finger in my face. "Don't forget."

Mum seemed a bit more anxious than usual. "Why not go tomorrow?" she suggested.

"Oh no, have you got one of your funny feelings?" I teased, laughing it off, putting her uneasiness down to lack of cigarettes. "Mum, don't worry, Olly's a good driver, we will not have an accident."

She sighed her big sigh at me. "Never mind, safe journey my loves."

CHAPTER TWO

Over my dead body

THREE MONTHS LATER

I sat down on the sofa. An older woman, a therapist, positioned herself in a single chair opposite, a coffee table between us.

"How's your mum, Elizabeth?"

"She's stopped blaming herself, finally."

"Excellent. I'm pleased you're back behind the wheel and conquering this driving anxiety."

"Me too." I grinned. "I'm putting it to the test this week, driving to Cardiff for a family get-together."

"Oh? First time since the accident, quite a challenge."

"Two hours, to be precise."

"We've got one session left, shall we save it? Come back in a few months' time and we'll see how you're getting on."

"I'll save it. You've succeeded in drumming it into my head that just because someone's driving it doesn't mean they're going to have an accident."

"No it doesn't, and if there were to be another accident?"

"There's no point worrying about the poo hitting the fan until it does."

A 17th century Grade II listed farmhouse nestling peacefully in two acres of panoramic South Wales countryside: home of Sally, as far away from the limelight as possible. I crept into the kitchen. Mum was sitting at the table, her hand poised holding a cigarette with ash twice as long threatening to drop onto Sal's handmade Indian table cloth. Next to her Di, dunking Hobnob after Hobnob in tea, both of them muttering and tutting at the newspaper. Sally, self-appointed head of the family, sat perched on the worktop like Buddha, barking instructions from a recipe book at Lel as she juggled egg boiling with ingredient grabbing.

"Sian!" Di rushed over and gave me a bear hug. "How was the journey?"

"I quite enjoyed it."

Sweating over the range, Lel gave me a back-handed wave. "Can't stop stirring, glad you made it in one piece Lovey."

Sally jumped down from the worktop, threw her arms around my neck and gave me her usual two cheek kisses then one on the nose. "Well done, Heart."

I walked over to Mum and gave her a hug, and she

squeezed my hand with both of hers. "Hello Lizbeth, we've been so worried about you."

Four names in four seconds. Elizabeth – my birth name. Sian – the name Dad decided to call me anyway. Lovey – Lel's nickname. Heart... I don't know why Sally called me Heart but she did, probably because it was different, like her contrasting eyes. She liked to be different, did Sal.

Sally Sunshine

That name was my contrary big sister's brazen response to Gary Glitter when he introduced himself and asked her who she was. I could picture her saying it with that great big dimple-chop grin of hers. Growing up in Borehamwood, home of EMI and other big names, working at Elstree Studios was a natural conclusion for young, ambitious Sally. The eighteen-year gap between us made her pretty much my second mum. Her job as a script supervisor meant my school holidays were spent hanging around on set with her and hubby Mike, not only Roger Moore's personal hairdresser but also mine. A ten-year-old girl with a James Bond hairstyle, neat – if you're a boy. Roger used to bring me sweets, and Christopher Lee gave me a signed copy of his Dracula album. One day John Cleese asked me who I was. Being a bit shy I said, "nobody". Unfazed that I wasn't part of the cast or crew, he stuck out his hand and transformed into Basil Fawlty. 'Well hello there Miss Nobody, nice to meet you.'

It wasn't always fun and games. On the set of *The Adventurer*, Sylvia Syms looked down her nose when she saw me, then Sal introduced me to leading man Gene Barry. "Elizabeth has been dying to hear your American accent," she cooed. "No I haven't" was my honest reply, causing them both to squirm. I didn't know she was paving the way for my being there until she grabbed me, yanked me to one side, flashed her one-green one-brown angry eyes and explained, in no uncertain terms.

Sal was so glam. Travelling around the world, spending weekends with Mike's clientele; Robert Wagner, Richard Burton and Michael Caine, to name but a few. She rose so high through the ranks of society that she paid to have elocution lessons and speak posh. She dropped that persona like a ton of bricks when she came home and reverted straight back to her common Borehamwood accent.

My big sister showered me with love and gifts, so many expensive gifts. Nothing pleased Miss Moneybags more than to squander her per diems on me at Brent Cross shopping centre. If I couldn't decide between the pink diamanté heels and the blue Dior sneakers, she'd buy them both. Sal: one of a kind, a proper – of her generation – free-spirited hippy. She often took me to Bhaktivedanta Manor in Aldenham, a temple donated to the Hindu religious organisation by George Harrison. We'd wander around the grounds barefoot, eating pulses and chanting 'Hare Krishna' at everyone. There, I learned the cow is a sacred animal. Next, we'd hop into her little red Spitfire and go for a burger, which I couldn't eat, knowing it was a sacred animal (I've struggled ever since), but she would laugh her dirty chortle and tuck into hers with a passion. Sal loved her food. Hence the family nickname 'dustbin.'

Sally and Mike were blissfully wed for twelve years before she finally got fed up with their extravagant lifestyle. Things came to an ugly head one rainy night. Mike was drunk and shouting, so she packed her bags, grabbed their beloved three-year-old son Dylan and told Mike to do them both a favour and row out to the middle of the lake. It doesn't sound bad, but you need to understand that their boat had a big hole in the bottom. Next morning Sally went back to patch things up and found him asleep in the car, wearing a suit and clutching a photo of Dylan. She banged on the passenger window to wake him, but he didn't respond. Then she saw the pillow stuffed in the half open gap of the driver's window and the vacuum cleaner pipe trailing out of it. She walked around the car, her eyes following the pipe trail, and that was the harrowing moment she saw that it was attached to the exhaust. He wasn't asleep.

That was my first experience of death, if you don't include my sleeping twin. Bless Sally Sunshine, and she was a ray of sunshine, still. Despite her own personal tragedy, she supported everyone. A life coach and bank to the whole family. She perched upon a golden pedestal and waved her magic wand over everything. She wangled David a career in the film industry, and with his help they bought Mum and Dad a retirement bungalow. She saved my house from repossession, took Lel on as a nanny for Dylan, put Di's girls through private school, paid for Steven's umpteenth gardening business and got John a top London lawyer every time he faced one of his many drug/drink/driving offences. She climbed the ladder of success from our humble council house to a five-bed mansion.

Sally Jones, famous within the industry as one of the top script supervisors in the country, worked on all the big movies with well-known producers and directors but was never too above herself to have time for everyone. Industry wannabes aspired to be her, and she helped them further their careers. She was their idol, and mine. Mum, Dad, John, Dave, Steve, Di, Lel and I were immensely proud of her. She was one very special human being. And bossy. And blunt. And quite rude at times…

The kitchen was full of sisterly hubba-hubba and the background jibber-jabberings of Radio 2.

"Salt and pepper!" shouted Lel.

"Did I say salt and pepper?" Sally moaned.

Lel bit her lip and shot me and Di a sideways glance. We stifled a laugh like cheeky children.

"Popmaster Sal," Di explained.

"Pop what? What are you whittling on about?"

"Salt and Pepper, the eighties band who talked about sex baby," she replied.

Sally shook her head at Di like she was the stupid one. "You are brain damaged."

It made me smile listening to Sally moan. It triggered a memory; the birthday card I sent her when I crossed out the J on Sally Jones and replaced it with M so it read Sally Mones. She didn't see the funny side. Nor did she see the funny side when I assumed she was David on the phone one time. 'Shouldn't smoke Marlboro Red if you don't want to sound like a man,' I said, sticking up for myself. I got off lightly. The worst I got from Sal was a flash of her angry eyes and a hoity sniff. I got away with it, because I was the little one, even at the age of forty-whatever. Everyone else in the family got treated like dirt on her hoity shoe if they dared cross the line. I sometimes fantasised that I was Cinderella, the twins were Anastasia and Drizella, and Sally Mones, the way she bossed them about, was in the Oscar-winning role of the evil stepmother. Busy chopping an onion, Lel didn't notice the water about to boil over, but evil stepmother Sally, or should I say Buddha, perched on the worktop, did.

"Bloody hell Lesley!" she rasped, in her twenty-a-day voice.

"What now?" Lel whined.

"Duck eggs!"

"Sorry, I haven't mastered the art of being in two places at once yet, your majesty!"

"Lady Muck and her bleeding duck eggs," mumbled Mum to me and Di.

Big ears Sally peered over her glasses at Mum. "If you can't say anything nice don't say anything, how many times have I told you? Smoke outside please."

"Have you seen how bloody grey the sky is?" Mum pointlessly argued.

Sally frowned. "There's a bloody blue one above it, Mother."

Mum rolled her eyes. "Like your namesake, your father's sister, she was bossy as well."

"Bossy? Me?" Sal looked bewildered. "Di, get the cut crystal wine glasses out," she ordered.

Mum's ash fell onto the table. Lel darted over, wiped the table cloth and scurried back to her cooking chores. Being Mum's carer, she felt the weight of responsibility for her.

Suddenly it occurred to me. "Oh my god Mother, you're smoking!"

"And chewing a Nicorette gum at the same time." Di raised her eyebrows at me. "Because she likes them Sian, honestly, hopeless."

"Shameless."

Di snorted with laughter. "She should audition for that TV series."

"She'd get the part hands down."

Mum didn't bat an eyelid.

"Don't worry Heart, it was my last one, I told Mum she could have it, save wasting it," said dimple-chop grin Sal, like that made it acceptable. "We're all giving up to support Lel."

"Speak for yourself," declared Di.

Sally flashed her angry eyes, then continued her speech. "I've been researching the internet and there's all sorts of herbal remedies, I've ordered five hundred Nicorette gum and a thousand nicotine patches."

"Blimey, I bet that cost a few quid," I said.

"Dirty bits of paper, Heart." Sal's typical response whenever anyone mentioned money.

Lel, sick to the back teeth of being the centre of attention, changed the subject. "How's Olly, Lovey?"

"Still seeing the chiropractor."

"I can't get over the lorry driver falling asleep like that," Di chipped in. "It's a miracle the two of you are alive."

Miracle indeed. I was expecting angel's wings and harps when I opened my eyes, not four lanes of stationary traffic facing us on the M25. Seconds before, we'd been cruising along minding our own business, then BANG! It was like a bomb exploding in my ear. A German juggernaut had hit us. We left the ground at 70mph and almost rolled before crash-landing backwards and spinning several times. One of my hands gripped Olly's chair, the other was glued to the grab handle, and both my legs were stretched out like Spiderman. Olly's arms wrestled with the steering wheel as the car sped toward the central reservation. I squeezed my eyes shut bracing for impact then...

Nothing. Two guys in separate cars behind watched it unfold and heroically managed to stop the traffic. They dragged me out of the car, then went back in for Olly. He wasn't dead either. He had been knocked unconscious briefly when his head hit the window. We had stopped six inches from the barrier. Miraculously, we didn't hit it. If we had I wouldn't be typing this now. The paramedics explained that nine times out of ten this type of accident is fatal, the lucky one in ten being seriously injured, yet we walked away from hospital with nothing more than cuts, bruises and severe whiplash.

Sometimes when I blink I see it, a gigantic orange indicator that filled the whole of my passenger window, but hey, injuries heal. Flashbacks, nightmares and an unhealthy dislike for foreign lorry drivers are a small price to pay in exchange for life.

"You always come up smelling of roses, Lizbeth." My concerned mum shook her head at me.

"She was born with a guardian angel, that's why," Sally pointed out.

"Who's that then?" Mum innocently enquired.

"Who do you think?" Sally tutted. "Her twin brother, Mother."

"And Olly's driving skills." Di looked horrified. "Imagine, Sian…"

"I know, the police called him the Stig."

"Imagine if you were driving…"

"Cheers Di." I laughed. Sally laughed too. Mum tutted and did that big sigh thing. Lel turned to face me, tears falling out of her bloodshot eyes. "It could have been so much worse."

Noticing how upset she was, Sal got down from the worktop and squeezed her shoulder. "Lesley, darling, you're so sensitive, they're here to tell the tale aren't they?" she gushed, demonstrating her beautiful soft side, the one usually reserved for Dylan.

Onion in one hand, knife in the other, Lel replied with her dry wit, "and these are onions Sal, aren't they?"

Saved by the bell. Sal's embarrassment quickly disappeared as she grappled her mobile out of her jeans pocket. She sniffed the air and fired up her 'posh' voice. "This is she." Her accent switched to common in a nanosecond at the realisation that it was my brother Dave. She listened, saying 'u-huh' a lot. "Of course me, darling," she dimple-grinned. "Whatever you want DB, it's your big day, u-huh, I'll let everyone know. Yes, your baby sister is here, yes she did drive." She winked at me. "Dave says well done Heart."

"Hi Dave, I'm forty-five by the way," I called out.

"Mañana Dave." Sal put the phone down. Her big fake dimple-grin faded. "I don't believe him. He's not inviting Steven to the wedding."

"He can't do that!" Di looked shocked.

"Can you blame him? He knows he'll get drunk and ruin his day," Lel pointed out.

"I'm sure he will," added Sal.

"But that's no reason not to invite him," I said.

"Yeah, bit harsh, not inviting your own brother," Di agreed.

Mum was vexed. "Over my dead body. If Steven doesn't go I'm not going."

CHAPTER THREE

The wedding

—————◦✕◦—————

A black Mercedes swung onto the gravel and pulled up outside the grand entrance of the Henry Thomas stately home. The car doors opened and out stepped my brother and his glamorous blonde wife-to-be, Welsh actress Sara. Lel, Olly and I walked over to greet them. Dave gave me a quick kiss on the lips and handed me his wallet.

"Sort the bar out for me, Liz. I've got a call with the director to discuss the schedule in five."

So it's Liz today. More often I was the little one, baby sister, kiddo or ratbag.

"Dave, it's your wedding day for fuck's sake." Lel was gobsmacked.

"I know, but we're shooting today, Lelly." A perfectly natural priority for Dave.

"The show must go on, Lel. Now come on, DB, or we'll

be late for our own wedding." Sara grabbed him by the arm and they dashed up the magnificent stone steps.

"Oll, have a word with Di, she's got news for you," Dave shouted as they sandwiched themselves into the last sliver between the revolving doors.

David 'Boom-Boom' Ball

Dave was always in a tearing hurry, like the white rabbit in Alice in Wonderland. My larger-than-life big brother with the equally big personality. The energetic, animated joke teller, bigshot film producer and family rock. The Jack-the-lad boy who had finally grown up and out of the football playing, limb-breaking days of his misspent youth and into a powerhouse. CEO of his own film production company, CF1 in Cardiff. With his 'boom-boom' catchphrase and no-nonsense attitude, DB was the man to be around in a crisis. The only thing missing was a blue cape. When John needed to get out of the army, Dave came to his rescue. When I came out of intensive care at fourteen, it was Dave who took me to Acapulco to recuperate. I spent a month in paradise while he was working on *Sunburn* with Farrah Fawcett Majors. Little old me had my picture taken with a 'Charlie's Angel' much to the envy of my school friends, thanks to my big bro.

Family was a big priority for DB, unless your name was Steven, apart from the years he went AWOL. I don't know why he went off radar, though rumour had it that bad blood between him and Dad had something to do with it. Funny, out of all my brothers Dave was the one who took after Dad the most. He was a businessman like Dad, fair-haired like Dad, handsome like Dad. He even had a moustache like Dad. Whatever the reason, for his disappearance I chose to prefer the non-family-gossip-grapevine version: he was working abroad. Up until that point he was the best birthday present buyer ever. For my ninth birthday I got a giant yellow bunny, bigger than me. On my tenth birthday he bought me a blue Sekonda watch and very nearly a gold necklace. I couldn't make up my mind, so he said I could have both (the carbon-copy Sally thing I was talking about) until wife-to-be Lyn dragged him to one side and had stern words. Lyn didn't like me, in fact she hated me and used to poke her tongue out and pull ugly faces behind my brother's back. Loathsome Lyn, Mum called her.

After the convenient 'no children' wedding I wasn't invited to, his head was turned by Mo, so the child-hater got the elbow. Mo gave him a daughter, Jo-Jo, but he didn't marry the lovely Mo; he surprised everyone by marrying someone else, the beautiful but oh-so-boring Jacki, who loved the cars, the clothes and the perfume but hated the long working hours, so instead of having kids they had a divorce. Next, he fell head over heels for Lorraine, aka Lollipop, who bore him a dashing son, Fraser. He didn't tie the knot with Lolly but he did muck out her horses and mow their eight acres until they drifted apart and sold the house. Fun fact – it was home to Vinny Jones later on. Shame, it was a fun era – for me anyway.

After a string of 'no, Daves!' he came bouncing back with the worst 'no Dave' to date: Nancy. That wasn't her real name, it was Lel's adaptation of the word 'narcissist' to be used by a circle of trusty members, in other words, everyone apart from Dave. The nameless one radiated self-glorification as she escorted me around their sprawling five-bedroom house. She showed me her daughter's freshly decorated room full of mod cons, then Fraser's afterthought of a room, not much bigger than a cupboard and a dumping ground for boxes. Big mistake. DB cottoned on she was a psychopath and the wedding was cancelled. They didn't have kids either, making her the (understandable) exception to the rule.

You see, on planet Dave the rules were, if you do get married you don't have kids, and if you don't get married, you do have kids. His next statistic, I mean lady love, was Eliane from Luxembourg who he affectionately nicknamed 'Alien'. Guess what? They didn't get married, which means at the ripe old age of fifty he became a father again. And again... two gorgeous boys a year apart, David Jnr and Freddie. Dave swore his Henry VIII days were over and Alien was the last one, and she was – right up until this new one...

If I got married I'd do it here: a picturesque choice of wedding venue. Ten acres of natural Welsh beauty with water-spouting statues and topiary trees dotted around, and a lake huddling at the bottom of the tiered landscaped gardens. It was a sweltering hot summer's day, adding to the dreamy atmosphere. Guests were happily milling around the grounds when another Mercedes pulled up. I figured it was someone important but no, out stepped Mum and Steven, who was waving a beer can in the air.

Olly laughed. "Look at those two, they're like the Royal Family."

"The Royle Family, more like," I replied.

"Sal forked out two hundred quid to hire that, because Mum refused to stay over," added Lel.

"She told me a hundred and fifty," said Olly.

"Pointless lie." I winked at him.

"Oi you, cheek!" Lel laughed, shoving me to one side.

We walked over to greet them. Mum looked around, visibly unimpressed. Steve's face lit up when he saw me. He brushed past Lel and gave me one of his special swaying cuddles.

"Hello, Sian. Loving the ripped jeans. Nice to see you've made an effort for your least favourite brother."

"Good to see you, Steve." Olly grinned. They gave each other a man-hug.

"And you, Oll, still as ugly as ever I see." Steve cackled loudly at his own joke, displaying the gap between his two front teeth.

He had this crazy cackle, my brother, which would erupt out of nowhere. Sometimes, if he'd been drinking, it resembled a seizure, the way his head rolled back and his shoulders shook up and down like that, and this was one of those times. Proving my point, he took a slurp from his extra-large can of Tennent's. He and Lel stared at each other in stony silence. The tetchy moment was broken by the appearance of Di and Sal, who snatched the can out of his hand and tipped the contents onto the ground.

"I don't believe you, Steven!" she snarled.

Sally crushed the can like in the scene from *Jaws* and threw it into her gold Gucci handbag. I so wished I had a paper cup to give Steve so he could play Richard Dreyfus to her Robert Shaw in *Jaws*. As usual, I was taking pity on my middle-child-syndrome brother, and I'm pretty sure I was the only mug who ever did. Me being the youngest by far and him being the middle child by far, I guess we had a kind of loner connection.

Bean

My nutty-goon of a brother Steve, according to John and Dave, resembled a coffee bean because of his dark skin and afro hair. He was the self-labelled family 'black sheep', and the most intelligent, talented, funny, complex waste of a life there ever was. They certainly broke the mould when they made Steve. One example was during the 1977 bread strike. Fearing they'd have run out by the time he got to the front of the queue, Steve did such a convincing impression of a loud dribbling wonky-legged person that he managed to wheedle his way to the front. He got his bread, stood straight, arched his back, thanked everyone, gave them a big smile and strode off like a normal person.

He was quite the entrepreneur when I was a kid and started his own successful gardening business which grew and grew, but so did the drinking. This became a much bigger problem after my brother John died. He took it bad. At the time of John's death they weren't speaking over something petty, and he couldn't get past that. Slowly but surely the drink won and he lost it all. Steve's life became a vicious circle of bingeing away his dole cheque in week one, getting barred from every pub within staggering distance of whatever hovel he was residing in, to being a hermit existing on porridge, devouring books and playing guitar for the remaining three weeks of the month. With Steve it was either deep, meaningful conversation or immature drunken lunatic entertainment.

The kids considered the bad behaviour of their naughty Uncle Dee-Dar (as tiny Teri called him) very cool. They each had a unique and special bond with him. Teri (or as Steve called her Tezzle-poo-pops-pum), Dylan, Amy, Lucy, Dean and Joe adored the bones of him, as did I. Unlike some of my family, in particular, Dave and some of his offspring. Lel got the hump sometimes, but only when they clashed like pissed peas in a pod.

I gave up trying to rescue him every time he got slung out of wherever he was living. He promised me he'd stay sober if I gave him a bed, but hard as he tried, he always ended up going down the same old rabbit hole. When he came home drunk (after having sworn he wouldn't go to the pub) and made Joe cry because he couldn't hold his fajita together and bits of salsa covered chicken dripped down his shirt, it was the final blow. He could break my heart, but he wasn't going to break my son's. I packed his things and threw him out. I vowed never to be the mug who fell for his 'I promise I won't have a drink' lie, and it was the best thing I ever did. After that, I was able to accept him for who he was and make the best of him, and when he was sober, he *was* the best.

It was Steve who picked me up when my makeup artist bubble burst. It was Steve who played mum to my kids while I re-invented myself and trained to be a fitness instructor. It was Steve who arrived on my doorstep and stayed for a month to help me move house. It was Steve who was standing by my bedside when I came round in intensive care. It was Steve who never failed to make me laugh with his contagious cackle. It was Steve who told me it wasn't silly to cry on my thirtieth birthday. It was Steve who encouraged me to aim for the stars. The kindest, most caring, supportive, loving brother you could wish for. Sometimes...

"Come on, Sal, play the white man, I'm having a livener to get me in the mood, I hate these stiff dos," Steve whined, in his defence.

Mum turned to Steve and scrunched her face. "What did I tell you? You bleeding idiot."

"Bean, if Dave sees you with that can he'll have you escorted off the premises," warned Di.

"I've only had one," he lied.

"You stink." Lel gave him the evils.

"Rich coming from you." He glared back at her.

"Same goes for you Lesley. Stay off the vodka," Di snapped.

"Me? What have I done?"

"It's what everyone's worried you're going to do, Lesley."

"Fuck off, Di."

"You fuck off. Do you want me to tell Mum what you did at Sukey's wedding?"

An awkward silence followed. I knew what was coming. Mum interrogated me, not Di.

"What did she do at Sukey's wedding?"

"She got drunk and told the groom Sukey had it off with someone on her hen night," I answered.

Mum scrunched her face at Lel disapprovingly.

"Then she tried to get off with the copper who turned up and tried to stop her drink-driving," Di rambled on.

Lel glowed red as a beetroot. "I did not, Di you liar!" she lied. "You're just jealous because you fancied him."

And so it continued, the all-too-familiar Tweedledum and Tweedledee bickering. Di deemed it her sole responsibility to keep Lel's naughty behaviour in check, but never out of malice, only love.

"Don't start you two, not here!" Sal scolded them.

"Yeah, chill out, girls," added Steve.

"That goes for you too, Steven." Sally glowered at him. "This is Dave's special day and I don't want any of you lot ruining it."

Famous last words if ever I heard them. My family +
alcohol + a wedding = disaster.

Mum did her big sigh. "Come on, let's go and get some
coffee in him."

We seated ourselves around a large oak dining table in the
breakfast area. Lel and Sal were engrossed in the wedding
schedule and stuffing their faces with Danish pastry nibbles
– Sal because she was a dustbin and Lel to soak up her
nerve-calming wine, masquerading as a cup of coffee. Di
and I were people-watching, sniggering and snorting like a
pair of schoolkids. She had great pleasure in pointing out
Olly, who was stuck listening to a mutton-dressed-as-lamb
guest, much to my annoyance. He was too nice to be rude,
my lovely Olly-Flower. Sometimes he could have done with
taking a leaf from the book of the one sitting next to me:
Mother. Unlit roll-up hanging out of her mouth, she elbowed
Steve and pointed towards said female guest.

"Ere, Steven, the sights you see when you ain't got a
gun."

Steve rolled his head back and cackled, took a lighter
from his pocket and attempted to light the fag he'd rolled
her on the sly. Sally, born with eyes in the back of her head,
snatched it out of Mum's mouth like a chameleon's tongue
catching a fly. She flashed her angry eyes at her and pointed
to the 'NO SMOKING' sign.

"Oh, and that other small point. You don't smoke,
remember?"

Di took a big swig of coffee, followed by another one, then another one. "Mm, caffeine. Just what the doctor ordered."

"I like your top, Di, it's nice. Purple suits you." I smiled.

"Do you? eBay, a fiver, I love it," she gushed, stroking it.

"eBay?"

"Sian, it's brilliant, I get everything from there, even the computer I use to buy everything from eBay I got from eBay."

We both laughed.

"Di, Dave said you had news for Olly?"

"Shit. Yeah sorry. I forgot."

Big-ears Sally glanced over her shoulder and shook her head disapprovingly. "Brain-damaged."

Di bristled. "Thank you for such valuable input." She turned her chair away from Sal and continued talking to me. "I got the director to listen to Olly's demo!"

"You didn't."

"I did – he asked if he was classically trained, so I said, hell yeah, Olly's played piano, violin and drums since he was four, and I told him about the Arthur Catterall Award he got when he was in the East Berks Orchestra."

"And?"

"He said, he's spot-on with his emotions, exactly what I had in mind." She flipped into dreamy mode. "Such a lovely guy, got horses as well…"

"Di, can we get to the end part, then you can tell me his life story?"

"He asked what he'd done. I had to be honest, Sian, and tell him Olly worked for a media company producing music for corporate videos and low budget TV adverts." She sighed, disappointed.

"Never mind, Di, at least you tried."

She smiled and dug me in the ribs. "He wants Olly to do the music."

"Bore off, Di, you're such a bitch."

She snorted with laughter. "Sian I promise! He wants Oll to call him in a month."

"No way, Di, you're such a star!"

The word 'promise' – a big deal in my family. It was the confirmation I needed that she wasn't teasing me. I flung my arms around my sister's neck. We both squealed with excitement, then she yawned and took another big gulp of coffee.

"I'm knackered, Sian."

"You look terrible, even the bags under your eyes have got bags."

"Oh no, do I look that bad?"

I rummaged in my bag and handed a concealer to my appearance-conscious sister. "Use this, it'll cover the dark circles."

"We were meant to be finishing at eleven, but they kept redoing the take." She lowered her voice and pointed at the mutton-guest. "It's that blonde American, what's-her-face, Rose something, always forgets her bloody lines."

"DB's the producer, why didn't he call it a wrap?"

"He can't, we're miles behind schedule. Sian, this job's been a mare, I'm so stressed out." She sifted through her pockets. "Where are my bloody fags?"

"You're always stressed out about something, and you need to stop smoking."

"Oh no, do I smell of fags?"

I laughed. "I'm making a point, you smoke too much because you're stressed and knackered all the time. You need to slow down, Di."

"Funny you should mention that, we're finishing this film in a month hopefully." She had a glint in her eye. "I've applied for a position as production secretary at BBC Cymru. I haven't told anyone yet, didn't want to jinx it." She glanced around the room, making sure no one was listening. "They rang me this morning, I've got the job."

"That's great news, Di, well done you."

"I'm going to give up smoking when I start," she announced, mighty pleased with herself.

Our hushed conversation was interrupted by the arrival of Dave and Sara, all dressed up ready to wed. Mum got up and greeted Sara, as always, by her *Pobol-y-cym* soap-opera name.

"Hello, Menna, you look lovely."

Sara cackled loudly and embraced her affectionately. "Hello, Mum."

"Rene, she hasn't played that part for five years, you old duffer," chuckled Lel.

Mum didn't care one iota. "She's Menna to me and she'll always be Menna to me."

One by one we rose to our feet and greeted each other. It was all very polite and friendly until Steve's smile faded into a straight-face, and he held out his hand to my brother.

"Dave."

DB, equally non-smiley, shook his hand. "Bean."

Sara broke the ice by throwing her arms around Steve. "Lovely to meet you at last, Steven. I've heard so much about you."

"All bad I hope."

They both cackled. My gappy-toothed brother had met his cackle-match.

"Right, you motley crew, let's do this," announced Dave. "It's all right, don't panic, you're allowed to bring your coffee," he teased, ruffling my tidy hair.

I'm sure we weren't allowed, but my lot did like to make their own rules. We walked off, happy families-ish, and made our way to the chapel. Sally turned to me and lowered her voice.

"Sian, I meant to ask, how's Teri?"

"Fine. Why?"

She paused and looked at Di, who glared at Lel, who shrugged her shoulders at Mum, who rolled her eyes.

"Are you sure she's all right?" Sally continued to probe.

"Err, yes, she's my daughter, I think I would know," I answered, sarcastically.

She glared at Lel. "Are you going to tell her what you told me?"

I started to feel niggled. "Tell me what?"

Sal turned to Di, the family chatterbox, and raised her eyebrows questioningly.

"No Sally. You're the one who blabbed, you tell her," Di responded angrily.

Sally turned her glare of attention back to Lel, the non-secret keeper, for support. Lel caved in.

"We know Sian," she patronised.

"Know what? One of you please tell me what's going on?"

"Someone put her out of her bloody misery." Mum rolled her eyes.

Di couldn't hold it in any longer. "Teri's pregnant," she blurted out.

CHAPTER FOUR

One big ordinary happy dysfunctional family

I spat my coffee out. "Are you kidding me?"

"Sian, I was going to tell you, I just didn't want to tell you here, like this..." Di tried to explain.

"Not now, okay?" Stern Sally, the one who had started it, scowled at Di like it was her fault, then turned back to me with her famous dimple-chop grin. "Don't worry, Heart, all shall be well."

All shall be well. Yeah right. Sally's answer to everything. What part of my unmarried pregnant daughter living at home and sharing a room with her little brother was there not to worry about?

"No, Sally! You can't drop a bomb and expect me not to say anything!" I snapped.

"I understand, I'm just saying, now is not the time or the place, darling." Sally the hypocrite was trying to appease me. I shook my head in frustrated despair and flounced off ahead of them in a mood.

"Come back, Heart!" I heard Sally shout.

"Sian, please, I'm sorry!" yelled Di.

"Lovey, don't be like this!" Lel called out.

We made it to the chapel in one piece, after narrowly missing a full-blown family row. Sally, honestly, timing! I could barely concentrate on a word the mumbling priest was saying. My mind was on other things, like how infuriating my gloating, know-it-all family were at times.

Dave and Sara gazed lovingly at each other as the priest joined them together in holy matrimony.

"Do you, William David Ball, take Sara Harris-Davies to be your lawful wedded wife, until death do you part?"

"I do."

DB took the ring out of his top pocket and placed it gently on Sara's finger. I glanced sideways and saw Lel wipe a tear from the corner of her eye. Di's bottom lip was quivering, and even Steve appeared to be choked with sentiment. I turned to Sal, and she winked at me and squeezed my hand endearingly. My angst dissolved and my heart swelled with pride. It was all rather emotional and romantic until Mum rolled her eyes and opened her mouth.

"Until the next time."

The reception was buzzing. Gold and silver banners,

balloons and decorations filled the grand hall. Olly and Dave were engrossed in conversation on the other side of the room. Olly peered through the crowd with a huge grin on his face and winked at me. I couldn't believe he was going to be writing the music for Dave's movie. It was like being in a fairy-tale. Waiters walked round with trays of canapés and champagne, and Steve and I hung around chatting. He helped himself to another glass whilst already holding one.

Di came over with the blonde mutton guest and a false smile. She gave me a sly wink. "Steve, Sian, this is Rose, she's our leading lady."

"Nice to meet you," I auto-smiled through gritted teeth.

Steve took her by the hand. "What's in a name? That which we call a rose by any other name would smell as sweet – Shakespeare, *Romeo and Juliet*."

Steve and his cheesy lines. Di and I gave each other a knowing look.

"Impressive!" she drawled in her loud American accent. "What's your name story, pray tell?"

"Funny you should ask. I'm known by my second name, Steven, my first name is Robert, after my father Bob, whose real name was William. Pleasure to meet you, Rose." He kissed the back of her hand.

"This is my brother, Rose," Di explained, hoping to diffuse any potential flirting.

"Oh wow, you're DB's brother!" she drooled. "He speaks highly of you."

"He does?" Steve seemed pleasantly surprised.

"You were in the army, right?" she quizzed him.

His face clouded over. "No, that's the brother he wishes was here."

Sore subject.

John-Boy

My tall, dark, strong and handsome ex-army big brother, who taught me how to fight and more importantly, how to defend myself. I would say, 'Goodnight John-boy.' he would say 'Goodnight Elizabeth'. Di would say, 'Goodnight John-boy'. He would say, 'Shut up, Di'. Makes me smile remembering how much it annoyed her that she couldn't be a Walton too.

I missed him when he was posted to Yemen. Joining the Royal Engineers Regiment sounded fun, but in reality it turned out to be a big mistake. He begged Dad to buy him out, but it was too much money back in the day so he was stuck with it.

The one thing that kept John sane was the camaraderie of his fellow squaddies and writing to Dave and Mum. One sunny off-duty afternoon the boys decided to go for a drive in the truck, but John opted to stay behind and write a letter. They laughed and called him a mummy's boy, but he dug his heels in so off they went without him. They never came back. The truck went over a landmine two hundred yards from the base. John heard the explosion and ran out, but it was too late. Nine lads, twenty-one years old. His army family, all killed.

Dave bought him out and got him a job in the film industry, but John didn't fair too well, finding himself a realist in a world of make-believe. It ended in fisticuffs between him and the transport manager, and it wasn't John who came off worse for wear, so that was the end of that career path. He went into the army a quiet, gentle soul and came out a tortured one. The tragedy haunted him the rest of his civilian life and he got involved with drugs and dealing. He sounds like a baddie, but he wasn't. He was protective of me and shielded me from that environment. I knew hardly anything about it other than the fact that he provided a service to his fellow tormented souls.

After a second stint in Wormwood Scrubs, he came out really gaunt. It was all he knew, army, prison, same difference. He hated being confined, yet he struggled being part of society. Where else was there left to go?

Shortly after his release I agreed to meet him at the Bull and Tiger for a brotherly/sisterly lunchtime catch-up. That was when he told me; "I'm going to get out of it, Sian."

"Not with me, you're not." I clinked his beer glass with my Pepsi bottle.

"Not like that, I'm going to get out of it – out of it."

"Where are you going?"

"Alpha Centauri." He pointed at the sky.

"Stop mucking about," I said, laughing.

He smiled, ruffled my hair and kissed me on the head. "Love you kiddo."

He wasn't mucking about. True to his word, the following

day, at the ripe old age of thirty-nine, John took his own life, his chosen route to the stars exactly the same way as Sal's husband Mike in his car.

Lel and I were strolling along Aberford Park when she dropped the bombshell. I reacted by stupidly thumping a tree and breaking my knuckle. John's fault, teaching me how to punch so hard. I was twenty-two and pregnant with Teri at the time. Di was pregnant too, but she miscarried and Sally suffered the burden of feeling somehow responsible for John's death because of what Mike had done. Dave and Steve rarely spoke afterwards. John was the glue between them, and I'm sure the stress of it contributed to Dad's cancer four years later. It affected him badly losing his oldest son; he wouldn't discuss it. Ever. If he had to, much to Mum's disgust, he would say he had died in a car accident, a half-truth which slowly ate away at him.

John turned up at mine after the pub that day, holding a small potted tree which he and two-year-old Dean planted in my back garden. At the time I didn't think anything of it, but John knew what he was doing. Now I drive past my old house once a year or so, peek at the colossal weeping willow and whisper, *Goodnight John-boy...*

I wandered outside to get some fresh air and found Mum posing for the photographer with with Sara's fellow actress friend Sue Roderick, who she insisted on calling Cassie, her favourite character in *Pobol-y-cwm*. For someone who *hated* having her photo taken it was a sight to behold. I couldn't wait to tell Steve, wherever he was. I asked around, but nobody had seen him. I cast my eyes down to the lake and spotted a faraway matchstick man. It had to be my loner brother, in stealth mode, having a cheeky drink. I headed on down to the lake.

Steve and I crunched along the gravel path sharing his champagne and a sneaky smoke. I'd become accustomed to gulping mouthfuls of Steve's drinks over the years, or tipping half down the sink to slow him down.

"I hope Lel doesn't see me." I took a quick puff of his roll up before exploding into a coughing fit.

"Yeah, shit news about Lelly-Bertus. She's doing all right though, hasn't had a fag for months, Mum told me."

"Actually I don't care. Why am I including myself in their stupid not allowed to smoke fiasco?" I coughed. "I'm not a real smoker. I need to de-stress. I can't believe everyone knew about my daughter being pregnant before me."

"I can't Adam and Eve it, Oll gets to be a grandad without being a dad. Jammy git's skipped the hard part, apart from putting up with you for the last five years." He rolled his head back and exploded into his contagious, shoulder-shaking cackle.

"It's not funny, Steve, I'm annoyed – with all of them, talking about me, behind my back."

He took a long slow pull on his turn of the roll up before handing it back to me. "Come on, Sian, you know what it's like. Teri's confided in Lucy, Lucy will have gossiped to Amy, because that's what sisters do, Amy's grassed to her mum, Di will have told Lel because they're twins and Lel will have blabbed to Sal because she can't keep her big mouth shut."

"I'm going to kill her."

"Ah don't, I think it's beautiful."

I prised the champagne out of his hand and took a big glug. "Because you're a piss-head."

"Less of the rudeness. *Mister* Piss-head, if you don't mind."

"Steve, you need to slow down. Dave will go nuts if he finds out, you need to keep a clear head. Tommy Daniels is here you know, he's chief usher or something."

"Screw Tommy Daniels. Do you know how difficult that is for me, Sian?"

"Oh shit, Tommy Daniels, isn't he the one..."

He snatched his champagne back and took an angry gulp. "On our wedding night, behind my back, Sian, and do I get any support from my brother?"

"No, because he doesn't know about it."

"He even called me Bean in front of that actress bird."

"That's funny."

"It's cruel, family's one thing, in front of other people, nah, it upsets me and he knows it."

"It means he loves you."

"He hates me."

"He doesn't. He has no tolerance of your drinking, Steve, he's paranoid you'll ruin his big day."

"He's a filmy prick, ever since he won them BAFTAs."

"So stay sober and prove him wrong. Come on, let's go back."

"You go, don't worry about me, Sian, it's awkward, Lel's not talking to me."

"You did knock on her door at three in the morning."

"She invited me for a drink!"

"At eight o'clock, Steve."

"And Sal had a go. It's all right for Dylan to have a few, you should have seen him at Sukey's wedding, the sun shines out of that boy's arse."

"And rightly so. After three miscarriages, can you blame her?"

"No, I can't, you're right." He let out a sigh of defeat. "I'm a bit of a twat, aren't I?"

"Yeah, but you're my favourite twat."

He cackled at that and squeezed me affectionately. "I do love you."

"I love you too Steve, which is why I don't want you making a fool of yourself."

"I won't, listen, forget about me, it's Tezzle pops you should be worrying about."

"Ugh, don't remind me, what am I to say?"

"Congratulations?"

"I'm serious."

"So am I! Darling, the last thing she needs is you having a go, anyway, pot-kettle, you were twenty when you had Deano."

"That was different."

"Here's one for you – why do you see the speck in your brother's eye yet fail to see the log in your own?"

"Because I don't understand Shakespeare?"

"The Bible actually. Look, it'll stop her getting off her face every weekend. It's the best thing, it'll be the making of her, Sian. Don't give her a hard time."

"All right, but I'm not saying congratulations – why are you such a wise old…"

"Drop-out?"

He was good at laughing at himself, was Steve. We passed a bench and he sank down onto it.

"Are you coming in?"

"I'd rather chop off my own leg with a blunt fork and roll around in salt and vinegar than listen to Daniels' piffling crap."

"Don't make me go through those revolving doors on my own, my phobia's bad today."

"Nice try, kid," he winked. "You go, I'll be all right, you know how much of a loner I am. Anyway, I fucking hate weddings."

He pulled a large can of extra strong Tennent's out of his plastic bag. Time to walk away.

The champagne was flowing, bottle after bottle, proper film-industry style. Di was surrounded by a circle of guests as she played *The Entertainer* brilliantly and effortlessly on the grand piano. Dave's first-born, Jo-Jo, glided onto the stage and delivered her best-woman speech, and we over-protective aunties laughed extra loudly in all the right places. She beamed with pride when everyone applauded her and gave a little bow like any good best man would before handing the microphone to Tommy Daniels. He stood with his back to the huge floor to ceiling window.

"Ladies and gents, I'd like to thank each and every one of you for making it today, especially the bride and groom..."

Everyone laughed and cheered. Apart from me and Olly. Over Tommy Daniels' shoulder, through the huge pane of glass, we saw Steve wobbling towards the old oak tree. He stopped, undid his flies and started peeing up it. *Tie a Yellow Ribbon* popped into my head.

"Oh – my – fucking – god," Olly whispered, manoeuvring out of his chair and slowly backing out of the room.

I scanned the grand hall. The guests were unconcerned, or turning a blind eye, and Dave and Sara were lost in the moment or pissed as farts, but either way they didn't spot him. Thank God.

The jollity continued. People were mingling, picking at food, drinking and laughing. Steve was back, on form, and in social mode, aided by the consumption of goodness knows how many cans of Tennents' on top of the champagne inside him. He was swaying and chatting happily to Rose until serious-faced Dave intervened. I overhead him say, "Excuse us Bean, we've work to discuss." He led her away by the arm and left Steve standing there, Billy-no-mates, as he often referred to himself. It tugged on my Steve heartstrings – that was cold.

"Ah, look at him," murmured Olly.

"Wish I'd taken a photo of him peeing on Daniels' speech," I replied.

Di appeared and saved the day. She grabbed Steve's hand and beckoned us over to them.

"Sian, Olly, family photo time, quick, I've got to hit the road after. I've got to go to Amy's."

"Oh my God, all that way, you shouldn't drive tired, Di, it's the biggest cause of accidents."

"I know, but she's thinking of having Henry put to sleep, she's so upset."

"So go tomorrow. She'll be more upset if you don't get there. Remember what the paramedics said, we were lucky to be alive, at best people end up seriously damaged."

"Sian, don't – thinking about that sends shivers down my spine."

We all huddled around the bride and groom as they posed. The photographer took several pictures, my favourite being Di's repulsed expression at Lel's aptly timed SBV (silent but violent) fart, or as Sal more delicately called it, traf – fart backwards, or Dean's brilliant invented name for it: poof-off. Everyone was happy and laughing, including Dave and Steve. Just one big ordinary, happy, dysfunctional family.

CHAPTER FIVE

The poo hits the fan

—◁✕▷—

August 2008. Nothing beats the crapness of a blaring alarm clock when you're fast asleep. Olly fumbled to turn it off and swung his legs out of bed like never before. The big day had finally arrived, and he was eager to ring the director and get the music ball rolling. Sunshine beamed through the gap in the curtains. The promise of a glorious day.

"Come on, Beak!" He clapped his hands. "Things to do, places to go, people to see."

Desperate for five more minutes I pulled the pillow over my head, but my mobile rang. No peace for the wicked. I grabbed it, opened one eye and focused on the screen. "Sally? What time is it, flower?"

Olly peeped at his watch. "Seven o'clock, aren't you going to answer it?"

It stopped ringing. "I was." I dropped my phone onto the bed. "I wonder what she wants?"

"Tea?"

"Why would she ring me for tea?"

I could tell by his face I'd amused him. "Would *you* like a cup of tea – you canehead?"

"Oh, right."

"I would hazard a guess your big sister and senior canehead misdialled. Ring her back and find out."

"When I've got my tea." I smiled.

My phone rang. I grabbed it off the bed and stared at the screen. It was Sally. Again. "Sal?"

"Hi, Sian, are you all right?"

"Fine, apart from tired because someone keeps ringing me, you?"

"I'm okay. What time did you get back from Olly's parents' do last night?"

"Midnight – I was going to have a lie in today, seeing as I've got no aerobics." Just because she was a morning person.

"Where's Olly?" she asked.

"He's here."

"Where are you?"

"In the bedroom."

"Are you sitting down?"

"Yeah, I'm in bed." I paused. "Why? Is something wrong?"

"Sian, I've got some bad news. I need you to understand, it's bad, but it's not the worst, okay?"

My stomach churned. "Oh no, is it Mum?"

"No, Mum's fine, it's Di..." she hesitated. "Sian, she's had a car accident."

I felt the blood draining out of my face and my heart start palpitating. I turned to Olly. "Di's had a car accident." He grabbed hold of my flailing hand and squeezed it hard.

"Sian listen to me, she had a head-on collision and she's in a coma..."

I heard a gut-wrenching groan come out of my mouth, then I wailed like a banshee.

"Sian, darling please listen to me, she's in a coma but she's alive, so there's hope."

I struggled to speak, but my mouth had completely dried up. "I had a weird feeling, when I got home last night, I rang to see if she'd got to Amy's, she didn't answer. I knew it, fucking driving when she's fucking knackered all the time, I fucking knew this would happen one day." I was so hysterical I could barely breathe.

"Darling take a deep breath, you need to try and calm down, Sian, please, breathe in."

I took a deep breath in...

"Now breathe out."

I breathed out...

"Where's Amy?"

"She's here next to me, we're at the hospital."

"Hi, Sian, Mum will get through this."

If she hadn't said 'Mum' I would never have known it was Di's daughter, Amy. Her usual bubbly tone was gone, her voice unrecognisably flat.

Inner strength took over. "Sweetheart, are you all right?"

"I'm okay, Sian. Tired – we've been here since two this morning."

"Oh my god, does your sister know?"

"Lucy's here, with me and Sal, Dave's here too, he was supposed to be going on his belated honeymoon. It happened around midnight, the police couldn't get hold of me or Lu, we were out, we were at a fucking party, Sian…"

Amy's voice wavered and she started crying. I heard Sally offering words of comfort in the background. Di had crashed at midnight. That was when I'd tried to ring her. It could have been my fault. I bet she was distracted by my call. I chucked my phone at Olly and disappeared off to the bathroom.

I stepped out of the shower, wrapped a towel turban round my head, put my dressing gown on and walked into the kitchen. Olly was pacing around talking on the phone. "Listen, Lel, get some painkillers in you and hang in there okay." He put the phone down and immediately put his arms around me. "You all right, my love?"

Numb and stiff like a piece of wood, I pulled away from him and towel-dried my wet hair. "I've got an interview for a new job, working for a chocolate company, I've got to see Lynette first, she's going to prep me on what I need to say and stuff."

Olly looked disturbed. "Is that wise, today?"

"No, I feel awful, but she's in a coma, what can I do?"

"Go and see her? I've cancelled work and spoken to Lel,

she's at Michele's in Elstree. I told her not to drive here, we'll pick her up en route to hospital."

I was so confused. I didn't know how to feel or what to think. I collapsed into tears. "What am I doing?"

"You're in shock, Liz."

"What about the dog?"

"Teri will look after the dog."

"You haven't told her."

"No. I didn't want to tell her while she's at work, especially knowing her condition we're not supposed to know about, so I texted and said pop home, we need a quick chat."

Oh yeah, that chat too. The one I'd been avoiding, waiting for Teri to tell me herself, or better, hoping was a myth.

A key turned in the front door. The dog ran off barking. I wiped my eyes, preparing myself as I heard my twenty-one-year-old daughter making a fuss of Izzy in the hall. Footsteps approached, and happy, smiling, innocent Teri breezed into the room, hair scraped into a bun, meat-counter-rules style. It mystified me how people saw a resemblance between us – my brown curly locks versus my daughter's silky blonde hair – but they did. Teri took one look at my face and her smile disappeared.

"You know, don't you?"

That's when I noticed the resemblance, when she opened her mouth. It sounded like me talking to me, a fun game we often played to confuse Dean. Not so fun when I discovered she'd used it on numerous occasions to ring school and say Teri was sick and not coming in.

"The family gossip grapevine couldn't wait to tell me," I confessed.

Teri ran into my arms, and we both cried.

"I'm sorry, Mum – and you, Olly, I didn't want you to find out like this. I told Lucy because I didn't know what else to do and…"

"It's ok, everything's going to be fine," I reassured her.

Teri pulled away, wiped her teary cheeks then looked from Olly's serious face to mine. "Then why don't you look like everything's going to be fine?"

Things to do, places to go, people to see, not what I had in mind. Longest journey ever. I spent the whole time tormenting myself. I imagined Di fumbling around in her handbag trying to answer my phone call and taking her eyes off the road…

Our conversation came back to haunt me: *'She'll be more upset if you don't get there. The paramedic said we were lucky to be alive, at best people usually end up seriously damaged.'*

'Sian don't – thinking about that sends shivers down my spine.'

And there she was, in the very situation that sent shivers down her spine.

It was quite a thing, the Spanish gene. Dean inherited it.

He reminded me so much of his Uncle John with his dark brown hair and dark brown eyes, the complete opposite of Teri. The milkman's, John would have said about her. I was twenty-three when my brother died, more or less the same as Dean now. I kicked myself for that thought. My sister wasn't dead, but even so, telling Dean bothered me. My practical joker of a son who saw the 'funny' in anything he shouldn't was going to have a hard time laughing about this. He was particularly close to Di, so I was kind of waiting for the right moment to tell him. Family meant everything to that boy. When he was twelve he asked if I would make him leave home when he was eighteen. I jokingly explained that mummy birds throw their young out of the nest and if they're not ready to fly...

He responded seriously with, "Mum, I will hit the ground."

But he didn't hit the ground, he flew, unlike me. Three years' worth of makeup artist training that amounted to nothing. Dean's career as a film industry electrician had kicked off and he was due to fly abroad in a couple of days. I badly didn't want to tell him, but I couldn't tell him while he was away either. Damned if I did, damned if I didn't. Thanks to Lel pointing out there never would be a right moment, I rang him en route to the hospital and blurted it out. He went quiet.

"Dean? Are you okay?" There was long silence followed by an alarm shrieking. "Dean? Say something."

"Yeah, I mean no, I'm not all right. Mum I've just walked

out of River Island with loads of clothes I haven't paid for."

So it would seem there are better right moments.

I sat on the edge of my seat in the family room staring into space. Olly marched up and down biting his nails. I turned to Lel, sitting beside me cracking her knuckles.

"I can't get over you being awake on and off since midnight, spooky, must be a twin thing."

"Huh?" She stopped cracking her knuckles. "Yeah weird, I had a clanger headache all night."

"I hope that doesn't mean she's hit her head – or has she?"

"I don't know, Lovey."

"Does Mum know?"

"No. Sal and Dave are going to go there and tell her to her face."

"Oh God, poor Mum. Does Steve know?"

"No, he's at Mum's."

"Of course, he told me at the wedding he was being evicted. Oh well, at least Mum won't be on her own when they tell her."

"That's why I went to stay with 'chele and Percy Pant-loaders for a bit, I needed a break, Steve can look after Mum for a change, earn his keep."

"Who's Percy Pant-loaders?"

"Her little boy, Matt."

"He must be about thirteen now?"

"He is, but I still call him that."

Olly's phone bleeped. "Amy texted, she's coming to get us, they must feel shit, they've been here most of the night."

"Why they didn't tell us last night?" I asked Lel.

"The police couldn't get hold of Amy or Lucy, so being her next in line of kin they rang me. My bloody phone was off, so they phoned Dave, and and he rang Sal. She drove them both to hospital, and decided it was best to let us have a decent night's kip first."

"I don't know how Sal does it, she sounded really chipper. She's so good at delivering terrible news, the way she said it kind of kept me from going down."

"Lucky you, Dave, bloody bastard, said to me, 'Di's had a car accident, there's not a mark on her, Lel, not a broken bone.' I thought, that's a relief. Then he said, 'but she's in a coma on a life support machine.' I almost passed out. It was such a fucking shock."

My brother and I, experts in the art of blurting.

The door swung open and in walked my (usually giggling) niece Amy, with a face like a zombie underneath her vivid red-dyed curly hair. She exploded into tears and ran into my arms. The four of us group-hugged and clung together for dear life.

"Come on, guys," she wiped her wet cheeks with her hands. "I'll take you in."

We headed off down a long corridor and approached the door to the ICU. Lel and I grabbed each other's hand tight.

"Ready?" said Amy.

Olly stared at me questioningly. I wasn't ready. He turned

to Lel, she shrugged her quivering shoulders. She wasn't ready either. Before we knew it Amy had opened the door. My hand flew to my mouth and my legs turned to jelly. Olly put an arm around my waist to steady me. Lel screamed out...

There was Di, lying there. Lifeless. Connected to a ventilator with a blood-soaked bandaged head and tubes poking out of every orifice. Her long bleach blonde hair had been cut short. Her famous gold hexagon glasses were gone. Sal and Dave were perched at the foot of the bed, tired and pale. Someone was leaning over, stroking Di's forehead and talking *at* her. I didn't recognise her until she lifted her head. Lucy. She had dyed her hair from the usual platinum-blonde to jet black.

"Look Mumma, Sian's here and Lel and Olly."

Poor Lulu. Her face was wet from crying, and she looked lost. It was such a shocking sight, seeing Di like that. I was unable to process it. All I could hear were the therapist's now meaningless words of comfort ringing in my head, almost taunting me: *There's no point worrying about the poo hitting the fan until it does.*

That was supposed to mean the poo wasn't going to hit the fan. But it had, well and truly. Big poo, big fan, big time. This was the kind of tragic stuff you read about in a magazine, feel fleetingly sorry for the family, then forget. This was the kind of tragic stuff which happened to other people, not to me and my Brady Bunch.

Lel was shaking uncontrollably. "Oh my God, I can't look at her, she's like a waxwork dummy." She turned her face away and started backing out of the room.

Dave looked concerned. "Come on, Lel, let's go outside and get you some air," he suggested.

"I'll come with you," whispered Sal.

They put their arms around Lel protectively and led her away. Sal winked at me and Dave squeezed my shoulder as they walked past.

Olly, Amy, Lucy and I hung around the bedside in silence. It was surreal, like being in a film. Any minute now the director was going to shout 'Cut!' and Di was going to spring upright and yank all those tubes out. I couldn't take it in – that this was actually happening.

"It doesn't seem real."

"I know, Sian," said Amy, leaning in close to Di. "Mum? Can you hear me?"

Di did not respond. Now who's had the last word? I kicked myself for that thought. Now who's the winner and who's the loser? Another ill-timed evil gem that popped into my head. Why was I being haunted by inappropriate memories of the past? Di and I became great buddies when she left home and moved away; all we'd needed was two hundred and fifty miles between us. We had our kids close together and that was when we bonded. She'd stay with me in Buckinghamshire and we'd take the kids to Thorpe Park or Chessington. I'd stay with her in Wales and we'd spend time at the beach. Either way, after the exhausted kids had gone to bed, the habitual ritual was to drink wine and laugh hysterically about the day's events, like the time the obese lady fell in a dug-out sandpit and couldn't get out. I loved the way my sister snorted with laughter at someone else's misfortune and squealed, 'That's so not funny!'

This was so not funny. Poor Di, she didn't look right. I examined every inch of her trying to absorb what I was seeing.

"Where are her glasses?"

"Smashed, Sian," said Lucy.

"Why has she got a cut behind her ear?"

The door opened. The consultant entered. "It's from the second impact, she suffered a hit to the back of her head." He shook hands with Olly, then me. "You must be the fourth sister your family were telling me about. You all look very similar." He smiled fleetingly but retained his seriousness.

"Is she going to die?" I asked him.

"We are doing everything we can for your sister, she's stable now, much better than she was."

"Better?" Olly asked.

"She's had several convulsions since she got here, she's been resuscitated three times."

"Can you believe this, right," Amy went on. "The person driving behind Mum was a paramedic, on his way to work!"

"He resuscitated Mum at the scene and managed to keep her alive until the ambulance got there," said Lucy, sounding full of hope.

I turned to the consultant. "That must mean she's not going to die?"

He didn't respond.

"God, a paramedic, what are the odds?" Olly shook his head in disbelief.

The consultant explained that she'd defied the odds by being alive, but her situation was grave. He asked us to return to the family room. He had the scan results.

Back in the family room, and this time we were all pacing around. The consultant walked in carrying a neat file of paperwork.

"You'd better sit down."

Like obedient dogs, we sat.

He opened the file. "The scan revealed Di has a severe frontal lobe brain injury, possibly caused by a bang to her head from the first collision. After the initial collision she was hit by another car and suffered a further injury to the back of her head which caused a DAI, diffuse axonal injury, a shaking of the brain."

I struggled to take in this devastating news. It sounded like he was talking about someone else, not my sister.

He continued, "The statement from the paramedic confirmed she was driving perfectly for miles, then veered off the road into the oncoming traffic. We're unsure at this stage as to why, perhaps something distracted her."

He looked directly at me. Paranoia kicked in. Was he hinting? It was her phone? Another unwelcome thought I didn't want to think. I felt sick.

"She will get better though, right?" pleaded Amy.

"I'm sorry to say it, Amy, this type of injury is the worst type of brain trauma, it's doubtful your mother will ever come out of the coma."

"But she's a fighter, she fought for her life, you told us yourself she's already defied the medical odds," I said.

"She's lucky to be alive, but the level of coma is deep. Her score is three, which means we're looking at a long-term comatose state, months, possibly years."

"Are you saying... she might never wake up?" Olly dared to ask.

"It's not impossible. You have to understand the longer Di is in this condition the higher the chance she'll develop an infection such as pneumonia, and she has no immunity to fight it. If she survives it will be a miracle, I'm afraid."

Nothing he said sounded real. Surely it was a case of doctors doing what they do, flippantly giving the worst-case scenario. Lucy curled into a ball in her chair and howled hysterically.

Amy jumped up and pointed at the consultant aggressively. "No, this is bullshit! You're doing my fucking head in!" she shouted.

"Ame, come on darling, keep it together." I was trying to console her, but she pushed me away.

"No, Sian! All this negative 'it will be a miracle' shit, miracles happen! One happened to you!"

"It did, Ame, but..."

"Stop!" She raised her hand. "I don't want to hear it, Sian!"

"Yeah, Amy's right, it's not impossible you said, for her to wake up? Please tell us she will wake up?" Lucy begged the consultant.

"That's right, Lucy, Amy, it's not impossible, but her injury level is severe. There is nothing we can do for DAI, and it's widespread across the whole brain. If she does wake up, I'm sorry to say this, she will likely remain in a vegetative state."

The worst-case scenario just got worse. Amy screamed at the top of her lungs, kicked her chair and ran out of the room. Lucy got up and wobbled badly, Olly grabbed her before she could hit the deck. I raced out of the room after Amy, who was running down the corridor as fast as she could. I found her rummaging in the boot of her car, bawling her heart out. She held up Di's purple top, the one she got from eBay. It was drenched in blood and cut down the middle.

"Look, Sian, this is what they gave me, and this." She grabbed her mum's blood-soaked white handbag, took out a pack of cigarettes and opened it, every single one of them, red. "Her belongings, they said."

Angry, she threw them back in the boot and kicked the car repeatedly. I grabbed her and held her tight and she wept uncontrollably until she slumped to her knees. She looked up at me, her big blue eyes red and heavy with agony, pleading.

"Help me, Sian, I don't know what to do, please help me..."

But I couldn't help her. And the pain was unbearable,

like someone had stuck a knife in my heart. A moment that will haunt me forever.

CHAPTER SIX

Sally's golden light

⸺◇⸺

Leaving Di suspended between life and death was heart-wrenching. Sally told us all to imagine her shrouded in golden light, a comment which under normal circumstances would cause family hysterics. This time no one laughed. Sal and Di shared the same spiritual beliefs. They had purple plates, rune stones, you name it. They devoured books on self-healing, ancient wisdom and all kinds of hippy shit. Sally was convinced that with the power of love we could heal Di. Begrudgingly we left her, shrouded in golden light.

Like lost sheep, none of us knew where to go or what to do next. Dave suggested sticking together for a bit, so we piled round to his and had a much-needed glass of wine. Sara, the incredible actress/chef, had cooked a giant Thai curry which was thoughtful and unexpected, and everyone tucked in. Together we were strong. Together we were able to comfort each other, and it felt nice.

Right up until Amy started spinning the blameometer. According to her, if Di hadn't been working stupid long hours, she wouldn't have been tired and none of this would have happened. Dave retaliated, suggesting Di wouldn't have been driving if Amy hadn't told her about Henry being put down. It kicked off so bad that Olly had to get in between them. I caved in and confessed to ringing Di at midnight, so if anyone was to blame it was probably me. Sal and Sara's attempts to pacify the situation failed miserably. Lel got pissed and began chain smoking, and Lucy stole her sister's car and drove off into the sunset. In bed that night I prayed I might wake up and find out it was all a bad dream.

But it wasn't a bad dream, it was real, and every day I woke up and had to be reminded all over again, day in day out. The whole thing was a shambles. The film got taken over by another crew despite Dave's best efforts at such a difficult time. Olly's music dream was not to be. Lel was smoking full-time and Sal was declining work offers because she couldn't bear to leave Di. She channelled her energies and money into healing her. She bought flowers and perfume to arouse her sense of smell, comfy clothes, blankets and soft toys for her to touch. She spent a fortune on Ginkgo, resveratrol and CoQ10 to promote healthy blood flow to the brain. She paid for the TV to be on so Di could hear life. Whether she could or not, nobody knew. Sal would sit with her on her golden pedestal, sometimes into the early hours, waving her magic wand, shrouding her in golden light, reading books about the universe, life, death, positive thinking, you name it, Sal read it. She spent so much money, but she didn't care. It was just dirty bits of paper.

Days turned into weeks, and nothing changed. Living miles away it wasn't easy for me to visit Di often, but the family kept each other in the loop. Sally rang from the hospital to share the latest.

"I've got some good-bad news. Di wasn't distracted. I've been speaking to the consultant. Further tests revealed she suffered a subarachnoid brain haemorrhage."

"A what?"

"A stroke, Sian! Di had a stroke while she was driving, on the fast stretch through Builth Wells, that's why she veered out of control and hit the car."

"Is that good, to have a stroke at the age of fifty-three?"

"No, but the consultant said she wouldn't have known much about it, so it's as good as bad news can get I guess."

"Too much stress, and smoking. She told me at the wedding she was giving up when she started her new job." I sighed.

"Don't do it to yourself, Heart."

"What about the other people involved?"

"Walked away with minor injuries, lucky eh? Anyway, it wasn't your phone call, you can stop blaming yourself now, Heart."

I cried tears of relief, then tears of shame for feeling

relief, then tears of sadness for poor Di. A subarachnoid brain haemorrhage! As if that wasn't rotten enough she hit a car and was hit by a second car and suffered a further DAI.

"Why couldn't it have happened when she'd got to Amy's and people were around?" I sighed. "She might have been saved."

"I know, I keep staring at her and wondering why."

"Di's bad luck, that's why."

"No, I mean, why did I call her brain damaged?"

"Oh Sal don't. It's just banter."

"Brain damaged – if I had a pound every time, it keeps going round in my head."

"Sally please, stop torturing yourself. I think we should stop blaming ourselves."

"I wish I could swap places with her."

"Don't say that."

"I do. I really fucking do." For the first time since ever, Sally, the brave one, swore, and broke down on me. "She doesn't deserve this, Sian," she choked back her tears. "Di is such a kind, selfless person."

"She is Sal, it's cruel and unfair, but you have to consider yourself, you're always at the hospital. I thought you were having a sleepover with Nirvana this weekend?"

"I had to cancel, I feel so bad. I've been teaching her how to ride a scooter with one leg, she was looking forward to showing me, poor little angel."

"Sal, go see your granddaughter, you need a break, you sound so tired."

"I'm burnt out, Sian, physically and financially, I don't know how long I can keep this up."

I stepped onto the scales and cast my eyes down. Nine stone one pound. I'd lost almost two stone in three months. I threw on some clothes and headed off to the clinic for my final 'driving anxiety' session. Oh the irony of it.

"Hello, Elizabeth, I see you've lost weight." The therapist seemed pleased.

I soon ruined it. "Remember our conversation? Not worrying about the poo hitting the fan until it did?"

Teri was in the kitchen smearing pickled onions with peanut butter when I got back.

"Morning, Mum." She arched her back, and a big baby bump protruded. "Me and Dan are viewing a flat this afternoon." She smiled.

"Morning. Great," I said, and I meant it – inside me somewhere, it just didn't sound like it.

She walked over to the fruit bowl and offered me a banana.

"No thanks."

She looked troubled. "A slice of toast then?"

"No, Teri, I'm not hungry, I've got to get on the road soon."

"Stop making excuses you're always not hungry, Mum!"

"How can I eat when my sister is lying there being fed through a tube in her stomach!" I snapped. Tears sprang into my eyes. Teri put her arms around me.

"Sorry, Mum, I'm worried about you, you'd be the same if it was me, wouldn't you?"

"No, I'm the one who's sorry, Teri." I squeezed my daughter tight. "I didn't mean to bite your head off, I just feel useless. I'm driving myself insane, picturing Di lying there, breathing through that horrible gurgling tube thing in her neck."

"What must be going through her mind?"

"Who knows? Triple cheese pizza?"

Teri pulled away, mortified. "I can't believe what's happened to this family."

Mum and I sat at Sal's kitchen table drinking tea. My poor little mum, she looked grey. Ever since Di, she'd gone downhill and was having tests and physio because her foot was numb. My sprightly eighty-five-year-old mum suddenly seemed very old.

"How's your tummy trouble?" I asked.

"If that's your polite way of asking if I've still got diarrhoea, yes I have."

"Me too. Emotional stress, my therapist reckons."

Mum sighed. "It doesn't go does it, the worry? It's always there, eating away at you like a bloody maggot."

"I still can't believe it, Mum."

"I can't believe you saying there's going to be a tragedy in that little triangle."

Oh yes. The throwaway comment I made when Mum was pretending to be deaf but hearing every word...

Lel entered the kitchen, shaking her head. "Another job I've turned down on Sal's behalf."

"What was it?" I quizzed her.

"Some big movie with that director, what's-his-face, the one who talks like Joe Pasquale."

"The skinny bloke. Joel Schumacher?"

"He's not skinny."

"He is, I've met him."

"No, you pleb, I mean the one I'm on about isn't skinny."

"Oh, you mean thingy-ma-jig – Michael Winner, or is he dead?"

"He's not dead, I don't think, anyway it wasn't him, he talks like Fagin."

"Ridley Scott?"

"Alan Parker, that's it."

"He doesn't talk like Joe Pasquale." I laughed. "Alan's got a soft quiet voice, I've met him."

"Oh I don't know Lovey, maybe he had a sore throat, whatever, I had to say she was ill."

"She is ill," said Mum.

"When are you going to wake her?" I asked.

"No need, I haven't had any sleep." Pale and drawn Sally shuffled into the kitchen in her dressing gown.

"Oh Sal, you look awful!" I cried in dismay.

Her face smiled, but her eyes didn't. She kissed me on the forehead instead of the usual two cheek kisses then one on the nose. "I haven't slept properly for weeks, I'm so tired, Sian." Weary, she plonked herself into a chair, folded her arms across the table and dropped her head.

"You had another call for work," said Lel.

Sal lifted her head like it was a lead weight. "What did you tell them?"

"I said you'd get back to them."

"What did you say that for?"

"You need to work, Sally, you need the money to pay Mike's stupid tax bill, otherwise things aren't going to get any better."

"I'm no use to anyone like this. You know how complex my job is. I can't think straight."

Mum squeezed her arm across the table. "You've got to pull yourself together my lovely, this isn't you, it's those bloody pills."

"I can't believe you're taking them, you hate pills," I said, surprised.

"I haven't had so much as a paracetamol ever since you… well, you know, and now I'm taking antidepressants."

"She's been on them for a couple of weeks," Lel cut in. "They're not for, you know – that." She pointed at her head, signalling the cuckoo-sign. "They're to help her sleep. The doctor said give it a month, see if they do any good."

"Well they're not, that's the third job offer I've turned down this week, Sian."

"She's not fit for work because she can't sleep, and she can't sleep cos of that stupid tax bill. She's not dealing with any of it, Sian, it's a vicious circle," complained Lel.

"Sal, you need to work." I tried to get her to see sense.

"Says the woman who quit after her first job.'

Touché. Excluding the sporadic day here and there my stint as a trainee makeup artist on *The Three Musketeers* in Vienna was also my last. I did like Tim Curry though, such a lovely guy and a brilliant actor. We'd sit around bored, flicking through his photos waiting for Kiefer Sutherland and Charlie Sheen to show up. Then onto set for more hanging around like a sucker fish, in case the actors needed a touch-up, similar to watching paint dry, thus allowing my idle brain to wander back to the real world: my kids, and how much I missed their little faces. Maybe I'd have got used to it if I'd stuck it out. Maybe I had ADHD before ADHD was a thing…

I sighed a big Mum sigh. "Sally, ring the poxy tax office and have it out, how can you be held responsible for something your dead husband did years ago?"

"I have to pay it, my accountant says, otherwise it'll get worse and go on for years. I could go to prison."

Lel tutted. "You're overthinking and making yourself paranoid. He said that's the worst-case scenario if you don't pay it, but you will, you can sell all your bloody houses if you have to."

"Then I'll be homeless. What will I do with all my stuff?"

Poor Sal, self-appointed head of the family, life coach and bank. All my life I'd never seen her this defeated. "This is so unfair, Sal."

"I'll be better off in prison, Sian, at least I'll have a roof over my head."

Lel lost it. "Sally! Stop saying that! You sound insane! This isn't about tax it's about Di, you bloody know it is!"

"Come on now, girls, stop arguing." Mum was exasperated.

"No, Mum," Lel went on. "It's not going to go away, she has to confront it, she hasn't been to see Di for weeks, Sian, she refuses to go, she can't handle it, you know why?" She turned to Sal. "Because you can't fix it, can you?"

Unemotional, unresponsive Sal got up from the table. "I'm going back to bed."

"I'm going to the hospital, why don't we go together, shroud her in golden light?" I tried.

"That's all I do, Sian, when I'm not asleep, which is most of the night."

"Come with me, Sal?" I persevered.

"I can't."

"See, I told you." Lel threw her arms into the air.

"Please don't be angry with me, Sian," Sal muttered.

"What do you mean Sal? No one's angry, we're trying to help."

She wasn't making much sense. Maybe Lel was right, this was more to do with my sister being in a coma than anything else. The Di thing hung over us like a black cloud. Feeling like she was dead but she wasn't. Talking about her in the past tense like she was gone, yet she was here. Death is final. You have to move on. But this? Chinese water torture with drip-fed heartache instead. Measured by the second, three months is incredibly long and slow. Our emotions were beyond stretched thin, but Di's grave situation only made the family bond stronger. We were forced to put our suffering to one side and dig deeper for Di, whatever the cost, which for Sal, was alarmingly high.

Someone was constantly at her bedside, mostly Dave, or Amy and Lucy, crying, pleading with her to wake up, telling her how special she was, how much she had to live for and how much we all loved her. But apart from surviving the occasional bout of pneumonia, which was a whole new level of frightening, nothing changed. Di remained fast asleep, in no man's land limbo.

Another month rolled by. As per norm Sal and Dylan came for Christmas, only this time it wasn't the norm. Usually when Sally and Joe were in each other's company no one could get a word in edgeways. Joe, my sixteen-year-old, six-foot baby, the spirited one who looked like me, loved a heated debate with my sister, the opposite of me. The Sally and Joe Show, Olly called them.

As predicted, no show. No deep discussions about atoms, electrons and photons. No energetic conversations on politics, or fiery banter of Sal trying passionately to convince Joe there was such a thing as life after death and him fiercely disagreeing. Sal had steadily continued to decline. She couldn't even muster a smile. For the sake of the kids I tried to keep things normal, playing games, as you do. We played Dean's favourite, *Atmosfear*. Everyone wrote their worst fear on a piece of paper, then put it in the secret tomb. She seemed to be doing okay until the end, when everyone revealed their fear. Mine was pigeons, Olly's dog poo, Dylan's bananas, Dean's spiders and Sally's – wait for it – homelessness. It wasn't funny, although Dean erupted into fits of laughter, slapping his knee repeatedly, and when Dean lets rip his crazy buffoon guffaw, it's contagious. We all found it hilarious, including Sal, in the moment. The rest of the time Olly and I tried to shake her negative mindset, but it was impossible. She said she couldn't work because her computer was broken. I suggested getting a new one, she said it wouldn't be compatible with her software. Olly advised getting new software and she said she wouldn't understand it. I proposed taking a course, and she told us she couldn't afford to because she wasn't working and she wasn't working because her computer was broken. Every solution to every problem was met with a brick wall.

Borrowing money wasn't an option either. I offered to re-mortgage my house. It wouldn't be enough, apparently. Excuse after excuse. I didn't know how to help. I'd never seen Sal like this. I came to the depressing conclusion that Lel was right. Coping with Di was near on impossible, throw into the shit-pot Mike's hefty tax bill, not working and not sleeping. Poor Sal, her problems made me shudder. For the first time ever, the self-appointed head of the family, life coach and bank couldn't fix it. Her magic wand was well and truly broken.

Tis the season to be jolly, not. Amy and Lucy spent Christmas day with their mum eating hospital turkey dinner by her side while Di lay there like sleeping beauty. All it did was prove how much we take everything for granted and when that's gone, to quote one of Sal's favourite hippie mantras; *love is all there is.*

CHAPTER SEVEN

The snow baby

—◦◦◦—

Hallelujah – Di opened an eye! It was February and it was bleak, but the sun was shining in my heart. I found myself singing 'I believe in miracles' in the bath. Amy and Lucy were beside themselves. Sally's golden light had worked, and with the sheer power of love we battled the angel of death. Di progressed from 'doubtful she will ever come out of a coma' to coming out of a coma. After six excruciating months, Sleeping Beauty finally woke up. Feisty Di proved feisty red-head Amy right; miracles DO happen.

Di continued defying the odds, from opening one eye, to both eyes, to moving her fingers. I left her sleeping peacefully, but I hadn't finished in the hospital yet. Next stop the abdominal aortic aneurysm ward (downstairs). I found the room, put some magazines on the bedside table and stared lovingly down at my poorly brother. Then I leaned over and kissed him on the head.

"Hello, darling, what a lovely surprise," said Dave, opening his eyes wide.

He attempted to sit up, wincing.

"Dave, careful, looks painful."

He hit the button on his morphine pump, then leaned back on his pillow. "Ah, much better."

"How are you doing?"

"Not bad by all accounts, the doc reckons I'll be out in a few days, with this for company."

He pulled back the covers to reveal a plastic bag attached to his side. My stomach churned at the sight of that and his huge Dr Frankenstein hacked-together cut. "Oh shit, Dave."

"You're not wrong there, kiddo." He laughed then flinched in pain.

"How long have you got to have the thingy on for?"

"It's temporary."

"A couple of days? A couple of weeks?"

"Twelve months."

"Serious?"

"Yup, the colostomy team are coming this afternoon to show me how to change it, so I can do it myself at home, and boom-boom, I'll be out of here. You know me, baby sis, I don't do sick."

"I don't recall you ever being in hospital."

"This will be my first and last time. Di saved my life."

"I heard. What is it with this family's luck? Di had a paramedic behind her and you collapse in hospital."

"Can you believe? I'm sitting next to her doing the crossword, next minute I'm waking up in a hospital bed! The aneurysm was about to burst. Doc reckons if I hadn't collapsed with the diverticulitis pain, they'd never have found it in time, I'd have been a goner!"

"You've got a guardian angel, you have."

"You're not wrong there kiddo. Have you been upstairs to see Di?"

"Yeah, she opened her eyes when I spoke her name, started doing that blinking thing again, and she was moving her mouth trying to speak."

"I've been teaching her every day, asking questions, she's advanced – one blink yes, two blinks no – to mouthing words. I tell you, it won't be long before sound comes out and she speaks."

"Do you think?"

"I don't think, I know. I've told her I've got a new movie in the pipeline and I can't do it without her. Di's a fighter, Liz, that'll get her on the mend."

"What happened about BBC Cymru?"

"Eh?"

I guess Di never got the chance to tell anyone, so I was the only one who knew. Did BBC Cymru know? Or did they assume she just didn't turn up for her first day all those months ago?

Dave winced in pain. Too much energy spent talking. I glanced at my watch.

"I'm going to let you rest and see Di before I go, she slept most of the time I was with her."

85

He gave me a weak thumbs-up and lay back on his pillow. "Thanks for popping in, little one."

My boom-boom brother Dave had almost died. Teri was right. The things that had happened to this family in such a short space of time beggared belief.

I sprinted down the hospital corridor. It was a funny, inexplicable thing, but every time I went to see Di, it was as though my legs couldn't get me there quick enough; I had an overwhelming urge to run to her.

I put my sterile gloves on, buzzed the double doors open and there she was, propped up on three pillows with a metal cage around her head, her blue eyes wide open and staring into space. Her once long blonde hair was short and completely grey. My appearance-conscious sister wouldn't like that. All breathing apparatus had been removed apart from a tracheostomy tube inserted into her neck. Her feet and hands, bound in splints, protruded from the bed. She looked so ill, and she was suffering, sometimes unnecessarily.

Fancy miraculously surviving what should have been a fatal accident to then choke to death on your false teeth because of the basic standard of NHS care. One time the hospital rang Lucy and told her to prepare herself: Di was about to take her dying breath. She rushed to hospital and discovered Di choking on her crown bridge plate. Mortified, Lucy managed to wheedle it out from the back of her throat in the nick of time, thanks to her nimble fingers, a wooden tongue depressor and her army medic training.

Then there was the rubber glove scandal. Di was sent for an MRI, but they forgot to remove the tourniquet afterwards, and her elbow swelled to dangerous levels. Chip off the old fierce block – Amy was furious when she discovered it had been left on all night, coupled with the horrifying fact that the tourniquet was a rubber glove, so tightly bound it stopped the blood supply to her arm. In her rage Amy wrapped it around the arm of the nurse in question and had to be physically dragged away by two doctors. They blamed the night staff, they blamed the day staff, but it was no one's fault. It was apparent that Di needed specialist help. Witnessing someone you love unable to fend for themselves, wholly reliant on 'carers' who aren't trained how to care – it's like animal neglect. Di was dead against that, yet here she was as defenceless as an injured dog…

I buzzed closed the double doors and walked over to the bed. Seeing my sister so incapacitated was excruciating. In the words of Bob Marley, you never know how strong you are until being strong is your only choice. The first thing I did was hide my pain behind a great big smile and tell her Amy and Lucy were all right. I didn't know what was going through her mind, but I knew that if anything, she would be worried sick about her girls. I also told her I'd scrubbed her kitchen floor until it was gleaming – we all have our fetishes and that was Di's. I stroked her stiff hand and kissed her on the forehead.

"You will get better, you're very strong. You know that, don't you, Di?"

Staring into space, she blinked once – 'yes' – in response.

"You had a car accident. Did you know that?"

She blinked twice, so I left it.

"I've got something for you." I smiled.

Karaoke queen Di loved singing. Pre-crash she was in a local cover band, so I had compiled a CD of her favourite songs. The first one came on, *Diana* by Paul Anka. Dad used to sing it to her when she was little. I sat in the chair beside her, holding her hand, choking back tears as I sang along, *"oh please stay with me Diana…"* I swear her blue eyes were smiling. After a couple of hours singing, talking *at* her and the usual blubbering, I had to wrench myself away.

"I'm sorry I have to go, I hate leaving you, I'm so proud of you, Di." She lifted her arm and wiggled her stiff fingers. I kissed her bandaged hand. "You will play the piano again, Di."

A tear slid from the corner of her eye. She mouthed *thank you* but no sound came out.

Thank you… It did my head in seeing that. It was heart-breaking. I wiped away her tear, kissed her goodbye and cried all the way back to the car.

Steve and I waded through a sea of cardboard boxes carrying my flat screen TV and carefully placed it on the pine cabinet. My fussy brother repositioned it until it finally looked perfect.

"There we go."

"Blimey, you can tell you're a Virgo." I laughed.

"Takes one to know one." He winked. We leaned back and admired it. "Thanks, darling you're too kind."

"You're welcome. You know what a tech head Olly is, we've had it two years so it's old now."

He placed an arm around my shoulder, pulled me close and gave me a brotherly squeeze. "I appreciate you coming all this way, you didn't have to."

"Don't flatter yourself, it was an excuse to be nosey." I glanced around the room admiring the décor. It was only magnolia but better than the usual complete stinking shite-hole of a dropout centre with paint-peeling walls. "Nice flat."

"Beats being homeless." Steve pointed the remote at the TV.

"Here's one for you – what's the difference between you and a Big Issue seller?"

"I haven't got a Scooby."

"A Big Issue seller's got a job." I laughed out loud at my homemade joke/poke at my brother.

"Ooh funny, a real rib tickler." He pulled a half-scowl. "Actually, Sian, been there, done that, got the T-shirt."

I laughed harder. It didn't surprise me. My nutty brother had done a bit of everything. Everything to do with being a dropout and everything to do with being successful. His claim to fame; dating a Miss World runner-up in the seventies. Astonishingly, *he* dumped *her* because she had too many teeth and reminded him of Bingo from Banana Splits.

"Nice to see you sober." I smiled.

"I can't afford to drink now I'm on the warfarin for me DVT." Steve continued 'flannel chicken' (as Sal called it) until the screen displayed the Snooker World Championship. "Yes!" He punched the air triumphantly. "I have missed watching this."

"Teach you for going on a bender and forcing Mum to kick you out."

"She didn't kick me out, she asked me nicely to fuck off."

"You seem to have landed on your feet."

"Thanks to Anglesey council. Anyway, Mum wanted an excuse to go and stay with Sal in Cardff."

"And now she can't leave. She was supposed to be there for a week with Lel. Have you heard the latest?"

"Sal's fallen off her golden pedestal?"

"And her magic wand is broken. Can you believe she's taking antidepressants?"

"Sian, it's beyond comprehension, she hates pills, has done ever since you... well, you know."

"She keeps saying weird things like she's going to be homeless and go to prison and stuff."

"It's terrible, I can't handle the things that have happened to this family in the space of six months, first Lel with her COPD, then Di, then Sal, now Dave."

"Have you been to see him?"

"No. How is he?"

"Putting on a brave face. I think the recovery process will be long, he's lucky to be alive, you should go see him."

"Yeah, I might."

"Lel told me you haven't seen Di for weeks?"

He ignored my question and began faffing around in a box. "Now where did I put the sugar?"

"She's trying to communicate by mouthing words, it's amazing, she moved her big toe the other day, Lel reckons – Steve?"

"Ah, here we go, found it. Fancy a cup of tea?"

Mentally drained by the drama and the monotonous, endless drives to see family who lived at opposite ends of Wales, Cardiff and Anglesey, I fell through the door shivering. It was icy cold outside. Olly and Izzy, my Bichon/Jack Russell greeted me.

"How was everyone?" he asked.

"Steve's in denial, Dave's got a colostomy bag, Sal's taking antidepressants, Lel's progressed to inhalers. Apart from that, fabulous."

"Oh Liz, Di's doing better than everyone by the sound of it."

"And Mum's foot's turning a weird green colour, she looks so old, Olly."

"She aged a lot as soon as they told her about Di's accident."

"You're not wrong, she's too old for all this crap."

"It's every parent's nightmare, losing a child – oh shit, sorry love, I didn't mean it like that."

"I know, and you're not wrong, the old Di's gone, it's like I have a new sister and I love her so much, she brings out the love inside us, doesn't she?"

"True, when the bullshit is stripped, nothing else is left, just raw love."

I felt sad leaving Di, but equally happy to get back to the sanctuary of home sweet home, and food. Di loved her food. One thing I could never do was eat in front of her at the hospital.

"I'm starving."

"Thought you would be," said Olly, pleased with himself. "I've made your second favourite pasta dish, Beak."

"Why not my first, Olly-Flower?"

He raised his eyebrows. "A tiny bit of butter, a tiny bit of flour, a tiny bit of milk, a tiny bit of stirring then a tiny bit of butter – definition of insanity."

Hearing the word 'pasta', my sweet sixteen-year-old Joe begrudgingly dragged himself away from Grand Theft Auto and blessed us with his hormonal grumpy-faced presence. "Mum. At what point in a man's life does he accept being called Flower?"

"When he becomes a man, Joe."

"But, Mum, a flower?"

"Remember Olly's homemade wine?"

"You mean the elderflower stuff in that dusty bottle?"

"No, I mean the Olly-Flower stuff in that dusty bottle."

"Whatever."

The habitual Sunday night rigmarole, returning from his dad's with attitude. Lucky old weekend fathers, getting the best bits for the least input. We tucked into Olly's version of Quorn black olive pasta, heaped with stringy mozzarella. Moody one minute, full of smiles the next, Joe piped up, "This is delicious, Mum, have you done something different?"

Ah, the normality of my own life and the joy of discovering that my other half cooked my dinners better than me. As I put the last forkful of food to my lips Olly whisked the plate away.

"Finished? Good. We have to go. Teri's gone into labour."

I almost choked. "Why didn't you say?"

"Strict instructions from Teri not to tell you while you were driving and to make sure you'd eaten first. Don't worry, I'm on it, we've got plenty of time."

Worried, Joe pulled back the curtain. "Have you seen it out there?"

Snow was falling thick and fast. Now having the opposite of plenty of time, the three of us whizzed out the door. The blizzard was so bad we made it to the hospital by the skin of our teeth. We found Dean striding up and down the corridor biting his nails. I left the boys to it and raced into Teri's side room.

Picture the scene. Archetypical builder Dan, Teri's muscly boyfriend, at the foot of the bed eating a Big Mac, and Teri screaming into a gas mask. My baby was having a baby. She was overwhelmed with relief to see me and with a blanket of snow inches deep outside, I was overwhelmed with relief not to have missed it. I wiped her sweaty forehead and stayed by her side for the duration while she dug her nails into my arm and swore at me like it was my fault. Bless her – my shy daughter, who never used profanities or displayed symptoms of someone with Tourette's unless there was a ladybird or some other small flying thing in the room.

Steve rang. It didn't matter that Uncle Dee-Dar was pissed, she was off her nut with gas, so they were on the same page. I put him on speaker and my brother/pisshead/midwife said all the right things. He talked her through it, telling her to stay calm and breathing with her. During that call she gave birth to a beautiful bouncing baby girl. The obstetrician carefully placed her in Teri's arms. Exhausted but glowing, with post-burger Dan standing proudly beside them. Teri gazed lovingly at Ella, smiled and whispered, "Ah, there you are."

My sweet innocent Teri. Hardly any pain relief either. She was tough, but I didn't know she was *that* tough. Tezzle-poo-pops-pum. I had a whole new level of respect for her. Ella, our cute little snow baby, so like her mum with her blonde wispy hair and big blue eyes, took me straight back to when Teri was born. Such a special moment. The boys rushed into the room and we all cried – tears of happiness for a change.

Spring sprang. Di was making slow but steady progress and Dave was on the mend. Ever the trooper, he had great pleasure informing me that he and his colostomy bag had been for their first meeting at Pinewood Studios. "Liz, I told them right at the start, 'ladies and gents we all fart, usually in these circumstances we manage to hold them in, unfortunately I can't'. I lifted my shirt, boom-boom, everyone had a laugh."

"Did it squelch?"

"Liz please, do you have to be so gross?" David pot-kettle-Ball replied. "Anyway, I got off the train and went to visit Di. Amy was there, poor kid sitting there with that toddler all day."

"Ah, Di loves seeing Meg, it cheers her up, they do scribbly drawings and stuff."

"I know, it's not that, it was the way Amy said, 'Meg, let's change Nana's nappy before we go.'"

"It is a nappy – isn't it?"

"No, Liz!" he snapped. "It's a pad, not a nappy!"

"Okay, Dave."

Amy, whenever she was there, which was always, changed her mum's 'pad' rather than have Di suffer the indignity of the nurses doing it. I think that gave her the right to call it what she wanted. Lucy on the other hand couldn't bear to do that, but she didn't mind picking Di's nose and cleaning her teeth, which made Amy gag. The things which upset some didn't upset others. We had to be mindful of each other's feelings at all times, or it would kick off.

Dave went on; "She's doing well with the spell chart. She spelt out 'crap', so I asked, 'Do you need one, or do you mean this place?' She spelt 'both' – did make me laugh, kiddo, she hasn't lost her sense of humour."

Seven months late for an interview has to be a record. My friend Lynette worked for an agency on behalf of a certain brand of chocolate. It was only part-time, but a necessary income boost to supplement my sporadic fitness franchise.

Now that I'd dropped three of my five classes following Di's accident I had no choice. A vile chest infection had left me exhausted, and I didn't have the energy for leaping around as a Moves Fitness instructor; I needed something a bit more sedentary.

Lynette spent the journey prepping me on what (and what not) to say as we drove to my doom to meet Stuart, my sweaty, red-faced, balding, overweight, stuffed shirt of a potential boss. She didn't sell him to me at all. It wasn't Stuart's fault he had to be formal and important and boring, all for something which equated to counting chocolate bars in supermarkets, who knew? Supermarkets had rules. No handbags allowed. No mobile phones. No heels. No adding up devices. No adding up device? Di, help! Throughout the interview Lynette had a *please don't let me down* expression on her face. I coped well until he got to the part about asking me what I could bring to the role and I heard myself say, "A calculator?"

Lynette fake laughed nervously. "That's her humour, Liz's playing."

Actually, I wasn't.

"You'll be given a brief to take in with you, and one of these." He glowed with pride, opened his desk drawer and handed me a branded pen.

"But I have to add up on my fingers? I've only got ten."

"It's a lot of data, you'll get used to it," he said, smiling.

I wanted to say, "Couldn't I sneak a teeny one in my school satchel?" but didn't. I spared him the egg on his face.

It wasn't his fault we were living in two different worlds, plus I needed the work. I put my corporate head on and answered his question; what could I bring to the role?

"I would ensure the store manager orders enough stock to enable me to increase the number of chocolate bars on the fixture so the maximum capacity can be sold thus drive sales for the company…" because that's what Lynette told me to say.

Willy Wonka clapped his hands approvingly. "Excellent, when can you start?"

Easy as pie.

On the plus side I could work the hours to suit me and complete the assigned calls within a given month whenever I chose. Not exactly a career, but too good an opportunity to miss. I was grateful to Lynette for sticking her neck out for me. My sweet friend, a special creature, and like all my friends, not the norm. Lynette came from the land of tea, cake and floral dresses somewhere up north and is, to this day, one of the funniest people I've ever met.

Day one of my training was also the first boiling hot day of the year; the sunshine helped, but I was still a tad nervous.

"Don't worry, Liz, leave the talking to me," said Lynette boldly. Our first call; Mr Patel's convenience store. Lynette played her part like the sublime actress/saleswoman she was, and explained to Mr Patel I was new to the role etc.

"A nice day for you too, my dear," he smiled at me.

"And for you," chirpy Lynette replied in her broad northern accent. "It must remind you of home. I bet you miss it, where you come from."

"I come from Luton," he responded without a smile.

"Of course you do, I mean, where you *really* come from, if you get me, it's in the DNA, isn't it, sort of thing," she said, digging a deeper hole with every word and an expression similar to someone on stage who had forgotten their lines turning to the wings for support. Worst teacher ever. I couldn't hold it in any longer, even Mr Patel started giggling. I couldn't remember the last time I'd laughed like that until my sides were splitting.

Once I got into the swing of it, I enjoyed it. My fellow corporate slave niece, Jo-Jo, called me 'the chocolate police' thereafter. Every week at the team meeting we were given a whole box of free chocolate. Whoop whoop! Twenty-four individual bars, all for me – to give to managers as an incentive. Not so whoop whoop, not so Charlie and the Chocolate Factory, but counting chocolate bars on my fingers and talking to store staff regarding banal crap was quite refreshing. How incomparably nothingy other people's problems were in relation to Di's. Hearing how gutted Maggie was about her chrysanthemums being blown over in last night's gale force wind – wow... I listened with morbid fascination, slightly jealous of her reason for being upset. Still, it was a welcome break from constantly worrying about my sister, although she was never too far from my thoughts.

Driving my car, I thought of Di lying there. Traipsing up and down supermarkets, I thought of Di staring into space. Eating dinner, I thought of Di, unable to eat. Wherever I went, whatever I did, I thought of Di, lying there, staring into space, every single day.

CHAPTER EIGHT

Life of Di

Di continued taking incremental steps forward. She progressed from spelling words on her ABC chart to making sounds, and was moved to a specialist hospital I shall name Millhouse, somewhere in Wales. It was a relief she was out of there after the rubber glove, the false teeth episodes and a whole host of other incidents.

Millhouse was better equipped to deal with brain injury patients and compared to some, Di seemed almost normal. Her tracheostomy tube was removed and she could breathe by herself, but she couldn't swallow and had to be fed liquid formula through a big syringe inserted into her bellybutton.

In the bed next to her was Janet, whose elderly parents visited her every day and had done since her accident. Janet had had a car crash when she was eighteen; she was now forty-three. For twenty-five years all she had done was roll her eyes around her head. We felt blessed that Di could move her arms and legs; she couldn't walk or stand, but she could sit upright in her special wheelchair a few hours a day. Getting in and out of it was an unpleasant experience for her. She screamed and hollered throughout the undignified, painful ten-minute hoisting process. All we could do was stand by and watch and offer words of useless comfort until it was over.

Di had advanced from making sounds to speaking. Her first words were 'Amy' and 'Lucy' – no surprises there, she loved them fiercely, for her girls were her everything. Her voice was deep and husky as if she'd smoked a thousand fags. Talking wasn't easy, but being the family chatterbox, not even a death-defying coma could shut Princess Di up. Vegetative state my arse. She didn't use unnecessary words such as *a, and, the, is, was*, but it was easy to fill in the blanks. Sometimes you could almost have a proper conversation with her, other times she spoke gibberish. She had splints on her hands most of the time, otherwise they would go into spasm and contort. Whenever she set eyes on Olly she would shout; 'Olly healing' repeatedly, and he would massage them with his hot hands until they straightened out. She cried a lot. She got confused a lot. Her short-term memory was shot, but her long-term memory wasn't too bad. The further ago it was the more clarity she had; how she had walked first, all over her wriggling baby twin sister, her Triumph Vitesse and how brilliant she was at playing the piano. Being reminded of the person she was always brought a wonky smile to her face and/or an outburst of tears. She was super appreciative of family visits and needed lots of cuddles. I grew accustomed to my sister's disability, yet at the same time my head and heart struggled to accept what my eyes were seeing. She should have died yet here she was, looking at me like the living dead. My sister had changed beyond all recognition. I couldn't help but wonder what was going on inside her super constantly calculating mind. All those times my superbrain sister had helped me with my maths homework, or should I admit, done it for me, without a calculator too. For what?

We had meetings with the neurology team about physio and stimulating Di's brain, and were told what we should and shouldn't do. I got a stern telling off for bursting into tears when I saw her. Her emotions had to be kept stable, they said. I did my best, but it was hard; she cried but I had to remain unresponsive. There was always someone keeping a watchful eye, making sure we were playing Connect Four, treating her like a cabbage and not getting emotional. The old Di was gone. The new Di belonged to them, not us. They claimed to have her best interests at heart. Perhaps they did. Perhaps they wanted a quiet life. Di was very vocal and would shout or bang her arm on the bed rail to get attention, and they would struggle to calm her. None of my family were trained in brain injury, but we didn't have a problem. All you had to do was put your face close to hers and get eye contact, and once you had a visual connection, her focus would switch to you, a bit like a child. It was a simple thing we did instinctively, but they didn't; they treated her like a naughty toddler much of the time.

One of the few pleasures Di had was a tiny sip of water occasionally. On one particular visit when she asked for water, the nurse on duty smirked patronisingly; "What's the P word?" A rush of anger washed over me, but I wasn't allowed to be emotional. For Di's sake I didn't say anything. I didn't need to. Di winked at me and replied; "Piss off." Brilliant. I whooped with delight and gave my sister a high five. Feisty Di was still in there and she didn't suffer fools, with or without brain damage.

It triggered a blast from the past. My first job after leaving Hillside school; Di rescued me and gave me a lift to work – late, because the bus had broken down...

"Come in with me!" I had begged her.

"What on earth for?" Di snorted with laughter.

"It's not funny Di, my boss will kill me, she's a monster, and she looks like Miss Piggy."

Together we raced into the building and up the stairs. Di waved at my boss and she waved back. "There you go, Sian, you'll be fine," she said, then kissed me on the cheek and headed back down the stairs.

As soon as she was out of sight, Miss Piggy ripped into me in front of the whole office. Di came flying back like a machine, arm outstretched, finger pointing until she was a hair away from her piggy face. "She said you would do that! Why did you wave at me, you two-faced cow, it's not my sister's fault the bus broke down! Talk to her like that again and you'll have me to deal with, understand?"

I glanced around the open-plan office, and my colleague's faces said it all. I could almost hear their silent cheers. Miss Piggy, rooted to the spot with fear, quietly agreed and treated me with the utmost respect thereafter. Like I said in her bio, feisty Di would defend me to the end. God help anyone who dared pick on me...

We became increasingly disheartened with the way Di was progressing. Why weren't they massaging her hands the way Olly did? Why did Lel have to turn up and discover Di in pain because they'd forgotten to remove her leg splints? In a desperate attempt to appeal to their better nature, Lel made a collage of pictures and memories and stuck it on the wall in her room, with a note titled 'Life of Di' to place alongside it, she read it out for my approval:

I am Di, I love animals and I love talking, so please talk to me about pets I've had. Henry, my faithful black Labrador, Wilbur, my pot-bellied pig and my horse Sonny. I'm grade eight at the piano and I want to play again so please massage my hands to keep them supple. I love all kinds of music so please make sure my CD player is on so I don't get lonely. Remember my splints need to be removed after two hours or they hurt. I sleep better on my right side and please can you put a pillow between my knees at bedtime as they get sore...

"What do you think, Lovey?" she said.

"Gold star, Lovey," I replied, flatly.

Bless Lel. It nudged them into making a bit more effort, at least when we were present. Meanwhile Dave had been campaigning to get Di a room in Oaktree rehab, a centre for patients with neurological conditions. It was better equipped for physio, plus they had a hydrotherapy pool and it wasn't a million miles away from Lucy's place and also Dave's house in Cardiff.

"I can visit Di every day, Liz, until I get back to work," he said. "But Sara's around and Lucy, there will always be someone near, we can sort out a rota. Fingers crossed, kiddo!"

Everything crossed – for Di.

The ups and downs of a crazy life. Teri and Dan took to parenting like ducks to water. Mother and baby were doing fine, but I couldn't look at my beautiful granddaughter without crying. I didn't understand it. I had so much love in my body for her, nothing to cry about. Olly said emotion is emotion, be it happy or sad, and Ella was a trigger for mine – all bottled-up and ready to pop. Poor baby had a lot of responsibility on her tiny head and she didn't even know it.

Dave and Lucy were over the moon when Oaktree agreed to reserve a place. Things were continuing onwards and upwards for Di, but on the Sally front they were spiralling backwards and downwards. She managed to get the tax office off her back by accepting Lel's twenty grand savings and cashing in her pension. It had two years left to reach maturity and would have been worth thousands, but the tax man didn't give a shit. *Que sera*, as Sal would say. It cost her dear, but she had her fingers in other retirement pies. In recent years she'd invested her life savings into property, the plan being to sell later on when they had increased in value. A good idea at the time, but not now the recession was upon us. The housing market crash meant the value of Sally's home, her holiday pad in Spain, her apartment in Florida and her dinky flat in Hull had minus zero equity, so she couldn't sell them. She wasn't working, so she wasn't earning to cover the mortgages, and steadily she sank deeper into debt and depression. The self-appointed head of the family, life coach and bank, couldn't cope with the stress. Dave mentioned the word bankruptcy, but she wouldn't hear of it. In her mind there was no way out of this nightmare.

When I was a teenager I stayed with Sal for a month to convalesce after being discharged from hospital. She bought a canvas for my bedroom; an enchanting forest scene with a caption underneath saying, 'Today I have grown taller for walking with the trees'.

Being a kid, I didn't get it. Now I got it. Sal had taken to disappearing for hours at a time, walking with the trees, a desperate attempt to make herself feel better, it didn't. She didn't have the mental strength to handle Di either, who had taken 'fierce' to a whole new level, shouting obscenities and smashing her arm on the bedrail. A normal consequence after traumatic brain injury, apparently, so Sal stopped visiting her. She wasn't sleeping at night and had taken to pacing around during the day. The words 'Sally' and 'depression' didn't belong in the same sentence. She had been a pillar of positivity all my life. Much as I didn't want to face it, I found myself googling 'nervous breakdown'. It said: A state in which a person is no longer functioning normally, typically brought on by stress and compounded by an inability to cope with stress.' It might as well have said 'Sally'. The doctors kept blaming her medication and chopping and changing it, but if anything, it made the situation worse.

Lel rang mid-morning. She was already reaching the end of her caring tether.

"I heard Sal on the phone to Joel Schumacher earlier, he offered her a million dollars."

"Shut up! Did she say no?"

"What do you reckon?"

She also told me Mum's green foot was turning black and she was falling over more. All in all, a very worrying time. By tea-time she really had reached the end of her caring tether.

"Sian, I'm so scared."

"Is it Mum?"

"No, Sally, she tried to swallow bleach."

It was a verbal kick straight to the stomach. "What?"

"Yep, said she wants to die. I don't know what the fuck to do, Sian, she won't listen."

"Do you want me to speak to her?"

"Would you? I know she ignored your letter."

"Eight pages straight from my heart to the bin."

"Aw, Lovey, I tried to read it to her but she walked away. Maybe you could try and talk some sense into her instead?"

After much background kerfuffle Sally came on the phone. "Hello, darling," she said, all normal.

Trembling inside, I tried my best to sound nonchalant. "Hi, Sal, Lel told me you tried to swallow bleach?"

"Yeah I did, it was yucky. I had to spit it out."

"You don't want to swallow bleach."

"No I don't, Sian."

"Then don't, it's not nice, Sal, it will burn you, why did you do it?"

"I don't know what came over me, Sian, I can't see any other way out."

"You need help, Sal, you're under way too much stress."

"I am, darling."

"You didn't read my letter, did you?"

"What's the point? I knew what you were going to say. I'm aware nobody likes me."

"Oh, Sal, why are you being like this?"

"Sorry – please don't hate me."

"I don't hate you. I'm trying to help, we all are."

"Is that why you're all talking about me behind my back?"

"We're not – well – we are, but not like that. Please don't be like this, what about your spiritual books, what about Ramtha?"

"What about it?"

"That helps, doesn't it?"

"I can't even look at it."

"Come on, Sal, what happened to 'all shall be well' and 'love is all there is'?"

It was her next answer which knocked the wind out of my sails. "Sian, I don't know what's going to happen, but whatever happens to me I want you to remember one thing – I love you very much, Heart."

My façade broke. I fell to my knees and begged like a child for her not to do anything stupid, but she hung up on me. I felt as though my heart was going to break in half.

I figured it might help lighten the situation in some small way if I took my six-month-old granddaughter to see Sal. She loved babies and doted on her granddaughter Nirvana.

I walked through the door and plonked Ella into her arms.

"Sian, don't." She panicked.

I was shocked by the sight of her. In a short space of time she had become unrecognisable. Mum said we had the same flashing angry eyes, except mine were boring hazel and hers were strikingly different. But they weren't sparkling with life today; they were dull with dark circles around them. My dustbin sister who I never thought would give up eating had lost so much weight her skin was hanging off her face. The dimpled chops were gone.

"Give her a cuddle Sally please."

"I can't. I'm too negative. I don't want to infect her."

"I'm not taking her off you, so you'll have to sort it out."

I walked off into the kitchen and left her calling my name. Mum was at the table, greyer than ever. Not being one to mince her words, she said; "You've seen Mad Mary then?"

Back in the lounge Sal was pacing around, cradling Ella in her arms, singing her a lullaby; she put her finger on her lips and smiled lovingly. Ella was fast asleep. It was the first time I'd seen Sal smile for months. I pried Ella gently out of her arms.

"I'm off to bed, Sal, goodnight, see you mañana," I whispered.

"Mañana." She kissed Ella gently on the head, "Such a pretty bubba."

I fell into bed with the enormous weight of Sal's financial problems on my shoulders. I racked my brains trying to find a solution – there wasn't one. It just went around in my head. I gave up trying to sleep and dragged myself out of bed at five a.m. to find Sally in the kitchen, sitting in her dressing gown, tired, anorexic, death warmed up.

"What will I do with all my stuff?" Her glazed eyes peered around the room.

"What stuff, Sal?"

"Everything, everywhere, there's so much of it. I didn't sleep a wink, Sian."

"I didn't either."

She stared at me with her dull, deadpan eyes. "Welcome to my world."

That scared me. Lack of sleep was how this whole

nightmare began for Sal. I was petrified of her world and becoming 'infected'. I tried to get her to eat breakfast but she couldn't eat, so I made her another cup of tea and listened while she talked about prison and dirt and flies and all sorts. She wouldn't comprehend rationality, so I gave up trying. I reminisced about the memoir she was writing. I hoped if I talked about that she would get involved and it might penetrate who she really was. Usually one tale would spark another, this was her life, it was so colourful. Now, for the first time ever, she showed zilch interest. Not a flicker of a smile, it was pointless. All I could do was try to normalise the situation and throw a few of her 'love is all there is, all shall be well' mantras into the pot. She stared at me in a way which suggested it wouldn't be.

Mum and her walking stick pigeon-stepped into the kitchen, eyeing my dishevelled bedhead disapprovingly. She stopped in her tracks; "Have you done your hair, Lizbeth?"

"Yeah, do you like it?"

"Didn't think so." She scrunched her face.

Mum's pet hate: messy hair. My cue to leave the room. Off I went upstairs acting like everything was hunky dory, but then I saw Lel stumble out of Sally's bedroom, white as a sheet.

"I found these in her bedside drawer." She opened her cupped hands, and they were cradling hundreds of tablets. "There's fucking shitloads, Sian, I think she's planning to kill herself."

Goose bumps shot up my spine then spread over my body, leaving me shivering with cold. "Lel, listen to me, you can't deal with this on your own anymore."

"Sian, I need to help Sal, but I need to get Mum back to Anglesey she's so ill, I don't think she's long for this world." She cried her heart out. "What am I going to do?"

"Take Mum home."

"But I can't leave Sal."

"Lel, you can't help her, none of us can. You need to ring the doctor."

It was as though Sal had isolated herself from everyone, like a dog when it knows there's something wrong and separates from the pack. A far cry from the lady who had picked me up unannounced from Cardiff railway station and asked no questions as to why I had a Harry Potter cake in a Sainsbury's carrier bag. The remorse of having ruined Joe's eighth birthday was overwhelming.

As soon as we got to hers, I broke down and confessed. I had stormed off after a row with his dad in town. What did she do? She took the cake off me. Five minutes later she re-entered the lounge carrying the cake, complete with lit candles, singing 'happy birthday' to Joe with that huge dimple-chop grin. My big sister had a unique ability to turn a negative into a positive. She never did negative, ever...

Poor Sal, she needed professional help. How hard Lel tried for so long, banging her head against a brick wall and getting nowhere. The thought of another sleepless night there filled me with anxiety. I was desperately tired. For the sake of my sanity, I needed to go home.

I dropped Ella off and went into rambling overdrive when I got in. I was losing my mind. I got a lot of verbal diarrhoea out of my system talking to Olly about Sal and absorbing his words of wisdom. He explained the pecking order was precisely why I or no one else in the family could help her. As Steve said, 'Sal's top dog.' Out of everything Olly hammered into my tired anxious brain there was one thing, and it's probably the one thing that saved me.

"Self-preservation, Liz. When oxygen masks are deployed in an aircraft you have to put your own mask on first."

"What about your children?"

"You're no good to them if you're not breathing."

He succeeded in drumming this into my head. I couldn't help Sally by taking on her problems and neither could Lel, especially with Mum poorly. I had to agree, there was no point us going down with her. I needed to stay strong to be of positive use to my family.

I slept like a baby after copious amounts of Olly-Flower wine – just as well. Lel phoned first thing and informed me that the mental health team had been round to assess Sally. They had concluded that she needed to be sectioned straightaway as she was a risk to herself.

"She looked over her shoulder as they led her away, guess what she said, Sian?"

"Lovey, don't…"

"You'll be better off without me."

My poor distraught quivering wreck of a sister. "Self-preservation, Lel," I chanted over and over, hoping I sounded more convincing than I felt. "You did the right thing."

"Yeah, self-preservation, I did the right thing, so why do I feel fucking shit?" she wailed.

I put the phone down and collapsed into a snivelling heap of tortured guilt. I cried all day. My Sally Sunshine. My second mum. My idol. Sent away like a lamb to slaughter, by us, her family. It really hurt...

Sal was admitted to the psychiatric hospital, and much as I hated it, there was a strange sense of calm in knowing she was in there. I recalled her "I'll be better off in prison" comment; perhaps this was what she wanted. Lel and Mum were able to go home, and Olly decided we needed a break, so he booked a trip to Canada for us and the boys to visit my cousin Pat and Pete. I couldn't wait. Now seemed like the right time. Sal was in safe hands, and Di was doing much better at Oaktree.

They had a proper timetable, for starters. Gardening in the morning, followed by physio, then painting in the afternoon. The bedrail arm-smashing had stopped and she seemed a lot calmer in herself. We played the 'good nurse/ bad nurse' game every time I visited her. I would point to one and ask what she was like, Di would smile and say 'lovely' or frown and say, 'bitch.' She was never wrong. There was no filter with Di; she was stripped of the constraints of society and developed an ability to see straight through people.

She would say spooky things like, 'Dancing Queen's coming on the radio,' in her disjointed wordy-missy way, and she'd be right. Her short-term memory had improved. I would ask who came to visit yesterday, she'd say Amy, Lucy, Dave or whoever and she was spot on. She'd come out with gems like, "Dad's been sitting with me all morning," or "John-boy was here yesterday". I spoke to one of the neuro doctors about that, and his opinion was fascinating. He believed people who had been to the 'other side' – plainly put, died and come back to life – developed clairvoyance and could communicate with both worlds. He pointed out that my sister had officially 'died' three times. I chose to believe it too. It was comforting to imagine Dad and John being with her when we couldn't be.

A year had passed since the emotional ball and chain of Di's accident and the growing pain of Sal's mental health. I was sick to death of feeling crap. Canada was calling, and I admit, I was looking forward to running away from it all.

CHAPTER NINE

Russian Roulette

———❋———

Dave took on the arduous task of untangling Sally's financial mess and getting her properties repossessed. He explained the only way out was to cut her losses and start again and, would you believe, she relented.

Dylan proved himself to be every bit his mother's son. He might have looked like his dad, but that great big heart he inherited from Sal. He didn't let the long working hours or the three-hour trek from Shepperton Studios stop him visiting his mum. He'd take her out for a few hours, but Sal was always eager to get back. On the way home he'd call me to help pass the misery of the M4 and let off steam. On this occasion he sounded baffled.

"I don't get it, Sian. Mum says she doesn't want to be in that place, but when I take her back, she seems – happy?"

He couldn't get his head around it. None of us could.

"I don't think she's happy, Dylan, I think she feels safe."

"Safe? In that fricking nut house?"

"She doesn't have to deal with her money problems while she's in there."

"I suppose. Explains why she keeps saying 'at least I've got a roof over my head'."

"Her fear was homelessness, wasn't it?"

"And we all laughed."

"Because we all have the same sick sense of humour, including your mum."

That cheered him up. He'd even had a chuckle with his mum for the first time in ages, he said, which sounded promising. Hopefully she would be out of there soon. I hated myself for it, but I couldn't bear to visit Sal; I don't know why. Actually, that's a lie, I do know why...

When I was ten my mum was taken away in an ambulance. 'Your mother's ill, try to understand,' Dad and Sally said, but how do you explain mental health issues to a child? She looked fine to me. Every day, Dad and I visited her. The journey was fun. Dad and I would sing carefree songs; *Little Brown Jug, She'll Be Coming Around the Mountain*. The gloom didn't descend until we arrived outside the grotesque Hill End Mental Hospital. These days they call them psychiatric units; back in the day life wasn't so kind. The revolving doors still haunt me, and I have to use the disabled entrance every time I go to John Lewis. Dad would grab my hand and tell me to look at no one but him.

I tried not to make eye contact with the groaning zombies, muttering to themselves and bouncing off the walls as we passed them in the echoey corridor, repeating Dad's words 'be brave' in my head. Sometimes Sally took me and we'd pretend we were on the set of a horror film. That helped.

Mum was diagnosed with severe manic depression. Visiting her was always a game of Russian roulette. Sometimes she shouted at Dad to get me out of that place, other times she was ecstatic and would grab me and kiss me with her Mommie Dearest red lipstick. I didn't want her to touch me but I didn't want to upset her because I was scared. I didn't like this woman; she looked like Mum, yet she was a stranger. I wanted Mum back. I remember her 'friends': Peter, who marched up and down the ward saluting. I always saluted back, mind. There was Winnie, with the cobweb-beehive and yellow teeth, she was nice to me, but the black-haired witch strapped to the bed opposite wanted to kill me. Not exactly *Jackanory*.

Mum was in and out of hospital, and it went on like that until I was fourteen and swallowed a handful of her tablets. To be fair, Mum's special cabinet did resemble our local sweet shop, Candies. There were so many enticing pots to choose – long skinny ones, small fat ones, red tablets, blue capsules, yellow pellets. Steve called them 'happy pills' and I vaguely recall thinking they might make me happy too, not that I was unhappy, just suffering adolescent mood swings once a month, so I took four, one from each of my favourite pots. After that, I honestly don't remember, apparently, I ingested hundreds. Dad told me he ran into hospital carrying me in his arms and that my heart had stopped beating. I was resuscitated and remained in a coma for three days. Mum and Dad tried to keep it hush-hush, but somehow Steve found out and rushed to hospital. It was strictly parents only, but he forced his way in and shouted my name over and over. I remember opening my eyes and thinking I was dead because I saw the blip, blip, green dot machine and Steve standing there – in a pink T-shirt? My eyes were whirling like Kaa's from *Jungle Book,* he later told me.

After several weeks recovering slowly in hospital, social services deemed I should go into care, but Mafia boss Sally refused. She said I was staying with her for a month, then going to Acapulco with Dave for a month, so there. Once a week they came round to interrogate me, same old, same old, grilling me as to why I tried to take my own life at such a young age. I shrugged my shoulders every time. In the end Sally got cross and told them politely that if they ever used the word 'overdose' again they were not welcome to come back. It wasn't my fault they didn't have child safety locks on pills which resembled Smarties, she told them.

Sal explained that I would always be protected, because I was born with a guardian angel. She nurtured me until I was strong again then handed the baton to Dave, but I am the reason she hated pills. I am the reason Lel cut short her visit to Canada. I am the reason Di left her amazing life in Australia. I am the reason Steve rushed out of the door wearing his wife's pink T-shirt with birds on it. I only went home to prepare for my trip to Mexico, plus I missed my friends.

I couldn't wait to see Sarah Taylor, who had the guts to pierce my ear three times with a stud, no needle, no ice, and together our names made Elizabeth Taylor, which made us special. And Lisa Hatton, who put the wonderful in my weird and wonderful childhood for believing upturned brooms were real horses. And Angela Moriarty, for being as bat-shit-crazy as me and having the best trigger laugh. And the girl with the cutest face and the hardest punch, Chelsea Toilet, bit of a weird name unless you're Oi-Ying Cheuk, newly arrived from China, and can't pronounce 'Tracy Tyler'. And one other special person, my man of steel. Kindred spirits we were.

'Gunfight at the OK Corral at the cinema this afternoon,' Dad would say with a mischievous twinkle in his eye, then we'd jump in the car and drive to Studio 70 in the village, nipping into Candies first. Dad would buy himself a quarter bag of toffee and I'd choose pear drops or tom-thumb pips, preferably the pips, so I could pour hundreds into my mouth and make cool long sucky noises throughout the film. I hated cowboys. I was in there for one reason: sweets. Dad would show his disapproval by furrowing his brow and stroking the ends of his moustache and that was all he had to do, he never had to raise his voice. No one messed with Dad's strict rules. If he said 'shut up' was a swear word, then 'shut up' was a swear word. He had the ability to switch from a demanding figure of authority to a child in a blink.

I hated the fact that he smoked, but I loved the way he extinguished his cigarette between his thumb and forefinger, then flicked it into the coal fire. I loved our Sunday drives to Elstree Aerodrome, collecting conkers, scouring for bird's nests, finding ones with dinky eggs in. The best part was driving through Trotters Bottom. There was a massive hump in the road, and Dad would stare at me with a twinkle in his eye and say, 'Ready to fly.' Then he'd put his foot down and drive over it so fast we took off, shouting 'wahey' as we flew through the air. I loved his driving, Mum hated it. 'Stirling bloody Moss,' she used to roll her eyes and say.

My dad was one of the brave volunteers who spent days digging to find the children of the Aberfan disaster. He grew up in the neighbouring Welsh mining village of Abercynon and it upset him deeply. I was only three, but seeing my heartbroken Dad cry like a baby is not easy to forget. He was my everything. He roared with laughter at my Margaret Thatcher impression, said I was better than Mike Yarwood. His story-telling was superb, especially the Canadian Mountie tales. The one where he got stuck in the snow and had to shoot his faithful Siberian Husky was my favourite. The minor detail that he couldn't have been a Canadian Mountie if he grew up in Wales then moved to London didn't bother me. I hero-worshipped him. He could do no wrong. With Mum, on the other hand, with all the comings and (hospital) goings, it didn't exactly help us to form a close relationship, put it that way, and that's how it was, right up until I became a mum.

When I had Dean, Mum stayed with me for a month, and that's when we bonded. I don't know how I would have coped without her. I lost the plot when my tiny baby puked double the milk he'd ingested. I raced into the kitchen, panic-stricken, and showed Mum his sodden blue blanket. 'Is he dying?' I screamed. The corners of her eyes crinkled up and the corners of her mouth downturned, but no sound came out – just a long wheeze. And there was my answer. How to belittle an emergency situation – ask Rena Ball.

From that moment on our strained relationship flourished, and Mum became my best friend. Or, maybe it was fairer to admit, I had grown up enough for her to talk openly about her breakdown and it came as no surprise. For the first time I understood how difficult her life had been. She got an infection after the birth of my stillborn twin and came so close to death that they told Dad to get the priest in. Against the odds she survived. The hospital said she had to rest and wasn't to lift so much as a kettle when she went home. Dad couldn't help, as he had a position of responsibility as MD of Alcon Aluminium and it paid good money. Someone had to bring home the bacon and pay for us lot. Rest was an impossible feat for Mum. She had six kids and a new-born to clothe, feed and water with no washing machine hence a line full of terry towelling nappies to deal with daily, plus a dad dying from leukaemia to care for, whilst holding down a part-time job as a cleaner and taking me with her… phew! And exhale. I felt exhausted just listening.

My trooper of a mum's coping levels gradually hit rock-bottom, and she needed help. Instead, they stuck her in a psychiatric hospital and used her as a guinea pig for all sorts of new wonder drugs, including the barbaric electric shock treatment. Having seen the film *One Flew Over The Cuckoo's Nest*, Sally begged Dad not to let them do it, but he was at his wits' end, and he didn't know Mum would suffer permanent memory loss. Poor Dad, and more so poor Mum. This brave London lady had been through the mill. It was going to take a lot more than a bit of puke on a blanket to ruffle those iron feathers.

She made up for the bad times. The grandkids wouldn't recognise the kind-hearted, loving grandmother I'm describing. When the new twenty pence came out she saved every one she got until she reached a hundred pounds, then opened a savings account, and she did that for each of her ten grandchildren. Once a week she gave a tenner to a local club, Band of Hope. Fifty-two weeks later they gave it back in a brown envelope which she handed straight to me on my birthday for God knows how many years. She liked a cheeky bet here and there and loved a competition, so she could give away her winnings. I loved my best friend dearly and made peace with that vague dark era until today. In truth, the Sally thing stirred up some deeply buried bad stuff and the cowardly bottom line is, while Sal was in that place, I found it easier to pretend none of it was happening.

Visiting Di I could handle, but it was a variant of Russian roulette. This game I called 'spin the wheel of fortune'.

Sometimes she was happy and euphoric and we'd sing songs and share memories; nothing pleased me more than seeing her wonky smile. Other times, she'd be aggressive or sad and tearful, and sometimes she slept throughout the visit. She looked so peaceful when she was sleeping that I confess to wishing for her not to wake up sometimes.

On one particular occasion I was welcomed with a wonky smile. Her blue eyes lit up and I could see the old Di shining through them, a harbinger of a happy visit. She asked for Sal, and I said she was working on a film. Ignorance is bliss, Dad used to say. Now I understood what he meant. Di was a bit teary, but they were sentimental tears. We cuddled and I told her how much I loved her, to which she always responded, 'I love you more'.

On the whole it was an upbeat visit, apart from the nurse on duty failing the 'good nurse - bad nurse' game. Meaning, I had to befriend the 'bitch' and lie through clenched teeth about how much my sister loved her in order to safeguard Di's wellbeing after I'd left. Hard, when instinct is telling you to bind her arms and legs, leave her in a room and see how she liked it. I swallowed bombs for Di, we all did. Well, we all did apart from Amy.

Di was sleeping when I left her, so I tiptoed away and prayed the bad nurse had a tiny heart in there somewhere. A session with Di was as educationally uplifting as it was emotionally draining. One thing it always did was bring out the love. To borrow Sally's phrase, 'love is all there is'; so true for Di, she didn't have anything else.

October 2009. Sal was getting better, according to the hospital, and was allowed out at weekends provided she stayed with family and wasn't home alone (or as Dave rephrased it, Macaulay Culkin). It was a mammoth weight off. That said, whenever she rang, I would stare at her name flashing on my phone. Sometimes it filled me with dread to the point I couldn't answer. Gutless I know, but I had to psyche myself up to cope with whatever she might say, which was usually very negative, poking the nerve of the Russian roulette era.

That day, seeing her name on the screen, I felt brave enough to risk taking a bullet.

"Hi, Sal, what you up to?" I asked, in my best fake 'everything's perfectly fine' voice.

"I'm at home."

"Who with?"

"No one."

"Why are you home alone?"

"The hospital told me I have to try," she sighed. "I had to wade through piles of nasty letters as soon as I walked through the door, all wanting money."

"Ignore them, Sal. Dave's dealing with that. Anyway, what's money, dirty bits of paper, your health is all that matters, Sal. How are *you* doing?" I said, desperate to keep up the positivity.

"Not so good."

My heart sank. "Why? I thought you were getting better?"

"I did too, then I tried to hang myself…"

There was a horrible silence.

"Don't worry, Sian. I couldn't even do that right because I'm so bloody rubbish at everything."

I was shocked to the core. I tried frantically to hold it together and say the right thing but I was floundering. "Oh, Sal, what – when – I mean, how?"

"With my dressing gown belt. I made a right hash of it."

I couldn't fake the niceties any longer. "For fuck's sake. You shouldn't be in that house on your own, it's not good for you, why did you do that?"

"I don't know why I did it, Sian, truly."

"Listen to me Sal, if you ever feel that way again EVER, pick up the phone instead and call me, okay? I'm going to ring Dave and get him to pick you up."

"Okay."

"Sally, don't do that ever again, please?"

"I won't, Heart."

"Promise me?"

"Darling, I promise. It made me realise I couldn't. How could I do something like that and leave a black hole in the lives of my family?"

That word 'promise' – a big deal in my family. It was the confirmation I needed. And she called me Heart, which was an encouraging sign. I felt instantly calmer. She hadn't called me Heart for ages.

Dave and Sara stepped up the effort of keeping a closer eye on Sal. They had a strict rule of no opening post, no reading emails, no answering phones, no negative talk policy, and they insisted she stayed with them so she wasn't alone. It seemed to do the trick and thanks to Sara's delicious cooking she was able to begin eating properly. There was no more talk of self-harm, thank the lord. At last Sal was on the mend.

Mum wasn't great though. I tried to get Sal to spend a weekend with her. I figured if she saw how ill Mum was, it would bring back the old Sal we all knew and loved, but she wouldn't. She refused to visit Di too. I couldn't get my head around it. Sal was getting better, but it was like she'd had a personality transplant. She didn't care about anyone or anything anymore.

The weekend before we were due to fly out to Canada, Olly and I did the rounds. We visited Di and while she slept we used the time wisely. Olly massaged her contorted hands and I sorted the travel insurance. She'd been at Oaktree for two months and settled in well, and most of the staff were nice, give or take the odd miseryguts. I watched her snoring, blissfully unaware of her damaged brain, and cast my mind back to that fateful Sunday morning in 1997.

My then brother-in-law Phil rang me at silly o'clock to share the news that Princess Di had been involved in a car accident. It took a while for my tired brain to work out he wasn't talking about my sister, silly me. Silly Phil, he kicked himself when he realised. I was one of the few people in the world relieved by that news, sad as it was. Little did I know that eleven years on it would have more significance.

It was always difficult tearing myself away from Di, and she didn't make it any easier. I swear my aura was emitting guilt, and somewhere in that strange brain of hers she knew I was going on holiday and didn't like it. Something was bugging her, because today was a particularly grumpy visit. She shouted, she cried, she swore, she dug her nails into my arm, she hit me.

"Di, whatever's wrong?"

"Sally!" she shouted, her blue eyes full of tears.

"I told you Di, she's working."

"Don't go," she pleaded.

I shrugged my shoulders at Olly, and he took over. "Di, do you want us to stay here 'til late, then drive all the way to your mum's, tired, and in the dark?" he asked, patiently, about ten times.

Somewhere in there, the real Di understood. Reluctantly, she let us go and with cumbersome hearts we headed off to our next port of call, North Wales to see Mum and Lel. Driving through the autumnal golds of scenic Dolgellau, a sense of calm came over me, followed by a weird pang of worry. I rang Lel.

"Lovey, is Mum all right?"

"Yeah, but she's in bed, she had a funny turn."

"What do you mean a funny turn?"

When we got there, I found out what she meant. Mum had had a stroke. I couldn't believe it. What the hell? One rotten thing after another after another. Luckily, it wasn't a bad one. Mum was a bit disorientated, but not enough to warrant hospital treatment. The paramedics would send a carer later to check on her. Thankfully, no more freaking hospitals for now, but Mum was weak, and this could be a sign of what was to come, they warned.

Olly went off to get food and I stayed with Mum, holding her hand while she slept, her face greyer than grey. We were due to go to Canada next weekend. I couldn't shake off the foreboding feeling: what if Lel was right, Mum wasn't long for this world? A tear came into my eye and I sniffed.

Mum woke up and smiled at me. "Hello, my love, how are you, Sal?"

"Mum I'm not Sal."

"I thought you were Sally and we were in heaven."

"It's me, don't you recognise me?"

She scrunched her face. "Of course I bloody do, what's wrong with you, Lizbeth?"

That made me smile. Mum was definitely all right.

"I had a horrible dream." Her mouth was so dry she struggled to get the words out. "I dreamt Sally died. She's not dead, is she?"

"No, it was a nightmare, Mum," I reassured her. "Let me get you some water."

I went into the kitchen and told Lel about Mum's dream.

"Weird. I was thinking about Sal and wondering why she's not answering her phone."

"She never does. I've been ringing her for days trying to get her to come and see Mum."

"Dave had to go away for the weekend, so he dropped her off at home."

"Macaulay Culkin?"

"She wanted to, apparently."

"Bollocks to her then."

"The hospital told Dave they would send someone to sit with her. She promised me she would phone and let me know she was okay, but I can't get hold of her. I'm worried, Sian, you know what happened last time she was home alone."

"She wouldn't do that again, she promised."

"I know but, Mum saying that, I hope it isn't a bad omen."

"Course it isn't, Sal's getting better."

"I think she's pretending to be better, it's what everyone wants to hear."

"I think she doesn't give a shit."

"Ah, don't be like that, Lovey."

I was pissed off. "She should be here, Lel, seeing Mum."

"I know, but what if she has, you know, done something stupid? I need to ring Dave."

"Well if she has, she's not getting any sympathy off me."

Mum was fast asleep, so I placed her water on the bedside table and crept away, adopting my usual stance at the lounge window and absorbing the breathtaking view of rolling fields and snow-covered mountains beyond. I had such a lump in my throat. What if this was the last time I would see my sweet little mum? Lel was on the phone to Dave talking about Sally. Stuff Sally. She should be here, with Mum. Mum was ill, like proper ill. Mum was dying. I was a million miles away in a despondent land of misplaced angry thoughts when I overheard Lel, out of the blue, say, "Where did they find her, Dave?"

I heard a bang, so I ran into the kitchen. Lel's phone was on the floor.

"Find who?" I asked.

"Sally..." she said, frantically running both hands though her hair.

She was shaking from head to toe, staring at me, wide-eyed and petrified, like a deer caught in a car's headlights, then she just came out with it:

"She hanged herself."

CHAPTER TEN

The worst news

And I thought laughing at John for telling me he was going to Alpha Centauri was bad...

My whole world collapsed. *She's not getting any sympathy off me...* My own pathetic words were echoing in my head and deafening me. I learnt the worst lesson the worst possible way – do not say things you do not mean, ever. The enormity of what had just happened was devastating. How she'd been the last ten months was nothing compared to a lifetime of Sal and who she really was. My idol, my Sally Sunshine. In that instant I knew I'd let her down. I felt stupid and small and insignificant. It didn't sink in. It didn't sink in at all. Only one thing sank in – Di, and Mum, somehow, already knew.

Olly appeared like a genie in the doorway, grabbed my hand and Lel's, took us into the lounge and sat us down. I felt so sick I kept gagging, while Lel was shaking uncontrollably. Olly knelt down in front of us and put his hands on our shoulders. I stared at him in the desperate hope that Lel was joking or perhaps I'd misunderstood, but his eyes told me everything. They were pained like never before and tears were falling down his face.

"Look at me, both of you. As a family we will get through this. Sally is okay now. She's found peace."

We agreed not to tell Mum; she was too ill to deal with such godawful news, the rest is a blur. I have no memory of saying goodbye to her. I don't recall leaving Lel. I do remember stopping at Amy's on the way home to be there for her in the moment. Amy and Lucy were close to Sal. She had put the pair of them through private school and was an influential part of their fatherless upbringing. Amy opened the door and took one look at my face.

"Oh God no, it's Mum, isn't it?"

I shook my head slowly. "It's not your mum, Ame."

"Oh no, Nana?"

"It's not Nana."

"Who is it then?"

Her eyes were pleading with me the same way they were that tragic day when I found her rummaging in the boot of Di's car. I so wasn't looking forward to saying what I was about to say next...

I don't remember the rest of the journey. I have no memory of telling my kids. I vaguely recall ringing Steve and him saying, 'not funny, Sian,' and hanging up, but I will always remember screaming 'Sally!' at the top of my lungs and falling to my knees in the back garden.

I lay in bed, sleep eluding me, staring at the ceiling, just staring and replaying her words. *I don't know what's going to happen, but whatever happens to me I want you to remember one thing – I love you very much, Heart,* and that eerily prophetic sentence when Di had her accident: *I've got some bad news, I need you to understand, it's bad, but it's not the worst.* She was saving the worst news for herself. Why didn't she ring me instead of doing that? Why, why, why, didn't she pick up the phone like she promised? In my peripheral vision a flash of white light kept zooming past, but every time I turned my head to catch it, it was gone. I didn't want to blink. When I blinked I saw Sally's galleried landing and her swinging from it. Never, ever again would she utter 'see you manana'. Sally had gone, and a massive part of me had died with her. All shall not be well.

My darker than dark thoughts were broken by Olly getting into bed.

"How could we have left Lel on her own?" I said.

"We didn't, Liz. Dot came round and told us she would stay with her. Remember?"

No, I didn't. "We're supposed to be flying to Canada Saturday."

"Oh, Liz."

"She's up there, Olly." I pointed at the ceiling. "I can see her the other side of it, pacing around with her hands on her head."

"What do you think she's saying?"

"I know what she's saying. I can hear her in my head, she keeps repeating "you don't understand," and she's pissed off because no one can hear. I can't stop visualising the galleried landing and her hanging from it."

"I don't think she did that."

"I can't imagine her doing that, she wasn't that brave."

"I get the feeling that however she did it, it was gentle."

"It doesn't make sense, does it? She told me she wouldn't do that and leave a black hole in the lives of her family. I think she's trying to get through to me Olly, I really do."

"So do I, and you know Sally, Liz, if there was a way to get through she would find it. We should go and see someone, like a clairvoyant or something."

"I didn't think you were into that stuff?"

"What choice do we have?"

Within two days of Sally's death Olly found a lovely, kind lady, Linda Monjack, in a neighbouring village and made an appointment for us to go.

"I've got a female here trying hard to come through to you both. She's talking about her funeral, I know this sounds silly, she's saying she hasn't had one yet," said Linda.

Wow. Impressive introduction.

"She's saying I was in such a muddle, now I've left such a muddle." She went on, "Looking at you is like looking at a younger version of this lady. She wasn't your mum but she was a mother figure she says. You and she were close – not in age, like this…"

Linda put her hands in a prayer position. Too choked to speak, I nodded in agreement. The next thing she said was unreal.

"What's happening to my throat?"

Her voice went croaky. She clasped her hands around her throat and craned her neck toward the heavens. "Sorry, you have to take this off me or I won't be able to carry on..." Her voice became so faint it literally disappeared.

She took a large sip of water and remained silent for a minute before continuing.

"Did she pass in tragic circumstances? Whatever happened affected her throat, her whole body jarred, there was an impact of some sort, yet she's telling me she was on her own."

She looked at us, confused. I went to speak, but she stopped me by putting her hand in the air. "No, don't tell me. She wants you to know she didn't suffer, it was all over very quick. This is going to sound odd, she's showing me stairs, was she found near stairs?"

Olly and I stared at each other, dumbfounded by everything Linda said.

"She's such a lovely energy this lady. She helped a lot of people when she was here, she was always there for them."

Yes she was, but no one helped her. Especially me. Hearing that was too much. I couldn't hold back any longer. Linda handed me a tissue and smiled at me affectionately.

"She loves you to bits, she's smiling now and showing me a photo of you and her, a head shot on a boat."

I knew that photo – Sal and me on a gondola in Venice when we visited Italy on our weekend off whilst working on *Musketeers*.

"Now she's in the air, she's showing me herself on an aeroplane. Did she travel a lot?"

I blew my nose and nodded.

"She's telling me she hadn't been well for a while. She was backwards and forwards to hospital and it made her tired, so did the tablets. She's showing me a capsule, red and white. She said it tipped her over the edge, she's saying, *One minute I was down there, the next minute I was over here.* They didn't get the medication right, if they had it would have helped her. She's saying two words, 'neglect' and 'irresponsibility'. The hospital let her go too soon and they won't want to be held accountable but they are. She's getting angry now, saying, *If I was down there I'd sort it.*"

I couldn't believe what I was hearing, yet I was strangely glad to be hearing it. It sounded exactly the sort of thing bossy Sal would say.

"She's telling me there's a picture of her holding a red rose?"

I wasn't sure. I turned to Olly. "It's on her computer desk top, the *Indiana Jones* crew one," he answered.

"She wants you to doctor it, blot the other people out and put it on her coffin. Can you do it?"

"I can try," said Olly.

"She's laughing." She smiled. "Saying now who's in a muddle?"

Linda continued, focusing her attention on Olly. "She's saying a big thank you to you. She's showing me you driving everyone around and saying *What would we do without him?* She's sending lots of love and says she would squeeze you, but you wouldn't feel it."

Olly's turn to be upset. He unashamedly shed a man tear.

"She realises she should have asked for help but she didn't know how and she's sorry people are hurting. She's saying she will continue to guide you in the right direction, like she did when she was here. She's showing me houses, saying you had plans, to do with houses."

Everything Linda said was on the nail. Sally loved *Sarah Beeny's Property Ladder*. It was her plan for us to buy houses together, renovate them and sell them on.

"She encouraged you to the hilt and always will. She's saying carry on with the plan, she will continue to help you both. I hope this has helped in some small way," Linda concluded.

Indeed it had. We thanked her for her words.

"One more thing," she said. "She's saying, *don't forget to talk to me and don't be sad.*"

"I'll try," I replied.

"Your sister has slipped away into the next room, she's behind the door, that's all death is."

We left Linda's temporarily lifted.

"I can't get over that, Olly."

"It was so specific, Liz. How could it not be Sal? It's all the proof I need."

"She didn't do it intentionally. I knew it. She would never do that to Dylan, she's hopelessly devoted to that boy. If she'd planned it, she would have left a note like John-boy."

"The message from Linda was her note."

I couldn't do that and leave a black hole in the lives of my family, Sally had said. She had promised, and Sally wasn't a liar, unlike Lel who told pointless lies. Everyone who knew Sally knew damn well she wouldn't promise something if she didn't mean it. None of it made sense, and none of it brought her back. *Que sera,* as she often said.

I stupidly didn't cancel Moves fitness that night. I only had two classes running now, and I couldn't keep letting my students down. Teri emailed everyone to inform them that my sister had passed away but class would be on as per usual.

On the way I got the collywobbles. I prayed no one would show. I half expected it. Who would want to face me knowing what Sally had done? But the exact opposite happened. So many people turned up that they were queueing to get in the door. The hall was jampacked. I sensed my nerves attempting to get the better of me but I was determined to keep a brave-face and not let grief win. Teri ogled me, concerned.

"No pressure, eh, Mum?"

To my surprise everyone was lovely, they didn't mention 'it' but they gave me cards and flowers. Trish, one of my long-term devoted students, plucked up the courage to raise the subject. She approached me and said, "I'm sorry about your sister, Liz, especially after doing so well."

"She was getting better. It doesn't make sense, does it, Trish?"

"No it doesn't, Liz, surviving the crash and coming out of her coma, at least she's not suffering anymore."

Of course, that's what they'd all assumed – Di! I didn't have the heart to tell her the truth. I didn't want to, I felt like a freak. Now I understood why Dad told people John-boy had died in a car accident. I spared Trish the humiliation and just agreed.

Summoning up some fake confidence, I jumped onto the stage. I could see Teri at the back of the class eyeballing me, but motor memory kicked in and took over. I learnt something that night: if you simulate happiness, it can take over and become real. Sally said to Linda "don't be sad," so I had to try, and it worked. Sal often came to my class and had a great time. I sensed the glow of her looking down on me, egging me on, and surprisingly, I enjoyed it.

Dave was baying for blood. The psychiatric hospital admitted that due to their own stupid incompetence nobody had bothered to go round to Sally's that fateful day after he had specifically told them he was going away. She might still be here if they had. I'd never heard my brother so distraught, ever.

"Liz, those bastards promised me they'd send someone to spend the day with Sal, I would never have gone away and left her if I'd known. What else didn't they get right?"

Sally's own words, 'neglect' and 'irresponsibility', were bang on. When I told Dave what Linda had said, that was it. Lel was instructed to make a list of Sal's medication, milligrams, dosage etc. For someone who noted everything from cups of tea to toilet trips per day, it was egg sucking. List lover Lel had already done it.

Suffice to say we didn't go to Canada. Thankfully I'd taken out insurance and they were happy to pay out provided I gave them a copy of the death certificate. I didn't want to do it, but Lel said if I didn't, she would, because it wasn't fair. I couldn't inflict that on her, so off I went to Sal's doctor to get a copy. There I sat, in the waiting room, possibly in the same chair my sister had sat in a week ago, all on her own, collecting her deadly medication. It was a wretchedly painful experience and I hated myself all the more for it.

The insurance company kindly pointed out that because I had taken the policy out after Sally's recorded death date, it wasn't valid. I tried to explain that she wasn't found until the following day. They were understanding and sorry to hear of my loss – however, I couldn't prove it wasn't premeditated so, unfortunately...

Arseholes. Two thousand five hundred dirty bits of paper down the drain. I didn't give a damn about the money. I cared more that they dared to suggest I did it on purpose. It made my blood boil so badly I replaced the image of me blowing up their offices with Sally, dimple-grinning about it.

I could hear her in my head laughing, and saying, "All shall be well, Heart."

Mike Roberts, the first ever technician to win a BAFTA for outstanding contribution to cinema, a good buddy of Sal's, passed away during the making of his last film, *Chocolat*. Following his death, Sal was a rock to his widow Eileen, and they bonded and became the greatest of friends. I was not looking forward to answering my phone one little bit when I saw her name on the screen. Eileen cried at me for ten minutes solid before she was able to construct a sentence.

"I can't believe it, Sian," she sobbed. "Not my Sal, she was full of life and so positive, please tell me it isn't true?"

She wasn't the only one shocked to the core. Stuntman Rocky Taylor, a long-time close friend of Sal's, also took the news very badly. Sally had been there for him following the most difficult time of his life after a stunt went horribly wrong on the set of *Death Wish 3*, almost costing him his life. They became more than close friends, and although it didn't last forever, the bond they had did. "Lovey, I spoke to Rock today," Lel, sighed. "He's torn apart."

Tributes came pouring in from around the globe. We were bombarded with messages from people who knew and loved Sally, and people who didn't. As I said in her bio, she was a mini celeb in her world. Friends, crew members, wannabees and well-known directors were shocked by Sally's 'suicide'. So much so that Dave and Dylan discussed the need for a memorial ceremony to set the record straight. I'm relieved to say that idea quickly went full circle. The catastrophic set of events which led to Sally's passing was not something any of us wanted or needed to be questioned about. Instead we did the complete polar opposite and arranged a close family service within a fortnight of her death.

Then, on the day of the funeral – as if the funeral wasn't rotten enough – Mum had another stroke and was rushed into hospital.

CHAPTER ELEVEN

House of Horrors

The wake, as expected with my family, turned into a brawl. There was no Sally (obviously) to lord over everybody, no fierce Di keeping Lel in check and no disapproving scrunch-faced mother. The key players were missing, and it seemed so wrong. Everyone drank far too much, and whoever had the brilliant idea that this was a good place to discuss whether Di should be told should have been shot. Dave was for it, flying the flag for Di's human rights. Steve was strongly against the idea. A disagreement between my two brothers, what a surprise. It was raucous, opinions were divided all over the place. Steve's angle was that it wasn't fair to dump that news on Di then leave her alone with a damaged brain trying to process it, but Dave, the new self-appointed head of the family, shot him down in flames. Di was to be told, end of story.

After the wake and copious amounts of strong black coffee, Olly chauffeured me and Lel to the hospital to visit Mum.

"Hello, my lovely," she smiled. "You look posh, have you been somewhere nice?"

"Yes, Mum," I lied, staring her straight in the eye, having just witnessed her eldest daughter being buried.

"Rene, you seem much better," Lel beamed.

"What am I doing here then?" she frowned.

Good point. Lel and I spoke to the doctor; he wanted to keep Mum in for the night to keep an eye on her, but once she'd had breakfast in the morning he was happy for her to go home.

And the award for best amateur dramatics goes to…

Me. Mum was fine, she wasn't dying. It was Sally who'd been dying, I just didn't see it.

One hospital down, one to go. It broke my heart watching Amy deliver the news to her mum. Di was inconsolable, banging her head on the pillow, shouting, "NO! NO! NO!" We tried to console her, but her arms were flailing, hitting us in the process. She cried herself into such a state the nurses had to sedate her until she had calmed down and was able to speak. "Sally not dead," she said, her big blue eyes darting back and forth from Amy to me. Amy, on the brink of tears, had to walk off. "Sally not dead," she persisted. "She here."

"When, Di?" I asked.

"Today."

"Today, as in, this today?"

She nodded.

"What was she doing, Di?"

"Crossword."

My family loved a brain-achingly impossible crossword, so that sounded feasible – enough for Amy to stop in her tracks and turn around.

"What was she wearing, Mum?"

"Dressing gown – slippers."

"What colour was the dressing gown, Di?" I asked.

"Blue."

"What colour were her slippers, Mum?" Amy asked.

"White."

Oh well, the brilliant idea of telling Di backfired anyway. Sally wasn't dead, to her. For the first time ever I felt strangely envious of Di's world. Believing Dad, John and Sally were alive was a much nicer place to be.

Back in the real world, a bereft, newly orphaned Dylan had the gruelling task of going to his mum's house to sort out her 'stuff'. "I had this great plan to stick post-it notes on everything," he said.

"How did that go, Dylan?"

"I um, went in the kitchen, picked up her gold handbag, then I um, put it back on the table."

He failed spectacularly. Bless him. They say the eyes are the window to the soul and Dylan's were so full of sorrow I felt actual physical pain in my heart when I looked at him.

"Do you want me and Olly to come with you?"

"Would you, Sian? I just can't do it."

I'd rather chop off my own leg with a blunt fork and roll around in salt and vinegar, but someone had to help him.

We drove through the automated private gates towards Sally's empty house of horrors and I had my first ever real panic attack. There was her black Mazda, still parked on the drive. I started hyperventilating so bad Olly had to stop the car and calm me down. After ten minutes' cognitive therapy I could breathe properly again. He told me to be an automaton, so I was. I pushed my emotions to one side and dug deep to find the strength to allow us to continue.

Walking through the front door was worse. The first thing to hit me was the stairs and the galleried landing, and in my mind, Sally hanging from it. I gawked at it fixated, until Dylan appeared from the kitchen and walked straight into my arms. We hugged and shook and cried and wouldn't let each other go for five minutes solid.

Surprisingly, he brought his newish girlfriend along to help. Not the nicest of dates I would imagine, hanging out with your bereft boyfriend and his grieving aunt at your dead potential mother-in-law's place where she took her own life. She said little, understandably, and spent the whole time standing around kind of frozen with a shell-shocked expression on her face. Poor thing, I felt sorry for her more than us.

Where to start in a five-bed house with a double garage?

My widely travelled sister had accumulated a lot of stuff in her sixty-four years on this earth. Antique furniture, rugs, china tea sets, art, objets d'art from around the globe, her gold Gucci handbag and a whole load of other designer bags for every occasion. Her precious oversized mirror she had especially imported from France. A thousand books, every script from everything she had ever worked on from *The Saint* to *Mamma Mia*. Don't even get me started on her jewellery and clothes.

I understood why Dylan's head had come off. Sally's biggest nemesis, 'stuff', a cause of great concern, was no longer her problem – it was ours. The whole thing was beyond upsetting, it was clear early on that Dylan and I were one hundred percent useless, so Olly took over the reins. His ingenious plan was to categorise: Keep. Sell. Charity. Dump.

Somehow, we muddled through. The contents of her bathroom, makeup, nail polish, face creams, perfume, toothbrush, everything, I swept straight into a black bin bag like the automaton Olly had asked me to be. The whole time all I could think about was Martin, the neighbour who had found her, and before I knew it, I was banging on his front door. He opened it, and when he saw it was me he quickly tried to shut the door in my face, so I stuck my foot in it. "Please, Martin," I begged. "Please talk to me."

"Leave me alone. I don't want any trouble."

I could see him panicking through the gap in the door. Resisting the overwhelming urge to kangaroo kick his door, I considered the consequences carefully before putting my foot in it, further. "I don't want trouble either, I've come to thank you," I lied.

"Thank me? I thought your family would hate me."

"Martin, open the door!" I pushed the door with a bit more force and he relented. Standing in front of me was a broken man. My frustration melted. Compelled, I put my arms around him and he cried. "What happened, can you talk me through it?"

He looked pained. "Do we have to do this?"

"Yes, we do."

"It will just upset you."

Did he actually say that? To me? I couldn't help but sigh and chuckle in equal measure. "Martin, I couldn't possibly be any more upset than I am."

"I'm sorry, I can't."

The thought of him knowing and not telling me was overpowering, and my composure cracked. "Please, Martin. I'm begging you. I will get on my knees if I have to." And I would have.

He heaved a sigh. "You really want to do this?"

"No, of course I don't, but I need to."

He sighed again. "Right, come on." He stepped outside and closed the front door.

"Where are we going?"

"I'm going to show you what happened."

We went into Sal's and he stood at the foot of the stairs, pointing to the turned balustrade halfway up. "One end of her dressing gown belt was tied to that and she was here like this." He laid on the stairs.

"She wasn't hanging from the landing?"

"No, nothing like that. She sat herself down, tied the other end round her neck and crept down the stairs gently like this." He gave me another physical demonstration.

Gently was how Olly had envisioned it. I felt strangely comforted by that.

"How do you know all this?"

"The police told me, after they'd dropped the charges."

"Charges?"

"Death by unnatural causes is a potential crime scene, and my fingerprints were everywhere."

I understood why Martin had been frightened when I knocked on his door. This kind man had a spare key to water Sal's plants while she was toing and froing between hospital and home. He'd gone to check on things as Dave had asked, and had the horrible experience of finding her.

"You were a potential murderer? Martin, I'm so sorry you had to go through this."

"That's all right. It wasn't pleasant but I'm glad it was me, not one of your family."

"When you found her, how did she look? What was she wearing?"

"She was lying on the stairs in her dressing gown and her slippers were placed neatly on the bottom step."

"What colour was her dressing gown?"

"Blue."

"Were they her gold slippers, the ones with the sequins on?"

"No, they were white."

Blue dressing gown. White slippers. I didn't know she had white slippers. Just as Di had described her. Bizarre. "What was her face like?"

"Her arms were by her side and she looked beautiful and very peaceful."

I wanted to believe that, I honestly did.

I was so engrossed in what he was saying I didn't see Dylan approaching. He'd been standing in the kitchen doorway and heard every word. Martin stumbled off the stairs and started apologising.

"Dylan it's my fault," I blurted. "I made him tell me."

"Good," Dylan held his hand out to Martin. "Thank you, my friend."

I wasn't expecting that. I thought I was the only one twisted enough to want the gory details. Apparently not. Such a great brave boy. A chip off the old block. I was proud of him on Sal's behalf.

As harrowing experiences go, eleven out of ten. Dylan and I were constantly distracted by painful memorabilia and the resulting meltdowns, but we picked ourselves up like automatons. For five days and nights solid we kept at it, broken, exhausted, until all of Sally's 'stuff' was gone. Dylan closed the door to his mum's house for the last time and we drove away following the big yellow storage lorry. Not one of us looked back.

CHAPTER TWELVE

Happy birthday, Mum

It became apparent that Di had reached a plateau and didn't appear to be getting any better. Not at Oaktree, anyhow. I don't know what I expected – something more than Connect Four and potting plants, I suppose. The good nurse/bad nurse ratio was erring on the side of bad. Di refused physio and they didn't push it. Her decision, apparently. Red tape and human rights gone bonkers, more like. The nappy ratio (or more appropriately pad) was a fiasco too. I thought Lucy was joking when she told me Di was allowed four a day, bearing in mind toilet problems was an area needing extra care because of her brain injury. I offered to buy them for her, but preferential treatment was against their equal rights policy.

At the next 'Life of Di' meeting Amy raised the nappy subject and also queried the whereabouts of Di's sleep system, which had mysteriously disappeared. It was an essential piece of equipment tailor-made to keep Di's body as pain free as possible through the night. The head nurse explained it had gone missing in the laundry. Oh, that's all right then. Sarcasm, the easiest form of wit, when you're beyond bereft and suffering mood swings ranging from bad to *really* fricking bad. I had to say it: "You mean, like a sock?"

She responded by giving me a curt smile. "It was soiled anyway."

We all knew why it was soiled, with a nappy ration in place. Amy and I stared at each other.

"Did you not think to replace it?" Amy enquired.

"Not an option I'm afraid, they're very expensive."

I looked at Amy's reddening face, I could see what was coming. She lunged across the table. "Are you android, or are you human?" She tapped her on the glasses repeatedly. "If you think I will give up because you say no about something my mum needs I'm going to appeal, and appeal again, until she gets it, so you might as well say yes now. Put that in the minutes of your meeting!"

That was the final nail in the Oaktree coffin. Majorly disgruntled Amy and Lucy got onto Headway, the brain injury association, and lodged an official complaint.

It's a strange sensation, buying a birthday card for someone and wondering if it will be their last. I meandered around Tesco trying to muster the enthusiasm to get Mum a present.

Having a stinking cold didn't help. She hated flowers, so that was out. She enjoyed a good autobiography, but picking the right subject was a challenge, Mum had strong likes and dislikes. As I said in her bio, she either loved you or hated you. If you chose wrong, being a bookworm she couldn't help but read it, which gave her more ammo to gripe about whomever afterwards. Literary self-harm, Steve called it.

They didn't have any crystallized ginger, and the chocolates looked naff, so they were a no go. My mind flashed back to the time I got her an expensive box. I ordered them early and the temptation was too much. Before I knew it, I had one, two then three. By the time I'd finished I'd dented half the box, I rang to order some more, but they were out of stock, so, I filled the empty sections with pink cotton wool balls. I even went as far as modifying the box with a gold pen: it read, 'Assorted Belgian chocolates and cotton wool balls'. I knew it would tickle Mum's wicked sense of humour. When she opened her present we were both in stitches.

"You soppy date, Lizbeth," she wheeze-laughed.

Those were the days. Not funny this time. I'd spent far too long sneezing in Tesco so I gave up on the present and grabbed a 'Special Mum' card, plus one for Joe, who was preparing to take his driving test. Tempting fate possibly, but I knew he would pass first time, unlike Dean. The day was slipping away, I needed to get my skates on. I dashed home, grabbed some bits and scribbled on the cards before shoving them at Olly to add his name.

"Wow." He eyed my spider-scrawl handwriting up and down. "I can almost see the impatience of the pen."

"I'm in a rush."

"I would suggest you're one step away from throwing the pen at the card and hoping it makes a mark, Beak."

November 2009. Mum was fast asleep in bed and snoring her head off when I got there. Beside her, doing the crossword, Steve.

"Sian darling, what a lovely surprise, you look shit."

My unshaven brother's delighted face quickly morphed into grief-stricken. As a family, it was impossible for any of us to greet each other and not collapse with the overpowering weight of Sally's loss, the worry of Mum and the ongoing intravenous burden of Di. He jumped up and gave me one of his special swaying cuddles, I felt him trembling. I grabbed a chair and parked it next to Mum, who was back in hospital following another funny turn.

"How long's she been asleep?" I asked, before blowing my bunged-up nose.

"All morning," he sighed, grabbing my snotty tissue and wiping his teary eyes. "Sal's still warm in the ground and now this. I can't get my head around any of it, Sian. If only she hadn't started taking those antidepressants."

"Don't go there, Steve."

"I fucking hope they rot in hell, the pond life who's in charge of pills at that shameful place."

"Have you seen Di lately?"

"No, Sian. I know everyone thinks I'm a bastard but I

can't handle seeing her."

"They don't. I don't."

"Dave does. Lel told me."

"Don't listen to Lel, she loves to wind you up." I laughed, hoping to hear Steve cackle. He didn't cackle, far from it.

"No human being should live like that. Di has no quality of life. Every time I see her, I want to put a pillow over her face. It kills me, Sian."

I couldn't argue. I understood where he was coming from. Time to change the subject. "What you been up to?"

"Paying my respects to Sal – my way."

"Thought as much." The newspaper was shaking, his hands were so bad.

"Yeah DTs have got me good and proper, Sian."

"Lel told me you've been on a bender."

"She can talk, fucking knocking back bottle after bottle of vodka night every night."

"Can you blame her for having a drink in the evening after Mum's gone to bed? After everything this family is going through?"

"She's supposed to be looking after Mum. I'm not happy about it, Sian."

"Why don't you look after Mum then?"

He was quick to shoot me down. "I can't. You know I can't."

"Neither can I, Steve, so what's the alternative? A care home, like Di, where no one cares?"

"Who doesn't care?" asked Mum, eyes wide open.

"MUM!" we both cried. "Happy birthday." We kissed

her on the head in turn.

Perfect timing. In walked Lel carrying a bunch of flowers. "Happy birthday, Rene." She scanned the sparse room aimlessly searching for a vase.

Mum scrunched her face. "What the bleeding hell did you get them for?"

"They're from Dave, don't be so ungrateful."

Mum rolled her eyes. "Why? Am I dying or something?"

"On the contrary, you old duffer, what do you think this is?" She held up Mum's overnight bag. "I'm taking you home."

Steve pulled a face and waved his hand in front of his nose. "Ugh, Lel, did you have to?"

"What?" she said, all innocent.

"SBV," replied Steve, still waving his hand in disgust.

"I can't help it, I had a dodgy Chinese last night. I'm sure it was the shitakes."

"Shit aches!" Steve rolled his head back and let rip his best cackle. "You need a pony, Lel."

"At least I don't fart the National Anthem," she said sulkily.

I laughed. "I'm so glad I can't breathe."

The door creaked open and the nurse walked in. Lel spun around and gave her a big smile. "Hiya, I'm Lesley, I called this morning. I've come to take my mum home."

Confused, the nurse beckoned us outside. Steve raised a hand opting to stay with Mum. She closed the door and took us to one side. "Your mother is on intravenous steroids, which is why she seems compos mentis, she won't be going anywhere today, I'm afraid."

Lel looked equally confused. "Every day I come here, every day I bring her clothes, every day you say Mum can go home tomorrow. This morning I thought, I won't take Mum's bag, I'll ring first, and you said Mum was good to go."

"No I didn't," replied Nurse Terse.

"Someone did," Lel retorted.

"I don't know who you spoke to but they were wrong."

"What is going on with this place?" Agitated, Lel threw her arms into the air and turned to me for support. "This is a fucking joke, Sian."

I felt the same. Two weeks ago we buried my sister, we were raw and prone to outbursts of anger, but this wasn't getting us anywhere. I took over and tried to keep things on the level.

"Let's move on from this pathetic conversation shall we. What do you mean, my mum *seems* compos mentis?"

"It's the steroids, your mothers on a high dose, they give a temporary sense of lucidity, she is actually very ill."

"So, whoever told my sister my mum was fine was wrong, and *you're* saying my mum's not well enough to go home?"

"No, unfortunately not, her blood test results came back this morning."

Lel cursed under her breath. "Come on then, out with it, what are you not saying?"

The nurse didn't beat around the bush or say it nicely. "I'm sorry to have to tell you this, but the test results show your mother has a cancerous tumour in her brain."

Happy birthday Mum...

Lel and I gawped at each other like lemons. That sentence did not register. This was not happening. Not my brave mum. I felt nothing. Lel, the same. Somewhere inside us underneath the numb, we were heartbroken children, devastated by that thunderbolt, but there was no room in our heads or hearts for any more grief. I tutted as if I'd been mildly inconvenienced by hearing such news. Lel's response was no better.

"Great. Now what?"

The nurse stared at us like we were the worst people, then continued her onslaught. "The answer is no, your mother won't be going home, she won't be going anywhere other than to a hospice, you'll have to get your own dinner tonight, I'm afraid."

That was the moment we looked at each other and laughed out loud like deranged lunatics – the preferable alternative to punching her in the face. Poor Lel. One minute she was going home with Mum, the next she was Macaulay Culkin. How life can change in a moment.

The super-supportive Headway people visited Di and assessed the situation. To be fair, Oaktree were doing their best within their limited resources, but their best wasn't enough. Di seemed to outgrow everywhere. To say her unique condition was challenging was putting it mildly. They concluded that her being there was detrimental to her needs and recommended a residential care home in Conwy County whose Avon unit claimed to do everything humanly possible to empower brain-injured patients to live their lives as freely and as fully as they chose.

We went to check it out and were impressed. It was nice, relaxed and casual. The manager was lovely, and it was a stone's throw from Amy's so she could visit Di any time of day or night with ease. A welcome break from trawling up and down the tiresome A470 from North to South Wales, passing the painful scene of Di's crash every time. It wasn't easy for Amy with little Meg and Sonny, her mum's horse, to look after. It was also nearer Steve's, so that would be interesting. It sounded perfect. Having only a handful of patients they were able to give Di a place immediately – and they didn't have a nappy ration. Yay!

Visiting Di at the Avon unit then on to the hospice to visit Mum became the new norm. Lel spent most of her waking hours going backwards and forwards between the two. I was worried about her, with her escalating COPD. Her smoking/drinking levels had no limits, especially with no Mum, no Sal and no Di keeping her in check. I was concerned about Steve too; he had spent a lot of his alcohol-free time at Mum's watching the snooker with her. She was an intrinsic part of his sobriety.

The three of us sat beside a sleeping Di. Lel was alternating puffs between her inhaler and the electronic cigarette I bought her, while Steve and I engaged in trivial conversation.

"My car's clocked two hundred and fifty thousand miles."

"Jesus Christ, Sian, you've been to the moon." Steve opened his eyes woefully wide.

"More like hell."

"Tell me about it," spluttered Lel, coughing/puffing her e-cig simultaneously.

"How are you getting on with that thing?" I asked her.

"Yeah," she replied.

"She hates it," said Steve.

"How long does the bus take, Steve?" I asked.

"About an hour, by the time they've gone round the houses, then half an hour on to Di's. Can't not, can I, when I've got a free bus pass, two for the price of one."

"How come you've got a free bus pass?"

"Because he's a registered alcoholic," Lel answered on his behalf.

"It's true. I admit to my sins, unlike you, eh, Lelly Bertus?" retorted Steve.

"Fuck off, Bean," Lel snapped.

Steve changed the subject. "I've been coming here every day, and it's got me thinking, we should try to raise the money and take Di to Dignitas."

"Digny what?" I asked.

"It's a place in Switzerland. They call it assisted suicide. It's basically euthanasia, it's legal over there. It's the humane thing to do, Sian. This country is bullshit, Di has no quality of life. You wouldn't treat a dog like this."

"It costs thousands, Bean," said Lel. "You might as well put a pillow over her head, it's a lot cheaper."

"Don't tempt me, Lel."

Mum was becoming increasingly frail, with every visit potentially the last. How nice it would be if Mum didn't die close to Sal and we could get Christmas out of the way and creep into a new year and pretend their deaths were far apart. At least Mum survived her birthday, something to be grateful for, I guess. We knew it was coming; it was just a matter of when. Sometimes she was compos mentis most of the time she slept. Mum frequently asked why Sal hadn't been, but Lel, Dave, Steve and I made a pact to say she was working away on a film and sent her love. It was nothing out of the ordinary, although she eyed me suspiciously when I said it. Mum had a sixth sense. She knew – I knew she knew – something wasn't right. And that's precisely why she didn't push it. Instead she would stare at me with sad eyes, allowing me to change the subject, usually on to Di and more lies about how well she was doing.

December 2009. One month after Mum's eighty-seventh birthday, I got home from visiting her and had an overwhelming urge to call, probably because she had slept the whole time I was there. Lel was going up in the evening and she promised to ring as soon as she got there if Mum was awake. As promised, my phone rang. I answered it and heard my mum's little voice say, "Hello my lovely, Lizbeth, tell me the truth, am I dying?"

"No, Mum, you had a funny turn."

"Why the bleeding hell am I still in here?"

"They need to get your strength up a bit, then you can go home."

"You don't have to lie to me, Lizbeth."

It brought a lump to my throat hearing that. Mum wasn't silly. She sighed her usual sigh but it was weak. "When am I going to see you, my lovely?" She sounded so delicate.

"Tomorrow, Mum. Promise I'll come tomorrow," I said, fighting back my tears.

CHAPTER THIRTEEN

Goodbye my friend

I had taken to turning my phone off at night, ever since Lel's "where did they find her" conversation with Dave and the resulting middle of the night calls from Steve dealing with grief – his way. For some reason this night I didn't, and it rang at the unearthly hour of seven am.

I turned to Olly. "It's Lel." He knew, and I knew, exactly why she was ringing. I stared at my phone, not wanting to answer, so I could have a few more seconds without knowing...

"Answer it, Liz – and brace yourself."

Bracing myself, I answered. "Lel, if you're going to say it, please don't, just tell me when?"

"Half an hour ago."

I couldn't speak straight away. I took a deep breath in,

swallowed my bomb of pain and chokingly admitted, "I promised I'd come and see her today."

"Oh, Sian, sorry – waking you up." Lel's voice was wobbling so much she could barely string a sentence together. "I know you said – it's just – after a few hours..."

"Ten minutes and I'll be on my way."

I did my famous blurting to Dean again. He was working on location locally and stayed the night. He was sleeping peacefully, blissfully unaware until I bowled into his room and came out with it: "Dean, Nana died."

He put the pillow over his head. "I don't want to hear it," he answered through sleep.

I swished a flannel over my face, threw on some clothes and walked into the kitchen. Olly handed me a cup of tea and thrust a banana in my face.

"It's a long journey, so just eat it please."

I forced myself to eat it, and it was like trying to digest a cushion. As I was struggling to cram it down, Dean came bursting into the room crying his eyes out, arms outstretched, straight into mine. "Oh God, Nana, I thought I was dreaming. Mum, I'm so sorry."

I was about to make the dreaded call to Teri when a text came through from her. I hoped it was the umbilical cord doing its usual text-each-simultaneously thing, not a case of bad news travelling fast. Apprehensive, I opened it – it read;

If bread has a little bit of mould on it, can I still eat it... toasted?

My right-hand woman insisted on coming with me, so I

picked her and Ella up on the way. Teri cried most of the way. Me? Automaton – until we pulled into Eryri car park and I saw my knuckle-cracking sister coming towards us. Hugging and crying; a normal occurrence these days.

"Do you want me to come in with you, Lovey?" she offered.

I won't lie, I was petrified and didn't relish the idea of entering Mum's room alone. Lel, my new big sister, held my hand and pushed open the door. There she was, my sweet little mum. My best friend. On her back. Motionless. Stiff. Her hair brushed back; she wouldn't have liked that. I walked over to her. Her skin was white and waxy and her eyes mostly closed but for a sliver. In the sliver, her irises were like marbles; there was no life in them. That's when it dawned on me. She was never going to open her eyes or smile or laugh her long silent laugh or scrunch her face like Wilfrid Brambell ever again. I threw myself across her, held on like I was never going to let her go, and cried uncontrollably.

"Lovey, let's go outside and get you some air – Sian, come on."

I was vaguely aware of Lel talking *at* me but I was glued to Mum. I stayed there for ages wallowing, until I heard Mum's voice in my head softly say, *Come on, my lovely, that's enough.* I froze. How stupid, clinging onto a dead body, Mum would hate it. Reluctantly, I let her go.

On the way home we called in to see Di. There were no family discussions this time about whether to tell her;

it was an unspoken, resounding no. I was worried eleven-month-old Ella would cry when she set eyes on Di, but to my amazement she did the opposite. Di reached out, and Ella did the same and gave her a big sloppy baby kiss. She cooed at Di lovingly and spoke gobbledegook to her.

"Beautiful," gushed Di.

The day before - the day before Christmas Eve, the day of Mum's funeral, also the day Dave found out his mother hated flowers. Bummer of a time of year. Christmas had been tinged with sadness for me ever since Dad passed a week after it, plus Boxing Day was his birthday, and now this. Did I say I felt like a freak? Understatement – cursed, more like. Two funerals two months apart, two of the most important people in my life AND my first Christmas Day without Sal. For those reasons I was determined to have a glass half full best Christmas Day ever. Today, the glass was half empty and I had the double burden of stressing about Joe. I couldn't bear for his first driving experience to be all that way on his own. It wasn't because I didn't have confidence in him, I didn't have confidence, full stop. I tried using the old "let's car share, it makes more sense" ploy; it failed. He reminded me of me, back in the day and my Fiat Oxo Cube, as Dave called it. Independent Joe was itching to drive and having none of it and off he went in his bang-bang rusty Peugeot.

It didn't help Dean calling him 'accident pro Joe' because he was such a professional at it, and reminding me of the time he ran into a metal post at school head first and knocked himself out. He lost so much blood his teacher had to have a week off with shock. Another time he got mugged and hit over the head with a baseball bat. Then there was the night he broke his jaw and had to have a metal plate put in. And whilst working at the Co-op he was accosted by an axe-wielding maniac demanding cigarettes. Joe unintentionally disarmed the masked intruder by asking which brand he smoked – funny, looking back. Being eight years younger than Dean the pair of us did tend to wrap him in cotton wool – a bit. I crossed my heart, my fingers and my toes for Joe to drive safely and not be like his non-accident-pro big brother who had two crashes in the first week after passing his test.

As always there had to be a funeral fiasco with my family. Eight months pregnant Lucy rang, saying she had got halfway and was having contractions. It reminded me of the time I was pregnant with Joe and had to drive myself to hospital when my waters broke because his father was over the limit. I'm surprised I got there intact – my feet were sliding all over the pedals. Poor Lulu. She was in such a fluster about being late I gave her the permission she needed to turn around and go home. It brought back the memory of Uncle John's funeral fiasco too. Sally and Di arrived late, as did Uncle John because they crashed into his hearse on the way and had to exchange details with the undertaker. I'll never forget that day. Everyone clapped as the dented hearse arrived with red-faced Sally and Di being towed by the RAC behind it.

I was dreading it when we pulled up outside Mum's church. To my horror, Joe was there. In one piece luckily, the bugger. Dave's children were next to arrive: Jo-Jo, Fraser, David Jnr and Freddie, on time, immaculately groomed and immaculately mannered. A testament to their dad's good-to-be-around-in-a-crisis character. Such mini-me pillars of strength. My brother's kids. One word: gorgeous. I loved those four little sparks of life.

My grief was thwarted upon seeing them and the surprising turnout of people. Loads of sad Welsh faces I didn't recognise had come to pay their respects to the London lady. My sweet little mum, she was loved by many. Outside immediate family, cousins Mig, Hugh, and his wife, Sue were there. My dad's lovely nephew and niece who I only saw at funerals or hospitals for the brain-injured.

Dave's eulogy for Mum was perfect. We laughed, we cried. Mostly cried. The boys – Dylan, Dean, Fraser, Joe and Olly – were pallbearers. They carried Mum's coffin to Lel's choice of song; *One Day like This* by Elbow. What a tear jerker, those lyrics...

Drinking in the morning sun... Lel – so apt.
What made me behave that way... Mum? I thought.
Using words I never say... Like duffer – perhaps.

Music, it's a killer...

Watching the boys carry Mum's coffin took me straight

back to that unusually hot, sunny October day eight weeks before. Sally was laid to rest in a tiny church snuggling in the valleys encompassed by the breathtakingly beautiful icing-sugar mountains of Snowdonia. The boys did exactly the same thing to *Every Grain of Sand* by her idol, Bob Dylan. Her favourite song and so heartrending, particularly these lines…

In the time of my confession, in the hour of my deepest need

When the pool of tears beneath my feet flood every newborn seed

There's a dyin' voice within me reaching out somewhere

Toiling in the danger and in the morals of despair

Don't have the inclination to look back on any mistake

Like Cain, I now behold this chain of events that I must break

In the fury of the moment I can see the Master's hand
…

I have gone from rags to riches in the sorrow of the night
…

In the bitter dance of loneliness fading into space
…

Sometimes I turn, there's someone there, other times it's only me

I am hanging in the balance of the reality of man

Like every sparrow falling, like every grain of sand

Hanging in the balance... Dylan's painfully apt choice of music for his mum. I seriously doubt I will be able to listen to it ever again.

Sal's little angel, Nirvana, drew a picture of herself riding a scooter balancing with one leg out and placed it on top of the coffin, and Dylan's heart-wrenchingly long eulogy about her being a mother *and* a father; too painful to repeat. Sally's passing was so fresh I honestly had no idea if I was grieving for her or Mum or both. When you're already at grief's rock bottom, you can't go any lower.

Christmas Day started well, once I'd gotten over my bout of 'ifs'. Ready to bite you on the bum with no warning. If I could go back in time and be the person I am today and not the coward I was two months ago, I could have saved Sal. My fear of mental health was a dot compared to the overwhelming longing to have her back and the overpowering torture I was suffering now. If only I'd realised last Christmas with Sal and Mum was *the* last Christmas, if, if, if... futile. One of grief's favourite words. I pushed it out of my mind. It helped that there were plenty of distractions: food, music, Joe, Teri, Dan, and Ella's first Christmas, and the need to make it special for Dylan, who came without his mum. Ever since Sally, whenever I set eyes upon that boy my heart physically hurt. Fortunately, we were blessed with Dean's company. I thought my big present under the tree was from Ella until I read the gift tag. Despite seemingly wrapped by a one-year-old, it was from twenty-five-year-old Dean. It made the day.

Every time I felt like crying I drank more Bucks fizz. Grief and alcohol, what a jolly euphoric cocktail. We joked about Mum's shock when she arrived at the pearly gates to be greeted by Sally and saying, "What the bleeding hell are you doing here?"

It was going swimmingly until I opened my present from Teri. Unbeknown to me, in cahoots with Lel, she had had Mum's rose quartz crystal heart ring, the one I loved but was too scared to ask for, put onto to a silver chain. Luckily it was close to midnight so I slunk off before I turned into a pumpkin. My borrowed happiness thanks to Bucks fizz had worn off and left me wallowing in self-pity.

I had Mum's ring, but the hand it had lived on had gone. All those times I never answered the phone because I was busy and forgot to ring her back. Things which seemed so unimportant suddenly seemed *so* important. I didn't care enough and it was too late to change that. Mum never ran out of care; if I had the slightest cold, she'd be there, standing over me with a blanket and a chicken Cup-a-soup. My unsurmountable problems shrivelled into tiny botheration's when I shared them with her. Just by laughing her long wheeze, or rolling her eyes then scrunching her face, she had the power to belittle them. Mum had a knack for dishing out one-liners which stuck like superglue. *You look like you're going to a bleeding funeral. The sights you see when you ain't got a gun. Until the next time.* Classic Rene. 'You've got a rocky road ahead of you my lovely,' she said, when I started my difficult journey as a single parent. I had a rocky road ahead of me now. Yes, we were expecting it, including Mum, she was ready, it's what happens – life is death, doesn't stop the heartache though.

I'll never forget her response when I caught her having a sneaky smoke in bed once.

"You do realise you could burn to death?" I said, trying my best to shock her.

"Ooh Lizbeth, what a lovely warm way to go," she smiled.

My battle-weary wise old Mum, she was unbreakable…

One day those wonderful memories would replace the heartache, but not today. I squeezed her ring hard and gripped it tight to my chest.

I cried myself to sleep.

Mum & Dad's wedding, 1944. The black and white days

Olly Flower and me

My Dean   Teri and our superhero Dan

John-boy, and looking uncannily like his uncle, my Joe

Beautifully different Princess Di

Big kid Lel and bubba Ella

Sal having Chianti with
Sir Anthony Hopkins

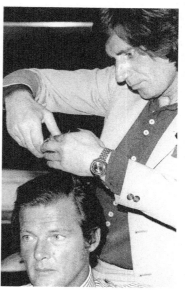

Mike, turning Roger Moore
into James Bond

Dave & Sara's wedding, 2008. The last pic of us all together as a happy family. Top row, left to right: Olly, Lel, Frazer, Me, Dave, Princess Di, David Jnr, nutty goon Steve. Bottom row: mini-me niece Jo, Mum, Sal, Freddie.

Cheeky Lel up close and personal with McCloud before she got the sack

Nutty goon Steve

Lucy, aka poor Lulu

Feisty redhead Amy with little Meg

Boom-boom DB gets a second BAFTA

A rare shot of the old duffer
having a cuppa

The sporadic makeup days. Me with Sir Alan Parker on the set of *Evita*

Sal on the set of *The Three Musketeers* with
Kiefer Sutherland & Chris O'Donnell

Sisters – left to right Me, Lel, Sal and Di

Sue Roderick (Cassie), Mum and Sara (Menna)

Dylan and the love of his life Sarah in happier times

Joe on the set of *The Monuments Men* with Bill Murray

Starry-eyed me, with Charlie's Angel Farrah Fawcett

My all-time favourite pic of Sally Sunshine in Skopelos
while filming *Mamma Mia*

CHAPTER FOURTEEN

Groundhog Day

Happy New Year. Actually, drop the happy, call it New Year. Olly got made redundant from the media firm he worked for. Not the most promising start. It should have been the end of the world, but I couldn't give a flying toss. He was too talented for them anyway. Death does that, puts things into perspective, nothing compares to the loss of loved ones. The mother in me was just about coping. Dealing with the everyday issues that come with having kids – automaton. On a deeply personal level the 'me' who was me was lost. It's an eerie paradox; surrounded by people yet feeling so alone, outwardly smiling whilst my insides were screaming. I felt guilty for not wanting to socialise, celebrate, or go places and be normal. My self-reproach served no purpose, it just added to my grief. Every day as dull as the one before. Not living but existing. Eating to stay alive. No joy in me, only darkness and pain. Another massive part of me had died and I didn't know how I was going to live in this strange new world but I would, somehow, because I had to, for Olly, my children and our new addition, Ella.

Many moons ago, when I split with my ex, I was down in the dumps and confided in my mum. She rang the next day, expecting me to sound more positive. I confessed; I still felt low. "You'll be fine tomorrow," she said cheerfully, willing me to feel better, but it wasn't happening. The next day I still felt rubbish and the next and the next. After several days she said, "This needs to stop now, my lovely."

"I can't help it!" It got my back up. My own mother void of emotion in my hour of need. The brave London lady who made us all; a proper, real, say-it-as-it-is, bulletproof Cockney with a heart of pure gold, said it as it was. "Don't go down that road, my love. If you do it's an awful long way back."

A mental roadblock appeared in my head and stopped me in my pessimistic tracks. Another superglue saying, and I knew why she was saying it. Mum had been down that road. There and then, I pulled my socks up and vowed never to do the same, no matter what life threw at me. Now, in my current frame of mind, my feet were hovering dangerously close to that road. The same road Sally went down – all the way to the end.

ECT had wiped Mum's memory of her dark days, but it had also taken the good ones with it. Birthdays, holidays, the multiple times she took me to Chessington Zoo – she didn't remember any of it.

"I often wonder what damage I've done to my children," she once said to me.

"Which children?" I asked.

"Steven, John-boy..."

"I had the same mother and I'm not an alcoholic or taking drugs."

She thanked me for that, and smiled at me with sad eyes, but she didn't cry. She couldn't cry. Another damaging side-effect of ECT.

Good job I wasn't a gambler like Mum. I would have put money on Di being first to go, given her hanging onto life by a thread. Runner up? Steve, one hundred percent. Mum was saving up for it. When the Band of Hope lady knocked on her door one time she said to me, 'Take the money out of Steven's funeral fund.' Did make me laugh. I thought she had Green Shield Stamps in that battered little red tin in her bedroom locker.

Next, I would say Lel. Her lifestyle was slowly knocking on the door of Steve's, plus she was full-time smoking again with the added bonus of COPD, reserving herself a seat on death row. But life is strange, and here they both were with me and boom-boom DB, surviving his own near-death experience, battling through the last eighteen months of hell, facing a new year with no Mum, no Sally and half a Di.

On a brighter note, Lucy gave birth to a little boy she named Dylan, after Sally's Dylan, after Bob Dylan. I asked her how Di had taken the news. She said, "Sian, she thinks she's had a baby."

Bless Princess Di. She did make us laugh at times.

On a not-so-brighter note, Amy and Lucy were concerned that the Avon unit was showing signs of being not all as it seemed. Here we go again. Again. "I can't put my finger on it, Sian," said Amy. "She's drowsy a lot of the time. Lu reckons they're drugging her."

I expressed those concerns to Dave.

"I can't get there, I'm snowed under prepping for this movie and having my colostomy reversal soon. I'll look into it and write a letter of complaint to the area manager, baby sis."

After a funeral everyone goes back to living their lives, but the harsh reality is, it's just the beginning. The Job Centre woman stared at Olly like he was barmy for saying he was a music producer. Always eager to help, our superhero, Teri's Dan-the-man-with-the-van, saved the day by getting Olly a job on his building site. I increased my hours and buried myself in chocolate bars and we were able to put food on the table... to stay alive... to put food on the table... Groundhog Day every single day. Why do we have to eat? I loved cooking when I had all the time in the world as a housewife, but now my kids had dwindled to fussy eater Joe at home, as a working mum cooking was just another chore to add to the list of dreary chores. Dean was jet-setting off to Belfast to prep for *Game of Thrones*, and Teri was becoming increasingly independent as a new mum. Steve had predicted that it would be the making of her, and he was right. Joe was driving himself to college and practically lived in his car. He was officially old enough to be thrown from the nest. I didn't envisage a problem with Joe. He'd been striving to fly ever since I gave birth and he flew out like Superman. Mind you, it didn't stop him dishing out contrary comments like, "Ever since I turned eighteen everyone keeps treating me like an adult!"

Empty-nest syndrome was looming with the added perk of being nobody's child. I had no Mum and no Sally to turn to. My hierarchy had gone. I was officially an orphan. And I was menopausal. Life as I knew it had disintegrated. No more Mum medicine. No more jam tarts, lemon slices and cups of tea. No more watching *Shut the Box* with her, Mum's say-it-as-it-is name for *Deal or No Deal*. I missed her big long sighs, her rolling eyes and her scrunched-up little face terribly. The sound of my phone not ringing and hearing Mum's voice say, "No, I won't leave a bloody message after the tone." There was one consolation: sad as it was, Mum and Sal were together, floating around in the bloody blue sky above the bloody grey one. Grief for Mum led seamlessly onto grief for Sally.

No more *Sally and Joe* show. No more duck eggs. No more drinking wine from cut glass crystal. No more Sally belting out G4's *I'm a creep, I'm a weirdo* at the top of her voice. No more stories. Sally's tales of her travels and behind the scenes stories of famous people, she told with great gusto, sound effects and everything, exactly like Dad, except Sally's stories were real. The moat disaster on *Willow* when Val Kilmer had to pull her out, a terrific tale. It was pitch black as she wandered off to find the Portaloo. "I was walking through a field, then suddenly I was doing breast stroke." She didn't just tell it, she animated it. Vintage.

She had dinner with Michael Caine, and Ronnie Biggs while he was in exile in Rio de Janeiro, and I loved the Sir David Niven story. He invited Sal to his hotel suite to have tea. A true English gentleman, polite and softly spoken, she said. They were having a delightful natter engrossed in the subject of life and death until someone knocked on his door and started talking shop. Sal was impressed at how gracefully he handled the intrusion into his personal time, not baulking as a lot of artists might have. She eavesdropped their conversation, in awe of his impeccable manners. When he eventually closed the door he turned round to face her, smiled and said, "Sorry about that fucking parasite, darling".

Then there was the evening she had with (amongst others) the Duchess of York. Sarah Ferguson was all airs and graces until they ended up in the toilet because she drank too much. After throwing up she begged Sal for a cigarette and, while smoking and hiccoughing and slurring, whinged on about how much the royals, quote: "Do my fucking head in".

On *Braveheart* Mel Gibson was dazzled by my sister; he didn't know what he would do without her, Sal was so good she could direct the film on her own, he told her. I answered the phone to him once or twice, so did Mum. I heard her say, "Mel who?" As if that wasn't bad enough, he went on to explain who he was, can you believe. I recoiled in the background listening to Mum say, 'Yes love, I did see you in Hamlet. I have to say, I preferred the Shakespeare version myself.' Mother, what was she like?

The night Sally met Omar Sharif at the Ritz in London, her husband Mike and Omar were waiting at the foot of the stairs as she glided elegantly down. She was wearing uncomfortably high heels in a desperate effort to impress and one of them got hooked in her flowing dress. The resulting tumble was the kind which goes on and it eventually landed her at the bottom of the stairs at Omar's feet. Hysterical, Mike said, "Omar, meet the wife". Omar helped her up, kissed the back of her hand, smiled politely, and in his thick French accent said, "Sally, my dear, never before have I seen such a *grande entrée*".

The festival in India was one of my favourites. Outside her hotel locals were dancing around a humungous fire and she figured it might be fun to join them. There was she, eccentric Sal, happily dancing the night away until the culture shocking moment she saw a tiny charred arm fall out of the fire. Turned out it wasn't their bonfire night but a grisly pile of dead burning children she was celebrating. Ah, so many anecdotes, I could go on all day...

Sally's storytelling was captivating to listen to; she was so good at it. Not any more. Sally's memories were now my memories. We human *beans* (as baby Dean used to call them) take everything for granted, you never know what you've got until it's gone, and they're just clichés, until they happen to you.

I didn't care much for this lonely new world. Thank God for the miniscule mercy of hands-free kits. I rang Joe to see if he wanted to come and see Di with me, but he was busy adulting.

"Sorry, Mum, I've got stuff to do, isn't it Ella's birthday soon? How old will she be?"

"You tell me."

"Um, one? Or is it two?"

"Seriously Joe?"

"What do I know about babies? Does one start at birth or not?"

I chuckled. "You're a teenager Joe, you know everything."

My firstborn came round to borrow a suitcase. Favour for a favour. I pestered him into coming with me before he disappeared to Ireland for months. "Bye, Izzy." Dean gave the dog a ruffle and a kiss as we were leaving. "Ugh, you smell like the contents of a Hoover bag."

I bent down and sniffed her head. "Mm, she needs a bath, her fur smells like a dishcloth."

"A dirty dishcloth that's been left out in the sun to dry all day."

Ah, the refreshing spontaneity of my kids. Impossible to have a permanent long face with them around. The pair of us guffawed our heads off.

Di's eyes lit up at the sight of Dean. She stared at his face wide-eyed and cried and cried and shouted his name a hundred times, and he cuddled her and cheered her up. He put his Panavision baseball cap and Ray-Bans on her. The pair of them howled when she knocked them sideways with her stiff hand, then pulled a silly face. Dean had a knack for making Di snort with laughter; it was incredibly sweet to see that hadn't changed.

"I struggle to understand her half the time," Dean confessed as we meandered back to the car.

"It's not easy, guess I'm used to it."

"What did she say that made you laugh your heads off?"

"She reminded me of the old photos of Nana and Grandad we had up in the hall, remember?"

"Vaguely."

"And you said to her, "Were you alive in the black and white days, Auntie Di?""

"Did I? What a prat!" He buffoon guffawed.

I laughed. "You were five."

"I remember the ones where you'd gouged their eyes out and drawn moustaches."

I squirmed. "The things I regret now I'm older."

"Old."

"Oi!"

"I thought Di seemed fairly happy, Mum."

"Mm, Amy and Lucy are probably paranoid. Can't say I blame them, after everything this family's been through. They must be worn out, they go there every single day without fail."

"Jesus, how do they do that?"

"It's their mum, Dean, you would do it for me – wouldn't you?"

"Of course I would, Heart," he grinned, immortalising Sal's now legendary nickname. "I'd also make sure you had air in your tyres, then I'd push your wheelchair over a cliff."

Hugh, Sue and Mig arrived as we were leaving. They often visited their disabled cousin, bless them. I contemplated why extended family, like my children, nieces and nephews, didn't share my urgency to see Di. I invited Dean for dinner but he politely declined in favour of being dropped off at the pub to get wasted.

"Thanks, Mum, but I need to get that image of Di out of my head, sorry."

Now I had my answer. Now I understood why other people made excuses not to go. That's how badly seeing Di affected them. I took for granted the power of the sisterly bond. I couldn't go two weeks without my Di pinger screeching at me to go and see her. She had lots of friends and filmy acquaintances who went to visit, convinced they'd get her walking again. Off they went, full of gung-ho naïve promise, only to leave in a state of shock, never to be seen again. How sad for Di. Her oldest friend Kath Groves wasn't afraid, nor was salt of the earth stuntman Rocky Taylor. As for the majority, the 'one-visit wonders', Olly called them. It required an unconditional love, the kind siblings have for one another. They say you never find out who your true friends are until you need them, never more so in Di's case.

Olly was tired. I was tired. We hardly saw each other. I'd taken to reading excerpts from *Ramtha, The White Book* by

J Z Knight, one of three things Dylan let me take from the 'keep' pile when we emptied Sal's house. My first keepsake was a big round cream rug. We were shopping when I saw that. I loved it so much Sal bought it and offered to keep it until I had a bigger house one day. I still didn't have a bigger house but... one day, until that day, it could live in my loft. The second; an ugly head, a wacko *objet d'art* no bigger than my hand. Sal always returned from her travels with a suitcase full of weird, wonderful gifts. We all turned our noses up at ugly man, so she kept him. Last but not least Ramtha; she'd nagged me to read it for years but I couldn't, it was deeply spiritual, way above me. Yet here I was placing it carefully on my bedside table like a holy shrine. Every night I'd flick through, open a random page and strangely find I was reading just the thing I needed to hear at that precise moment. No wonder Sally raved about this book. It was like magic and so comforting. When the words did resonate, they wrapped my damaged mind in cotton wool and took it to another dimension, far beyond the grief. I couldn't read more than bitesize chunks, but the bits I did read my spiritually unaware mind absorbed like a sponge. It said something like:

All matter, including your body, is made up of atoms, if you coagulate atoms together, those atoms create what is called gross matter. Gross matter then creates molecules. Molecules create tissue. When you die, you move immediately into infrared. It is the psychic realm. From the psychic realm the shaft of light appears and you go down it. Then you hit the light.

It made me think about death. I mean *really* think about death, in a different way. This chunk was fascinating, it went along the lines of:

As we start to awaken and become more sensitive, we start to see into the subtle patterns a lot more easily. They can produce flashes of white light in our peripheral vision. We can see these when we are naturally sensitive to seeing/ feeling energy in times of intense grief. This is all just energy, we are made of energy, and the other side is not as far away as you think.

Sometimes when I went to bed, I saw flashes of white light in my peripheral vision. It first happened the night of Sally, when I sensed her walking around on the ceiling and Linda said, "your sister has slipped away into the next room, she's behind the door, that's all death is." Behind the door or, above the ceiling, perhaps? I liked what they thought and I wanted to think it. Going down this road was much preferable to the alternative, going down *that* road. Mum wouldn't want that. Sally wouldn't want that. Bossy Sally, still managing to have the final word. Poo-pooed Ramtha (and doxycycline) became my essential bedtime friend.

Olly's new bedtime friend was Rightmove.

"I think we should do it," he blurted out, out of the

blue one night, while I was mind-deep in hemisphere enhancement.

"Excuse me?"

"You gooseberry fool," he grinned. "Sally told Linda we should carry on with the plan. We should sell this house and buy a property to renovate, Liz."

"Without Sal?"

"There's some interesting places for sale and I learnt how to lay bricks today." He smiled.

"Playing with Lego doesn't make you a property developer." I turned the lamp off. "Goodnight, Olly."

We couldn't do it, not without Sal's help. That great plan died with my sister. The idea of moving home had excited me before, but now it filled me with utter dread. How could I sell the house my children grew up in, that Mum had stayed in so many times and Sally had helped me decorate? The mere thought of leaving behind those precious memories was too much for my exhausted brain to deal with.

CHAPTER FIFTEEN

The dreaded Sally thing

Life goes on, with or without an aching heart. Counting chocolate bars was consuming my life and practising new routines for my fitness class was a breeze with the right mental ingredients – focus and concentration – of which I had none. Consequently, my Di pinger had gone off two weeks late, so I took my aching heart for a much-needed overdue trip to the Avon Unit.

No sooner had I entered the building than I heard Di shouting "Nurse!" repeatedly from her room, several rooms away. The place was like a funeral parlour. Where was everyone? I walked into Di's room and found her banging her arms on the bedrail to the point where they had bruises and cuts on them. She looked disturbed. What on earth was going on?

"Di, have you been calling the nurse for a while?"

She nodded, so I stroked her head until she had calmed down and told her I'd be back in a tick. "No banging, okay?"

"Okay," she agreed.

Off I went snooping. I tiptoed along the corridor, poking my head into the other patients' rooms. No sign of any staff anywhere, just the sound of laughter resonating, so I followed the trail and found them. I spied from a distance and saw every single member of staff having a lovely little get-together in the rest room. I slunk off back to my sister and told her to call for the nurse, at five-minute intervals. I timed it. Thirty minutes later – bear in mind that Di was meant to have someone with her at all times – I heard footsteps approach and hid behind the curtain.

"What's the matter with you now?" said the voice.

I couldn't believe my ears. Good nurse, bad nurse. Epic fail. I stepped out from my hiding place. "She's been calling you for half an hour, that's what the matter is."

The bad nurse jumped out of her skin, her face flushed red. "Oh, I, I didn't know you were there," she stuttered, looking guilty. "Sorry, we're a bit short-staffed."

"Why is there a bed sheet on the floor?" I grilled her.

"She fell out of bed the other day, so we put it there to be on the safe side."

"What do you suppose a sheet will do?" I could feel my temper rising. "How did she fall out of bed when she has bed rails?"

"She's very strong, she's managed to hoist herself over it a couple of times."

She started faffing and fussing over Di, straightening her bed, pretending to be a good nurse. Just as I was about to snap, my saviour walked in: Lel.

"Hi, Fu Manchu, everything okay?" She winked at me, then turned to the nurse. "You can leave us to it now, go and have a break."

The nurse scurried out of the room. Lel shut the door and took one look at my face.

"I know Sian, that's why I've befriended them all," she bristled. "This place is the worst one yet. They haven't got a clue what they're doing."

"Fu Manchu?"

"Oh I don't know, it's Chang Fu something, whatever, it's just easier isn't it."

I couldn't help but chuckle at Lel's innocent yet befitting disrespect.

"Sian, last week I asked one of the new carers, who looked about twelve, where she had worked previously, expecting her to say Gwynedd Care or somewhere. Guess what she said."

"Chinese takeaway?"

"Fucking New Look."

"Jeez, I didn't mean it!" I was annoyed. "Why didn't you tell me?"

"I didn't want to worry you, what with Mum and Sal, Olly losing his job, and you're so busy with aerobics and being the chocolate police."

She was so upset that my pent-up mood softened, and I gave her a sisterly hug. "How you coping?"

"Not bad." She puffed her inhaler. "I've decided to get a dog for company."

"Good idea, just what you need."

"I've been going to Llaneilian Point, it's so nice there. Sian, there's *loads* of dolphins."

"Do you mean, you saw *a* dolphin – once?" I laughed.

"It's not a pointless lie, honest, that's why I thought I'd get a dog, I'm there all the time, come down, see for yourself."

"Sounds incredible."

"It is. Listen Lovey, we need to get Di out of here. I overheard one of them say 'what goes on in that vegetable brain of yours?' the other day."

"Right, that's it." I grabbed the door handle, ready to kill.

Lel put her hand over mine. "Don't do it, Sian. You can't afford to lose your rag, it'll make matters worse for Di while she's stuck in this hell-hole."

Amy and Lucy weren't paranoid. Millhouse was paradise and Oaktree heaven by comparison. We had high hopes for this residential care home, which claimed to do everything humanly possible to empower brain-injured patients to live their lives as freely and as fully as they chose. In my naivety, I believed they would make her legs work again and un-spasm her contorted hands. Di was talking and sitting up, so I suppose we naturally assumed she would continue to make progress until she was walking and eating and, well, became Di again. February 2010, eighteen months post-crash, we were beginning to realise it wasn't to be. Di was never going to fully recover or play the piano again, whether she was in Millhouse, Oaktree or the Avon Unit. Dangling between two worlds was as good as it was going to get, so she needed to be somewhere where she was given the right love and care, and that was not this place. So far the Avon unit had been the absolute worst. They had promised the earth but delivered zero. There was no stimulation whatsoever, however much of a functioning brain Di had she was bored out of it.

On the way home I rang Dave. He was pig sick when I told him.

"You need to call Headway ASAP Liz."

"Amy and Lucy are on it, and they've reported them to the Head of Neuroscience from somewhere or another."

He tutted and sighed. "Shite state of affairs."

"Talking of shite, haven't you got your colostomy reversal soon?"

"Funny you should say that, I went there today, I've got to keep it on for another six months."

"That's ages away!"

"What can I do? Got to be patient, haven't I? At least I'm alive, eh kiddo."

"Ah Dave, six months will fly by," said the hypocrite.

"True, you know me, I don't do sick, thanks for the positivity, little one."

If they remove it, I un-positively thought. Each time he went there they moved the goal posts.

After a laborious journey back from Di's I almost forgot the most crucial thing in the world – Ella's first birthday tomorrow. I stopped at the supermarket, grabbed a card, a giant number 1 candle and a disgustingly drab cardboard cake. I queued at the checkout, wondering what excuse there could be when in a shop for not bothering to buy food when you're aware you're going home to an empty fridge? Grief? Menopause? Both? It certainly didn't help with decision making, or remembering which appliance was called what.

Joe had become accustomed to me telling him his tea was in the tumble dryer or his socks were in the microwave. "Dinner's in the washing machine, yeah Mum" – one of his favourite lines to try and put a smile on my face. And it did. Best medicine and all that, laugh at adversity, don't go down *that* road.

I made a positive decision to bother and left my place in the queue to find something decent for tea for a change, creature comforts and homeliness. A nice family meal to bring us together and stop Joe going to that place teenagers go – out. Fussy Joe and Olly's favourite, winner-winner-fake-chicken dinner.

"Shall we have veggie fajitas tonight?" I rang and asked Joe excitedly.

"Or, counter offer – oven chips? I'm out tonight, Mum, sorry."

"Oven chips?"

"Yeah I bought some, and some eggs, easy food, you're forever rushing, and you never stop to eat when you've been to see Di."

My Joe, finally leaving the underworld of adolescence and blossoming into a kind and thoughtful grown-up version of the boy he always was. Oh well, just me and Olly.

"Do you fancy fajitas for dinner?"

"Sorry, love, the client's bought pizza, I'll be stuffed when I get in." Took me right back to Di and how she loved veggie pizza with triple cheese. "Couldn't get me some Radox muscle soak could you, Beak? I'll be back late, bath and bed for me, living the dream eh."

Oven chips then – for one. Or, counter offer – nothing, followed by staring at mindless babble on TV followed by bed. Food – overrated when you're bereft. I was getting used to the gaping hole inside me these days. Anyway, special day tomorrow. Something to look forward to – watching other people enjoy eating cake.

Teri, Dan, Joe, Olly and I leapt up from the table in my poky but cosy kitchen/diner and cheered as beaming baby Ella blew out the giant number 1 candle on her disgustingly drab cardboard cake.

"Happy birthday, dear Ella, happy birthday to you..."

Amy got a response from the Head of Neuroscience. Apparently it wasn't the first time he'd received complaints regarding the Avon unit and he recommended a residential care home called Hafod-y-Green. Being the closest, Amy took herself off to check it out.

"It's so nice there, Sian, perfect for Mum," she sighed. "I spoke to the manager, but she fobbed me off and told me they were full."

"Why does everything have to be a fight?"

"It got me thinking, Sian. Mum's better off out of it."

"Oh, Ame, don't say that."

"It's true, Sian. I'm sick of watching her suffer all day every day, Lu feels the same and Mum keeps saying she wants to die."

"She's said it to me a few times. We have to face facts, it would have been better for her if she'd died in the accident."

"She should have died, she defied the odds didn't she?"

"Too feisty for her own good."

"I looked into the Dignitas thing Uncle Dee-Dar was on about. Me and Lu went to Mum's doctor, they said assisted dying is illegal in this country, but there is something they can do."

My ears pricked. "What can they do?"

"All I have to do is say the words."

"What words?"

"Stop feeding Mum." Amy's voice wavered. "I'm legally allowed to starve my own mum to death." She sounded so distressed. "How much do you suppose it will hurt her, Sian?"

Once again I couldn't help her. All I could do was let out a big sad sigh.

"Uncle Dee-Dar said say the word and he'll put a pillow over Mum's head while she's asleep. He says she'd have been better off dying in a coma or being a vegetable like Janet. He keeps banging on about it, Sian."

"I hope he isn't serious, he's mentioned it too many times for my liking."

"Don't worry, he hasn't been for ages, he's so upset about Sally and Nana he can't handle it. He's not even watching the snooker."

"Don't let him visit her on his own, whatever you do."

"It gets worse, Sian, I found out Mum's heart stopped beating."

"Oh God, Steve didn't go there, did he?"

"No, the dickhead manager at Avon resuscitated her. Imagine how pissed off Mum must have been when she came around."

"Why would she do that?"

"Because I never signed a DNR form, can you believe? I didn't know anything about a stupid form. I've spoken to Mum's doctor about it now, so everyone gets it, do not resuscitate her."

"I can't believe we're having this conversation, Ame."

"It's so sad, Sian, but while Mum's still with us I'm not standing for it. I'm going to see that Head of Neuro guy in person and make him support my request for a bed at Hafod-y-Green."

Di was heavy on my mind. I couldn't bring myself to look at Ramtha. As usual Olly was flicking through Rightmove. How hard it must have been, to go from living the dream and sitting at a keyboard writing music to shovelling sand and cement. Every day the same old Groundhog Day of tired aching muscles. For the first time in a while I found myself focusing on someone other than me, or my half dead/actually dead family. Olly had been more fired up than me about the prospect of buying properties with Sal and renovating them.

Over his shoulder, something caught my eye.

"Show me that pink house," I asked.

"You don't want to see that one."

"Why don't I?"

"Because it will require a lot of Lego bricks."

"I'm sorry."

"I'm teasing," he grinned.

"The thought of moving, it scares me so much, it gives me bad anxiety."

"You don't need to explain. I'm wishful thinking, being on a building site is back-breaking, all that hard work for someone else to make a profit."

"I'm sorry, Olly, I wish I could carry on with the plan, but I can't."

"It's too big a project anyway. Dan reckons the kitchen needs a knock-through into a conservatory to give it a dining room, amongst other things."

"Like being way out of our price range?"

"Exactly, goodnight Beak." Olly yawned and turned the lamp off.

"Flower?" I turned the lamp back on. "I suppose, it wouldn't hurt to look…"

TWELVE MONTHS LATER – February 2011

Teri, Dan, Joe, Olly and I leapt up from the table in my half-built Lego kitchen/dining room/conservatory and cheered as beaming Ella blew out the giant number 2 candle on her handcrafted scrumptious sponge cake.

"Happy birthday dear Ella, happy birthday to you…"

Right on cue, my phone bleeped. It was a text from Lel regarding tomorrow;

Happy second birthday Ells Bells
xxx see you manana Lovey for
the dreaded Sally thing ☹

The dreaded Sally thing was finally upon us. It wasn't as formal as a normal court, but equally intimidating. The five of us hung around in the reception waiting for the coroner like suspects on trial for murder. Me, Dylan, Dave, Sara and knuckle-cracking Lel.

"You'll get arthritis if you keep doing that," I pointed out.

"I've already got it," said Lel, nervously sucking the life out of her inhaler.

"How's the house, kiddo?" My brother asked, readjusting his colostomy bag under his shirt.

"Still pink," I sighed. "Been there almost six months already."

"Get away!" He looked surprised. "Hang on a minute, where's Bean?"

"Don't know, Dave," Lel answered. "I texted him to say I was on my way, knocked on his door, called through the letterbox, nothing."

"I hope he's all right?" Sara, looked worried.

"Course he's all right," scoffed DB. "He'll have been on a bender."

"Paying his respects to Sal – his way," I said.

"Have you heard from him, cariad?" Sara asked Dylan.

Lovely, caring Sara (or Menna), who in her own words, married my brother for the 'worse' part of better or worse. She always called us 'cariad', Welsh for sweetheart.

"Huh?" Dylan came out of his trance. "Oh yeah, he texted and apologised, saying, 'you don't need me, you've got enough of my siblings doing your head in'."

"Guy's a total waste of space." DB shook his head angrily.

The coroner arrived and shook our hands, and we entered the courtroom. A policewoman and the court usher were positioned beside a desk guarding something. It was on display for us all to see: a clear plastic bag containing the evidence. Sal's blue dressing gown belt.

It wasn't pleasant, the coroner's spine-chilling step-by-step account of events. We discovered 'it' had happened early Saturday evening. I pictured Sal waiting for the mental health team, pacing around, beside herself, having been left on her own all day. We were in there a good couple of hours reliving the painful experience of Sal's tragic demise, each of us grilled. I expressed my confusion over Sally's death, how she had told me she wouldn't do that and leave a black hole in the lives of her family. Dave informed the coroner that Sally was suffering delusional thoughts that we were conspiring against her and talking behind her back, which was out of character. Lel had done her due diligence and provided the coroner with a list of Sal's medication, and Sherlock Steve had armed her with the knowledge that one of the side effects of those red and white pills was suicidal tendencies.

The coroner had undertaken extensive investigation himself. Antidepressants put a blanket on your emotions, he explained: you don't feel anxiety, but you don't feel joy either. Delusional thinking can occur and is frighteningly common. He asked if we had any questions; I did. I asked a question "for a friend": if a fourteen-year-old took four antidepressants at once, could it possibly create a delusional fog which caused suicidal thoughts? It possibly could, he said.

The coroner surprised us by talking about Sally and her life as if he knew her the way we did. He described her as a high achiever who had helped a lot of people in her short life. To ask for help herself would be to admit she had failed. He told us how people suffering suicidal thoughts often experiment with different ways. One of the easiest ways to die accidentally is from hanging; loss of consciousness usually occurs within five seconds. I thought about what Linda said: "One minute I was down there, the next minute

I was over here". It made sense now.

It was hard going, yet it was plain to see that the coroner was an intelligent man doing his difficult job as fairly as he could. He summarised by saying he was one hundred percent satisfied after gathering the evidence that Sally was not the sort of person to wilfully take her own life. It was his professional opinion that the psychiatric hospital was responsible for my sister's death. It was disturbing, but at the same time a burden lifted. He recorded 'medication mismanagement' as the cause of her death, and that was the moment we all burst into tears, including the young policewoman who had been called to the scene by Martin on her first ever assignment, to untie a ligature from a dead person. We weren't the only ones suffering.

The meeting concluded and we rose to our feet. The coroner shook our hands in turn and announced awkwardly, "Before you go, I'm sorry, I have to ask this by law, I'm sure you don't, but do any of you want to keep the ligature?"

I did. I don't know why. To hold it for a bit? To make peace with it? Because I'm sick in the head? It didn't matter anyway, I never got the chance. Boom-boom Dave answered on everyone's behalf,

"Absolutely not."

We decided to go for lunch before we went our separate ways, to commiserate/celebrate the tiny glimmer of light in the forever darkness of a life without Sal.

"Justice," said Lel.

"You know the first thing I'm going to do?" declared my brother.

"What are you going to do, Dave?" I asked.

"Tell Cameo's to remove that shit off the internet or I shall sue their arse."

"What shit, Dave?" quizzed Lel.

"The agency Sal was with, they put a blog online saying how sad it was to hear of Sally Jones' suicide. It's the first thing that comes up when you put her name in Google."

Hurrah. Sally didn't wilfully take her own life. Yes, it was a result but equally frustrating, sad and regretful. It didn't stop her being dead. Her words came back to haunt me. *Please don't be angry with me, nobody likes me, don't hate me Sian,* and that heart-stabbing line she said to Lel, *you'll be better off without me.* It wasn't Sally talking, it was the tablets. I remembered that comment she made about the bleach-swallowing episode: *I don't know what came over me, Sian.*

I know what came over her. Antidepressants, that's what. I remembered that comment she made about the dressing gown belt incident: *I don't know why I did it, Sian, truly.*

I know why she did it – antidepressants, that's why. The kind that cause not a rash or a tummy ache as a side effect, but suicidal thoughts. Sally took a trip down that road and was given the wrong directions. There by the grace of God go I, and millions of others who have felt the weight of the world on their shoulders at some point in life. A weight that for Sally wouldn't lift, worsened by the medication they gave her. We put our trust in an archaic system, poorly equipped to deal with mental health. If only I'd realised all this before it was too late I'd have flushed those disgusting deadly red and white pills down the toilet.

"I wish I could turn back time and be a better son," said Dylan.

"I wish I'd been a better sister, Dylan," I replied.

"How do you think we feel?" cried Dave, his face reddening with anger and hurt. "Us two went away and left her on her own that weekend." Sara hung her head in shame.

Lel leapt up out of her chair. "Fuck this." And off she went.

"Come back, cariad!" Sara pleaded with her.

"I'm going for a fag!" she called out.

"Leave her, Sara," I said. "She blames herself. She's the one who signed the section papers."

"Ah no, this isn't fair, you all did so much." Dylan's eyes were full of sorrow. "You got her eating again, Sara. I can't thank you guys enough for looking after Mum the way you did."

"Dylan's right," I said. "And you, Dave, you worked tirelessly to sort out her finances."

Humbled, Dave and Sara burst into tears. I felt so sorry for them.

"Oh Liz!" Dave was bawling his eyes out. "We only went away to finalise the papers for Sal's apartment in America. We got Spain repossessed, Hull was nearly there.

I was looking forward to coming home and telling her the good news. We were so nearly there…"

Such an intense mixture of emotions, up one minute, down the next. Together we walked to the car park; Lel was leaning against her bonnet, smoking.

"You okay, Lelly-Bertus?" Dylan put a loving arm around her shoulder.

"Yeah," she sniffed, wiping her eyes. "Let's try to stay positive, it's what Sal would want."

"Hey look, over there!" Dylan pointed. A dazzling vibrant rainbow had cast a glow over the brightening sky.

"It hasn't even rained!" Sara was dumbfounded.

"Hey, wait a minute, that's reminded me, hang on." Dylan raced over to his car and came back waving a rainbow-patterned sun hat. "I forgot to say, Steve sent me this to bring with us today as a mascot. Mum gave it to him when he landscaped the garden for her."

"Weird, it hasn't rained," DB was mystified.

"It's not a rainbow, that's why," Lel pointed out. "It's Sally."

Dylan put the rainbow hat on his head and blew a kiss towards the multi-coloured arc in the sky. The five of us stared, mesmerised, gawping in awe. God rest her soul. Self-appointed head of the family, life coach and bank to everyone. Sally Sunshine was shining – for us. Hopefully, now her spirit would be at peace.

"Wow, look at that!" said my never-said-anything-remotely-spiritual-before brother. "It's a Sally-bow!"

CHAPTER SIXTEEN

The pink house

⸺⋈⸺

TWELVE MONTHS EARLIER
February 2010

"Wow, look at that!" said Olly. "It's a rainbow. Maybe it's a sign."

"Yuck, it's not only pink, it's got those hideous things on it," I whinged, oblivious to the rainbow. I was pointing at the huge metal butterflies on the side of the house while we were waiting for the estate agent.

"Yeah but, it's detached." Olly had a twinkle in his eye.

"And out of our league. Three hundred and fifty grand, why are we even here?" I moaned.

"Because you said it wouldn't hurt to look."

It wasn't too crummy inside, to be fair. Once you got your head around the fluorescent green walls and red banana-leaf carpets.

"This lounge is huge," beamed Olly, wide-eyed.

I couldn't deny it was the perfect room for Sal's big round cream rug. The layout was cock-a-doodle and it was a bit psychedelic, but it was clean. It needed painting, and a knock-through into a conservatory to make the poky kitchen a large kitchen diner. Alex, our friendly estate agent, showed us what else we could do, a few tricky layout changes, all of which would increase the value by twenty-five percent. "They'll accept something around the three hundred mark," he informed us.

I laughed. "Still way out of our price range."

"We can borrow two hundred and seventy-five, max," Olly sighed, disappointed.

"They had an offer of that amount six months ago," Alex confessed.

"Really?" said Olly, excited.

"Which they refused, presumably," I said, not so excited.

"They did," Alex confirmed. "But they haven't had any offers since and the market is pretty dead, so – try it, you never know your luck."

We found a cosy corner in a local pub to sit and calculate the impossible over a strawberry beer. To make it work we needed to buy the pink house for two hundred and seventy-five thousand, way under value and previously refused. Then we had to sell our mid-terraced shoe box for a whopping two hundred and fifty thousand, way over value, in a dead market. It was never going to happen and I have to say, that suited me down to the ground.

"Look at this stupid menu." I launched it across the table to Olly like a Frisbee.

"Ugh, I can't stand Yves Saint Laurent food." He adopted a plum accent. "A spliced atom of brie, served in a petri dish, with a smear of jus, and a fleck of chef's toenail clippings."

I laughed out loud. "And we have to give our table number and order at the bar. Look at the queue, it's meant to be upper-crust here, it's like a cattle market."

"You think that's bad? Next they'll be giving out flat-packed tables and handing everyone tool kits. Let's go."

"Counter offer – oven chips?" I suggested.

Teri, Dan, Joe, Olly and I leapt up from the table in my poky but cosy kitchen/diner and cheered as beaming baby Ella blew out the giant number 1 candle on her disgustingly drab cardboard cake. "Happy birthday, dear Ella, happy birthday to you…"

Since the Fu Manchu incident, Lel's 'New Look' discovery, and the Head of Neuroscience saying he'd received complaints regarding the Avon unit, I couldn't stand the thought of Di in that place. My two-week pinger hadn't gone off, yet here I was, breezing through those revolving doors. My phobia was well and truly cured, thanks to the sheer volume of hospital and care home visits which consumed my life.

"Excuse me?" said a rude sounding voice behind me.

I spun round and saw the once lovely manager looking annoyed.

"Oh, hi, only me." I smiled.

"You can't come here without an appointment," she snapped, positioning herself in front of me, blocking my path.

My back went up. I was still bristling over the sheet on the floor from my previous visit. Now I needed an appointment? We were told we could come any time of day or night, it didn't make any sense. "Since when?"

She ignored me and continued her rude onslaught. "Who authorised you to come here?"

Lel's words of wisdom, "don't lose your rag", went straight out the window. "ME!" I shouted, through gritted, angry, get-out-of-my-way teeth. I didn't know what had changed or why, but if she thought I was coming all this way and leaving without seeing my sister...

I brushed past her, went into Di's room and slammed the door shut. Di was fast asleep. I got straight on the phone to Amy, no answer. I tried Lucy, no answer. I rang Lel, no answer, I rang Steve, no answer. I didn't want to ring DB, he was snowed under prepping for his new movie. Damn it. I punched the wall.

Di yawned and opened her eyes. A ladybird landed on her leg. She stared at it and didn't flinch – a first. Di, a massive animal lover but with an equally massive aversion to small flying things, particularly ladybirds. The old Di would leap around cursing and shouting at whoever was nearest as if it were their fault. It didn't matter if it was a stranger either. Teri the same, she'd inherited her ladybird Tourette's gene from Di. I'd laughed at them both doing that, many times over the years.

Unfazed by the ladybird, Di closed her eyes and went back to sleep. I rang round again, and this time Lucy answered. I blurted out my annoyance.

"Sian, she's being a cow-bag, ever since I told her we've reported them." Now I understood what had changed and why. "It's obvious, Sian, they're drugging her to stop her shouting. Let me guess, was she asleep when you got there?"

"Has been ever since, she woke briefly, didn't flinch when a ladybird landed on her leg."

"There you go." Super intelligent Lucy, like her mum, did not suffer fools.

"At least while she's asleep she's unaware of the fact she's in hell."

"Ah, Mum's all right, Sian, she told me Nana's always in the bathroom and helps her dress and wash every morning."

"Because she doesn't know my mum's gone," I reflected sadly.

"I forgot to tell you, the other day she said to me, 'why didn't you tell me my mum was dead?' I asked how she knew and she said, 'My mum told me'. Can you believe that?"

"God she's spooky."

"Makes sense, doesn't it? Nana looking after Mum while she's stuck in there."

"I couldn't agree more, Luce."

I put the phone down, it rang straight away. "What

news, Lel – no I haven't spoken to Amy – ooh she's ringing me now."

Like buses, nothing for ages, then three at once.

"I saw that Head of Neuroscience guy in the flesh!" Amy was brimming with enthusiasm.

"Crikey, Ame, how did you pull that off?"

"I went to the hospital where he's based, Sian, it was impossible, he was either operating or in a meeting, so I waited in my car for hours and did a stake out." She giggled and I was glad. I hadn't heard Amy's infectious spasmodic giggle for a long time. "I figured he has to go home at some point, right? I pounced on him as he was getting in his car."

"How did you know it was him?"

"There's a picture of him in reception."

"Stalker!" I laughed.

"Sian, he was such a lovely guy, we spoke for ages about Mum. I told him everything, and he's going to write to Hafod-y-Green to support getting her a place. He's also reporting the Avon unit to the Higher Health Board. I'm so excited."

"Me too. Well done, sweetheart, keep me posted."

We said our goodbyes, and my phone rang again. Four at once. It was Steve. He'd been on my mind ever since Amy told me he was on a downer. Time to have words.

"How are you, bro?"

"Oh you know, up and down, Tower Bridge."

I'd never heard him sound so low. "Everything's temporary, a wise man once told me."

"Ha, you remember."

"I've never forgotten, Steve, it's helped me get through many a rough time. How's the snooker championship?" I was pathetically attempting to make small talk and lighten his mood.

"I can't watch it, Sian, it's not the same without Mum." His voice faltered.

I sighed a big long Mum sigh. "Ah Steve…"

"I miss her so much I can't handle it, Sian, or Sal, or Di. I've told Amy, say the word and I'll put a pillow over her head."

"Steve don't, it's not for us to play God."

"No one should live like that. She should have died in the accident, Sian. She didn't die of pneumonia. She's not a vegetable like Janet. She has enough savvy to be aware how trapped she is in her own body. Can you imagine how frustrating it must be?"

"Yes, but she's sleeping peacefully right now."

Steve was losing it and I was happy to be his punching bag. Anger turned inwards causes depression, I once read somewhere.

"Then there's the dreaded Sally thing coming up and DB walking around with his bag of bloody shit."

"Ew, is it bloody?"

He cackled his head off. "Fucking bag of shit then."

"They've pushed his colostomy reversal back six months."

"Yeah right. I had a mate who had one of them, they

kept telling him the same, it's bull, they're lying, Sian, he'll
be stuck with it for life."

"Don't, that's my fear too – listen, come and stay for a
bit, we can cheer each other up."

"Thanks, darling, I could use a break. I'll have a gander
at train timetables and let you know marijuana." Steve's
adaptation of Sal's *mañana*.

"No you won't."

"Yes I won't."

"Please."

"I will, when I'm feeling better, sorry for ranting darling."

He didn't need to apologise. One thing my family and I
were: true to ourselves, well, most of the time. I watched Di
sleeping peacefully, and my mind drifted back to the time
she stayed with me and was on the phone to one of Dave's
snobby vegan fanatic wives/girlfriends and being extremely
phoney about herbal this and herbal that. Unfortunately
we'd quaffed a couple of bottles of wine, so she was in no fit
state to be talking sensibly.

"Amy and Lucy are fine. How's um – um –" she said,
fumbling around for a piece of paper and thrusting it into
my face. I wrote on it: *Ben*. Di carried on chatting. It went
like this,

"Sorry, I was just having a sip of my herbal tea," she
fibbed. "I was about to ask, how's Ben?" She turned to me,
a look of panic in her eyes. "Hamish, that's what I meant,
sorry."

That's what I meant, sorry. Funniest line ever. What

part of Ben sounds like Hamish? I burst into uncontrollable hysterics. How could my silly sister believe for one second someone with the surname Dover would call their son Ben? She glared at me red-faced, waving her fist, trying not to snort. Attack of the memories. Nice, when they were nice. That particular one, has to be in the top ten sister-wind-up's chart.

We tried our luck and fell at the first hurdle – our offer on the pink house was declined. We put ours on the market anyway because Olly said "We have to carry on with the plan", but we fell at the second, third and fourth hurdles. The highest offer we got was two hundred thou.

"I've got an idea," said Olly, racking his brains, as he often did when it was time to sleep.

As usual, I was deep in hemisphere enhancement. "Hmm."

"Let's give this house a fresh coat of paint, snag the bits that need it, fix the hole Dean punched in his bedroom door when you told him about Sal, see if it makes a difference."

Dog with a worn-out bone Amy took herself back to Hafod-y-Green, having heard nothing in response to the Head of Neuroscience's letter of support. Despite receiving his request to offer Di a place, the manager Ellen, was reluctant.

"What happens next, Ame?"

"I've done what happens next. I went back today and begged her. I told her I wasn't leaving until she did something to help, so she agreed to visit Mum and see how bad it is for herself."

"And they'll be on their best behaviour."

"I told her that, Sian, she totally gets it. She's going to go posing as a relative."

Umpteen viewings later our trusty estate agent walked through the door as we were walking out of it with another time-waster, I mean potential buyer. Awkward. We left getting out of the way a teensy bit too late. The lady smiled as she passed me and I heard Sal say, *That's your buyer and she's going to give you the full asking price.* Six days passed, nothing, not a dickie bird. I was not convinced.

Day seven, Alex rang. "We've got an offer!" he declared, ecstatic. "Two hundred and twenty, the best one yet, isn't that great!"

"No," I replied, happily. A, I didn't want to move. B, we couldn't afford to move unless we got the full asking price of two hundred and fifty and C, I thought I'd put Sally to the test.

As promised, the manager from Hafod-y-Green visited Di posing as an old friend. Ellen reported to Amy that she was appalled by the state of affairs at the Avon unit.

"She told me she's never seen anyone so petrified and agreed to give Mum a bed, Sian. I just burst out crying and gave her a massive hug."

"Great news." I tried to sound enthusiastic.

"You don't sound pleased."

"No, I am. Well done Ame, sorry, it made me feel horrible her saying Di was petrified."

"I said the same, but she said we weren't to know. She did specific brain tests with Mum and that was her conclusion."

"I shudder to think what goes on behind closed doors in that place."

"Concentrate on the positive, Sian, Mum's getting out of there, and I can't wait!"

"How long?"

"It'll take a few months, but I'll be there every day and Ellen's going to keep visiting to keep an eye on things, and Nana's there every morning, did Lu tell you," she giggled. I laughed. It was hard not to when Amy let rip her infectious spasmodic giggle. "I don't care what people say, Sian, I believe Mum. She might be brain damaged but she's not stupid."

"A damaged superbrain probably equates to an average one, like the rest of us."

We both giggled.

I couldn't visit Di as often what with packing to move home... Yep, the impossible happened. The smiling lady increased her offer to the full asking price and our previously rejected offer on the pink house was accepted. Sally was right. I couldn't believe it. The thought of moving petrified me, but I figured it was meant to be. *Que sera*, as Sal would say. My life was in the hairy, scary hands of Fate.

I volunteered to do the loft. Mug. I didn't get very far. Sally's sacred rug was there, waiting to be rolled out like a red carpet in my bigger house. Ooh, the first tinge of excitement. Soon ruined by my second find, a birthday card. It said, "I'm so lucky to have a sister like you, all my love, Sal." I don't recall her buying me a card like that. Sal was a chip off the old Mum block in the department of sentiment. The third find was a Sony Walkman with a tape of me and Di singing and laughing. The fourth was a letter from Mum when she was in Hill End saying, "Can we be friends when I come home?"

A tidal wave of grief hit me. Upset for Di. Sadness for Mum. Anger for Sally. That's the thing, when a parent goes it's heart-breaking but it's meant to happen. Sally was a completely different kettle of grief. A ghost train ride of anger, then relief, then guilt, stopping briefly at forgiveness en route to *love is all there is* before heading back to anger.

"How you getting on up there, Beak?" A voice called out.

"Yeah, doing great," I fibbed.

The big day came: Di's moving-out day. They didn't want her to go, and why would they? Di was one of two remaining patients worth thousands every week. The fat cat who got the cream was soon to have rotten egg on its face. Amy, Ellen and the ambulance arrived to take Di to her new home at Hafod-y-Green. Would you believe the not so lovely manager had the audacity to try and stop them?

"You won't believe what happened, Sian." Feisty Amy was spitting bullets. "That cow of a manager tried to block the entrance to Mum's room and said she couldn't go because they'd reassessed her and she was a mental health patient."

"A mental health patient!"

"Can you bloody believe it? Ellen was so cross, she snapped at her and said she was taking Mrs Hadden as arranged."

"I wish I'd been there."

"Don't worry, Sian, I lost it." She giggled. "I said, if my mum is a mental health patient then it's all your fault, because she came here as a brain-injured patient!"

"Good on you, Ame."

"Then the cheeky hag said Mum wasn't allowed to leave the building! Can you believe the audacity of the woman? Sian, I was so angry. I said, "Watch me". Then I shoved her out of the way, grabbed Mum's bed and wheeled her out really fast."

"Shame you didn't run her over."

"I was going to, but she cowered out of the way so I shouted over my shoulder, "Then I'm going to come back and burn this shithole down!" She burst into a spasmodic giggle fit. "Ellen looked at me a bit weird."

"That is a bit weird." I laughed. "But I am proud of you, Ame."

"And Ellen's taking action against them with the Higher Health Board. She said she wished there were more people like me. She said I was fierce and loyal, Sian."

"You are, sweetheart."

Fierce and loyal, like her mum.

It was now October 2010 and I didn't have time to reflect or wallow in sadness on our moving day, despite it being the first anniversary of Sally's death. Chaos reigned. We sprung a huge leak under the kitchen sink and had to unpack two boxes of towels to mop it up on our hands and knees while the buyers were coming through the door and tripping over us with their stuff. Perhaps it was part of Sal's heavenly masterplan to keep my mind occupied on this grim day.

"Good luck with the move, little one," said DB. "Thinking of you, and you can think of me."

"Why, what's happening?"

"You were right, six months has flown by. I went for my reversal op this morning."

"No way!"

"Yep – no way, they want me to keep it on for another six months."

Oh dear, as Steve and I had feared. "That's when we've got the dreaded Sally thing, Dave."

"I can't afford to miss it."

"You won't miss it." *You might not be having it at all*, I thought.

Stressful to say the least, but we did it. The kids mucked in and by the evening we were dead beat. One more box to unpack, the 'odds and sods' box. There he was, ugly man, with the horrid scraggly grey hair and whiskers poking out of his nostrils. A strange *objet d'art.* but Sally loved him. I loved him now, so I hung him, pride of place, on the fireplace mirror.

"Really Mum?" Joe pulled a face.

"Beauty is not in the face, beauty is a light in the heart, Joe."

"Whatever," he replied, stuffing his face with chips. Cold chips naturally, washed down with a crate of Peroni.

There was a knock at the front door. Joe wandered off and came back into the lounge. "I wonder what this is." He held up a huge envelope. "It's a letter addressed to Joe & Co." He opened it, it was a card from Steve, with a little ditty poem.

Our relationship is special, I hope it never ends,

Although you three are miles away, you're my bestie special friends.

All the best in your new home, can't wait to come and piss you off, Steve xxx

Bless, he timed it Virgo perfect so it would arrive on our first day. It's the little things...

I flopped onto the sofa and gazed lovingly at my big cream round rug. Surprisingly I felt okay, not sad. It was a new beginning and what Sal wanted. I sensed the glow of her dimple grin and the glow of Mum scrunching her face and saying, "I don't know why she bothered putting it on the floor. She's not going to let anyone bloody well walk on it.'

I couldn't wait to visit Di at Hafod-y-Green, and what a breath of fresh air it was. Nestling away in four acres of stunning Welsh countryside, the place was a haven; better still, Di's room overlooked the farm, so she could watch the horses out of her window. When I got there the giggling Filipinas were giving Di a manicure, she'd had her hair done and a facial – a first! She looked so happy, radiant and glowing I couldn't believe my eyes; I was overcome with joy. Tears of years of bottled-up emotion rolled down my face. I could feel the long-suffering Di burden melting away. These cute little people worshipped her, they considered her brilliant and brave and funny and they had all the time in the world for her. It was a welcoming sight. She had her very own Oompa-Loompas.

I met Ellen for the first time and she was lovely too. She showed me Di's agenda and explained how she was never, EVER, on her own. She had 24/7 care. If she woke in the night and needed anything, anything at all, the Oompa-Loompas were there by her side to give it to her. At long last, life was finally on the up for Princess Di.

CHAPTER SEVENTEEN

Tickety-boo

Within six months of the move, Olly and Dan had knocked through the kitchen and built a Lego dining room/conservatory. We had ripped the banana carpets up and literally thrown magnolia paint on the walls. Change, the thing I was petrified of, turned out to be a blessing in disguise. Moving home enabled me to let go of some things, like Sally's garden umbrella, which upset me because it was turning green with algae. Intense grief would still hit me like a truck out of nowhere. Usually it was when I'd put mascara on, or I was eating, or cleaning my teeth, or every time we went in a coffee shop as Teri pointed out but, like it or not, the past gets further away, ghosts start disappearing and new people take priority.

For Ella's second birthday, this time, I bothered to get her a handcrafted scrumptious sponge cake. We had come a long way from the disgustingly drab cardboard afterthought cake days. Di remained content at Hafod-y-Green, two and a half years post-crash, so far no drama. One more painful hurdle to overcome, Sally's inquest, tomorrow...

In March 2011, a couple of weeks after the 'dreaded Sally thing', I woke up feeling like a normal person. I'd forgotten what that felt like. We had discovered that my sister hadn't intentionally taken her own life, and it mattered, a lot. The emotional Sally baggage I'd been carrying for best part of a year and a half had finally lifted. I wasn't the only one feeling upbeat. Lel rang and left a broken message on my answer machine, I got the gist,

"Lovey, I'm here with the dog, watching the dolphins, and I was ringing to tell you, for the first time in a long time, I feel tickety-boo."

No coincidence Lel saying that, and me feeling normal, following Sal's inquest. I couldn't wait to share the news; I felt tickety-boo too. I called her back, but she didn't answer, still experiencing her exhilarating dolphin fix no doubt, so I left an equally jolly message. Phone still in hand, I rang Steve for the umpteenth time. He didn't answer, again, so I left a message, updating him about Sal's inquest, again, and asking if he'd sorted out a bloody train ticket, yet again. I couldn't wait to see him. For those of us on this plane of existence, quote Ramtha: life is for living.

"Sorry I missed your call, Lovey, signal's shit up the top of Llaneilian point." Lel sounded puffed out. "How are you?"

"Tickety-boo, Lovey, you?" I replied, full of the joys.

"Well I was – I don't know how to say this, Sian – it's Steve. He um, collapsed, he's in hospital. Amy told me."

"Is he ok, is it bad or…"

"I'm not sure, you know what it's like with him."

Oh I knew all right. It wouldn't be the first time Steve had ended up in casualty after nearly drinking himself to death and suffering the consequences, like deciding to clean his guttering and falling out of the bedroom window, or falling down the apples and pears as he called them, but he always bounced back after a night in hospital. It was probably much ado about nothing. On the other hand…

"Do you want me to ring the hospital?" Olly offered.

I hit the buttons, handed him my phone and waited patiently on the apples and pears, heart in mouth, silently praying for Steve to be okay.

"Hi, I'm calling regarding Steven Ball – he's not there?" Olly gaped at me. I mouthed the word *Robert*. "Sorry, I meant Robert Ball – I'm not his next of kin, no." Olly gaped at me again. I mouthed the word *brother*. "I'm his brother – can I get there, yeah sure – about three hours – it's not worth it? Okay."

Instantaneous relief, it obviously wasn't bad. I listened, Olly said *okay* a lot before finally handing me back my phone.

"Why is it not worth it? Are they sending him home?" I asked.

Olly looked at me, deadly serious. He shook his head, whatever that meant, it wasn't good.

"Tell me!" I shouted, hysteria rising inside me.

"It's not worth it because he's not in a good way, Liz."

"What the fuck Olly! What are you saying?"

"They said he'll be gone before we get there."

"But – he was supposed to be sorting a train ticket and coming to stay with us."

Olly didn't say any more. He didn't need to; his broken face said it all.

I screamed and hurled my phone at the wall. It smashed into smithereens. Here we go again. Panic-stricken, I ran into the kitchen and rummaged through the bin. I wiped teabag juice off my crumpled packet of doxycycline, then barricaded myself in the bedroom. Did I say I felt like a freak? Did I mention I was cursed? The very evening of the very morning I finally felt tickety-boo I found out my brother was dying. How was I supposed to process that, let alone tell my kids? Joe and Steve were thick as thieves. I couldn't believe this was happening. First Di, then Sally, then Mum, now this? I felt insane.

Steve had suffered a fatal embolism. The hospital told Olly he was only alive because of machinery. He died the next morning. My brother hadn't been on a bender; he'd been in hospital. That's why he didn't answer the door to Lel. That was the reason he didn't go to the dreaded Sally thing, Amy confessed.

"He was in and out for a couple of weeks, Sian, his DVT flared up, he had a scan which was fine so I picked him up, dropped him off at home, then he collapsed."

"I can't fathom it out. If he was fine, why did he collapse?"

"I don't get it either, Sian, he was in good spirits, said he was going to retire from drinking."

"Why didn't he tell me he was in hospital?"

"He told me not to tell anyone, he didn't want me to worry you, after everything that's happened, and what with the Sally thing."

I was trying to be strong for Amy, poor kid had been through enough, but I couldn't hold back any longer. I cracked. "That makes me so sad."

Amy's brave front also collapsed. "Sian, I should have told you, I'm so sorry…"

Why, oh why, was life so cruel? And why did the hospital send him home to die? I couldn't get my head around any of it. Too many unanswered questions only one way to find out.

Walking into the warden's office/guest quarters brought back the memory of when Olly and I had had the pleasure of staying there, the night of Mum's funeral, little over a year ago.

"I've sorted you and Oll a room, Sian." Steve had been chuffed with himself. "It's the warden's office but I had a chat with the manager, Cerys, and explained about Mum, she said she'll stick a bed in there for you, ain't that sweet?"

I'd have preferred a B&B. I didn't relish the idea of staying in Steve's warden-controlled holiday camp for recovering alcoholics, but it was free and it was kind, so we had no choice. It was rather cosy until we were abruptly woken by a ridiculous ear-piercing buzzer followed by a coughing and spluttering which seemingly came out of the walls.

"What time is it, Cerys?" grumbled a thick Welsh accent.

"Good morning, Geraint," came the bright cheerful response. "Seven o'clock, same as usual."

The buzzer screeched again – and again. "Bore da, Cerys," croaked a Welsh female voice.

"Bore da Myfanwy bach, are you all right?" replied the bright and cheerful Cerys.

"Yes, sorry about that, I was on the toilet."

"God's sake," I moaned. "How long is this going to go on for?"

"Look over there, Beak." Olly pointed at a numbered chart on the wall, each number with a little red light next to it. There were twenty of them.

"I don't believe this." I groaned and pulled the pillow over my head.

"What number's Steve?"

"Twenty," I muffled. That tickled him, he creased up and did a mean impression of Gladys Pugh. "Hi-de-hi, campers!"

We got into the swing of it after number ten, anticipating what my brother had to say, twenty ear-piercing buzzers later.

"Morning, Cerys, I slept very well indeed, thank you," announced Steve in his polite English way. "By the way, my sister and partner are in the guest suite. I asked Reece to turn the Tannoy off so they can have a nice lie in – hang on a minute – you're speaking to me through the Tannoy."

"Oh dear," said a sheepish Cerys.

Steve's contagious cackle roared through the Tannoy. "Morning Olly and Sian."

Back in the horribleness of now, Cerys was in pieces about Steve, as were the residents. Everyone loved him; he was such a character and such a helpful member of their community. She told me Sue, his neighbour, had found him. It was a struggle getting it out of Sue, she was so flustered. I eventually discovered Steve had been admitted to hospital because his leg had swollen. They had given him a CT scan which came back clear and he was sent home after a course of intravenous antibiotics.

"Had he been drinking?" I asked.

"Lord no, the doctor had told him to stop or it was going to kill him. He came home from hospital, he'd even bought my favourite biscuits, love him. We had a nice cup of tea and a chat, he told me he'd retired from drinking and was starting his life over, he was so happy..." Tears welled in her eyes as she gazed at the half-eaten pack of custard creams on her coffee table. Then she had a mini breakdown.

"Do you want me to go, Sue, this is upsetting you?"

"Not at all, I understand you need to know. It's just so sad, I still can't believe it, let me catch my breath," she said, fanning herself. "He went off to the laundry room with his washing, oh Sian, he had a real a spring in his step..." She stopped and had another mini breakdown.

"Sue, do you want to show me? Would that be easier?"

She nodded, so off we went to the laundry room.

"He had a cut on his forehead here," she demonstrated. "He smashed it on the machine as he bent down to put his washing in."

My hand flew to my mouth and my eyes filled to the brim. The shock wore off and reality sank in. I was reliving my brother's final steps.

"He didn't hurt himself, Sian, the paramedic assured me, it would have been lights out first, then bang."

I'd seen and heard enough. I thanked Sue and headed off to Steve's flat – as I was his next of kin, Cerys had given me the keys. Five minutes later Lel turned up. After the abnormal norm of hugging and crying, the pair of us wandered around like lost souls, not having a clue where to begin. Fortunately, unlike Sal, Steve didn't have too much stuff. I stared at my old TV perfectly positioned on the pine cabinet and detected a well of deep sadness stirring inside me.

"Look what I found," said Lel. "He must have just written this, the pen's still here."

She read it out loud, and we laughed and cried throughout.

Retirement

And so the day has finally dawned and the twilight years they start. Don't think you've worked hard all this time to become a boring old fart.

Just to reach this graceful age is an achievement by itself.

There's plenty more for you to do, you're far from on the shelf.

There's betting, bonking, snoring hard and lots, lots more besides. And bundles of great laughter left to split your rotting sides.

In this wondrous new beginning, new horizons you'll not lack. With the fortunes of technology to ease an aching back.

I know you'll carry on with zest and ne'er give up the fight. But I'm afraid to say your thermal vest won't help your ailing sight.

There are those with reservations as retirement is nearing. That's daft, it's a celebration, despite the loss of hearing.

The truth is, you look good, colourful and well. No one would notice, no one could, that you've lost your sense of smell.

Life is now one long break lazing on the heath. Lap up another juicy steak, shame about the teeth.

The world is now your oyster whilst you're out and you're about. With a swagger and good roister as your hair starts falling out.

There's much to look forward to, with the free time that you've got. Do all the things you dreamt of, whilst your bones begin to rot.

The lake of life is now all yours without the slightest ripple. Such calm sedate retirement as you become a cripple.

Enjoy the evening of your years and a sense of new adventure. As you wave goodbye to all your fears with the onset of dementia...

"Waste of talent," Lel sighed. "What inspired him to write it?"

"His retirement – from drinking."

I stumbled across Steve's favourite book: *The Dictionary of Cockney Rhyming Slang*. I opened the front cover, he'd scribbled on the inside: *Thanks Mum, for this terrific book, I leave it to Joe.* It also said; *To Ramona - Sinead Rowan, at my funeral, pretty please, Sian.*

He knew...

Lel and I sat on the grass at the top of Llaneilian Point staring out to sea. The largest pod of dolphins swam by and a massive Sally-bow filled the sky. I imagined myself throwing those deadly red and white pills in the sea. I imagined Di hadn't been driving that night; instead she'd had a random op like Dave and they discovered her subarachnoid haemorrhage before it could burst. I imagined my sprightly mum hadn't gone downhill and Lel hadn't started smoking again. In each case I imagined a different outcome, one I desperately wanted. Every cell in my body yearned to have my crazy, funny Brady Bunch back and there was nothing I could do about it. A stream of warm tears cascaded down my face. If that wasn't devastating enough, just when my nutty-goon of a best friend/brother retired from the booze to start his life over, it had been taken, how spectacularly tragic. Or, how spectacularly nice for him to go out on a high and not have to suffer the shame and indignity of falling off the wagon. I preferred the glass half-full version, it gave me comfort, along with knowing he was reunited with John at last, and Dad, and Sal, and Mum, punching the sky, watching heavenly snooker with her up there somewhere.

"Tickety-fucking-boo," snivelled Lel, through her tears.

"Why?" I sobbed. "I don't understand life."

"If we weren't tickety-boo how would we have coped?" said my wise, puffy-eyed sister.

I didn't plan to do it, but an overwhelming urge diverted me to the hospital, Ysbyty Gwynedd, on the way home. I headed toward the giant cross, an image forever engraved on my heart. I knew exactly where to go. The last place I'd seen my lovely dad; the chapel of rest. I strolled along the hospital corridor. Yuck, that smell of pee, antiseptic, get-well flowers and questionable food smells mixed with a stainless steel tang blasted me right back...

Dad was lying in his hospital bed semi-conscious as Lel and I walked tentatively over to his bedside. I grabbed his bony fingers, and he opened his eyes, smiled at me, then flicked his imaginary cigarette into an imaginary coal fire. "I've given up smoking, Sian," he whispered in my ear.

And they were the second last words he ever said.

I couldn't help but laugh at the irony in that. I'd been complaining about it ever since I'd worked out it was going to kill him. One night, hanging around the streets of Manor Way with my mates, inhaling crisp fresh air, I came home to a lounge engulfed in smoke. I strolled into the room fake-coughing. 'Where are you, Dad?' I spluttered. 'You'll end up in a morgue in ten years' time,' I said, my desperate fifteen-year-old attempt at getting him to quit his forty-a-day Senior Service habit. Out of the mouths of babes and sucklings comes forth truth...

On his deathbed, just before the ambulance came and whisked him off to Ysbyty Gwynedd, Dad got emotional on me for the first time ever and whispered in my ear,

"Sorry for smoking, Sian, and I'm sorry I didn't protect you from your mother's illness, I haven't been a very good father."

"Dad, I wouldn't change a thing. My life has made me the person I am today, you've been the best dad in the world."

"Really?" he smiled, through childlike tears.

Being face to face with the big gold cross jolted me back to earth with a bump. I pushed open the door to the chapel of rest and crept inside. The place was like a morgue, I stupidly thought. Perhaps something to do with the fact that it was a morgue.

"Can I help you?" said a voice.

Startled, I let out a little whimper.

"Sorry, love, I didn't mean to make you jump, we're closed," said the caring gentleman.

"Oh – I wondered if I could see my brother, Steven Ball."

He looked puzzled. "We don't have anyone here called Steven Ball."

"I mean Robert, he's named after my dad Bob whose real name was William," I said, feeling silly.

"Ah, Robert Ball." He pulled a sad face. "You haven't made an appointment have you?"

I shook my head.

"I thought not." He sounded slightly uncomfortable. "I'm not supposed to, but..." he tapped his head with his finger. "I'll see what I can do. We don't keep them here you see."

He came back five minutes later and asked if I wouldn't mind giving him fifteen minutes so he could get Steve 'ready' for me. Only in Wales, the kindest, sweetest folk.

"He's ready for you now love, behind that curtain." He put a comforting hand on my shoulder. "Do you want me to come in with you?"

I shook my head.

"That's fine, but I have to warn you, your brother was an organ donor."

"I know, he felt strongly about helping other people."

"So we've taken both his corneas."

"Oh – that's um – nice." I sort of smiled, disconcerted.

"It's the only bit of him we could use," he chuckled then coughed awkwardly.

"Will I see?"

"No, so long as you don't open his eyes."

It felt wrong, the way you'd feel at a pantomime if you opened the curtain, only a million times worse. I was aware of taking quick, shallow breaths. Legs trembling, I opened the curtain with my cold clammy hands, secretly hoping they had the wrong man, so I could shake off the horrible notion I was some sort of modern-day Grim Reaper.

His mouth was open enough for me to catch a glimpse of the familiar gap between his two front teeth; it was definitely my brother. In at number three on the current death chart, six months shy of his sixtieth birthday. Steve seemed content lying there, in fact he was almost smiling. I half expected him to sit up and shout 'Joking!' but, he didn't. I gazed at the wide-open gash on his forehead. I pictured him falling, hitting his head on the washing machine, and sensed a deep sorrow brewing. Lel's words popped into my head: *We need to put the fun in funeral for Steve.* She was so right. He was a happy soul and he knew how to put the fun in funerals.

Like the funeral fiasco of my mum's sister, Auntie Doris. My stressed-out cousin had asked Steve which hymn to play; he suggested *Onward Christian Soldiers*. I mean, fancy asking my brother a question like that when he was three sheets to the wind. The next day he confessed to his moment of drunken madness. I told him not to sweat, as no one in their right mind would play it at a funeral. There we were, the grieving relatives, Mum, Sal, Dave, Steve, Di, Lel and I, sitting in the front pew and on it came. I'll never forget the utter bewilderment on Sally's face as she turned to me singing "marching as to war", loudly. I had to bury my face in my hymn sheet to hide my cackling. Steve the same. The most inappropriate funeral song ever, and everyone was singing it, oblivious...

I spoke to the nice gentleman about Steve. He explained that his 'massive haemorrhage' didn't show on the scan because it had come out of nowhere, like a lightning bolt. There was nothing anyone could have done. He was putting his washing in the machine, contemplating his retirement from alcohol, then bang, gone. I shook the nice man's hand and thanked him for bending the rules to let me say "see you marijuana".

"I'm sorry about your brother, would you like a lock of his hair?" he offered.

"Is that what people do?"

"Sometimes. It can be comforting to have a keepsake." He handed me a pair of scissors.

"You mean, me do it?"

"You don't have to, if you don't want to, my love."

"No, it's fine."

I took the scissors and disappeared behind the curtain like Sweeney Todd.

CHAPTER EIGHTEEN

A cursed freak of a Grim Reaper

To save Steve the indignity of a pauper's funeral, I paid a grand for him to have a coffin in preference to a cardboard box. He wouldn't have cared diddly-squat, but I did. Lel and I were taken aback at the size of Steve's posse. So many people young and old alike, all crying their hearts out. He truly was someone special to everyone, not just me. Hugh, Sue and Mig were there – as usual; we discussed meeting somewhere other than a funeral – as usual. There was only one VIP missing, my brother Dave, who against all odds was finally having his ill-timed and potentially cataclysmic colostomy reversal.

The surgeon had told DB the op was a risky procedure. Things get stuck together inside, the effect can be like unravelling starchy spaghetti, and if the bowel leaked it could prove fatal. Furthermore, he strongly advised against it. David 'I don't do sick' boom-boom Ball was having none of it. This wasn't a 'Tesco bag for life' he told Sara. In his mind it had always been temporary and two years was long enough. He'd promised his boys a long-awaited return to football, swimming and play fights, all the things you can't do with a stoma bag. Not having it reversed was not an option, it was a life gamble, and he was prepared to risk it.

Sara read out a brotherly eulogy for Steve on behalf of DB. It was incredibly sad saying goodbye to another brother and at the same time wondering if my other brother would be alive by the end of this funeral.

My turn to speak. Lel was too shy. I headed down the aisle towards Sara, who was staring at her phone. Not the done thing at a funeral, unless it's something urgent. Please God, no more terrible on top of shattering on top of devastating news. My heart was racing, until she lifted her head and I saw the biggest swallowed-a-banana-sideways smile on her face. She showed me the text. it read: *Sorry my darling, you won't be making that claim on the life insurance just yet* ☺ *xxx*

Hands shaking, I dropped my eulogy paper. It fluttered around in the cold church breeze like a butterfly before landing in the christening water in the font. I pulled it out like a dead fish, screwed it into a ball and threw it over my shoulder. Everyone laughed. The fun-eral had begun. Turned out I didn't need it, it was easy, the words fell off my tongue. The place was in hysterics as I shared Steve's many hilarious moments, including the 1977 bread strike and the time the extremely posh Grosvenor restaurant in Borehamwood refused him entry. He went around the back, climbed through the kitchen window, poured himself a glass of cooking wine, helped himself to a plateful of chicken from the fridge, seated himself at the workstation, stuck a napkin into his collar and tucked in. He even left a fiver tip on the side. Then there was the embarrassing moment when he interrupted the vicar's speech at his wedding to ask if anyone had any Vaseline to ease putting the ring on his wife's fat finger. Honestly, I felt like a stand-up comedienne performing on *Live at the Apollo*.

Lel and I were determined to put the fun into Steve's funeral, and we succeeded. I could have sold tickets. It was a fantastic send-off. The one moment of sadness was at the end when we played his beautifully touching choice of song, Dylan's *To Ramona*, especially when she sang this bit...

The pangs of your sadness
Shall pass as your senses will rise
The flowers of the city
Though breathlike
Get deathlike at times
And there's no use in tryin'
T' deal with the dyin'
Though I cannot explain that in lines

Back to reality, back to having a heavy heart and feeling positively un-tickety-boo. This house was supposed to be a death-free fresh start, but I couldn't shake the horrible perception that it was tarnished now. Every time I walked through the front door I envisioned the red cross of the Black Death on it. I was exhausted, struggling with juggling chocolate policing by day and aerobics by night. I made the decision that at the end of that term I would give up my two remaining classes. I loved it; I just didn't have any energy left.

Lynette warned me that chocolate headquarters were on my case. Ugh, the mundaneness of work. I'd lost heart since they'd slashed the hourly rate and halved our expenses yet doubled the workload. I had the misfortune of meeting my boss once, and she insisted on accompanying me on a store visit to assess how 'bad' I was at my job. I recognised her straightaway. She had stepped straight out of the eighties and into Tesco, fresh off the *Dynasty* set. Cruella De Veal I secretly called her, a fitting mickey-take since her surname was Veal. I didn't know what I'd done wrong, but it was embarrassing, she told Lynette. I had ruffled the shoulder pads of the big cheese. Never mind all the good stuff, and the fact that I had increased company sales by seventy-five percent, that didn't matter.

I racked my brains, and the only 'embarrassing' thing I could recall was my recent run-in with a grumpy store manager when a whole pallet of chocolate had been delivered in past its sell-by date. He started droning on about not ordering any more stock because *my* company was rubbish. The say-it-as-it-is Rene gene reared its head. I cut him dead: "It's not my company actually, furthermore I don't care." I'd been half-expecting to be hauled over the coals ever since he'd shuffled off in a mood.

Ms Veal couldn't wait to get the condolences out of the way so she could deal the blow, and it wasn't that. It was far more sinister. Every month I filled out my report and sent it to the client (a certain brand of chocolate) and my expenses, which I sent to the office. This month I had made the godawful mistake of sending my report to the office and my expenses to the client.

"We have a professional image to reflect to our client, this isn't good enough, blah, blah, blah..." Cruella told me off like I was some sort of juvenile brat as opposed to a grief-stricken human who perhaps couldn't concentrate at the moment or listen properly to what she was piffling on about. I couldn't help but prove I was just that – a juvenile brat. "It's not my fault they have similar pre-paid envelopes," I said, laughing.

"It's not funny, Elizabeth, it's embarrassing," she growled.

Laughing aside, I was never too far away from flipping my lid. I'd had enough of my life being riddled with corporate cancer. "You think that's embarrassing? Try watching your big sister have her nappy changed. That's what I call embarrassing!"

Way to go, Rene gene. That killed the conversation. Good. Sack me.

Grief makes you observe things through different eyes. My exciting half-built conservatory/kitchen was a dirty building site, and I hated it. Property development sounded fun, but in reality it was hard work and extremely stressful. I needed creature comforts like a door to my bedroom instead of a dust sheet, and to be able to walk around barefoot without treading on a nail. I realised too late I wasn't great at living like this, I was malfunctioning, doing stupid things like sending the wrong envelope to the wrong company. The simplest of things like what to cook for tea became a Mensa challenge. Not a lot was going on upstairs apart from voices in my head. "Why not make carbonara tonight, Heart? Joe loves it," Sal would say.

Sometimes we had full-blown conversations. I'd ask her why she did what she did, and she'd say, "do we have to keep going over this?" I'd say, "I can't help it, I miss you so much." She'd say, "not as much as I miss you, Heart." Then I'd cry and sense her presence with me and feel blessed for having a life, and an Olly, and my children, and an Ella.

Lel, on the other hand, didn't have a life. We all deal with grief in different ways. I immersed myself in chocolate bars, Lel mooched around in a dressing gown praying to her angels. She needed a hobby, something, anything, to keep her occupied, so I sent her a candle-making kit; she loved candles. Her visits to Di were slacking off too. To be fair, so were mine, Di was settled and had her Oompa-Loompa family. She was in good hands and was sometimes more upset than happy to see us, that was my reason. Lel's excuse was she didn't trust driving her deteriorating chug-a-lug, but it wasn't true. It was because she'd taken up a new hobby – daytime drinking. We skyped each other regularly to 'check in' but it gradually tailed off to once a week, then fortnightly.

One time I wasn't in the mood for her bullshit. I got straight to the point.

"Why have you got puffy eyes?"

"I don't know, Lovey, it must be the cucumber," she slurred.

"Not the litre of vodka you've had? I thought you'd stopped smoking?"

"I have, Lovey."

"Lel, you're putting tobacco in a Rizla paper as we speak, or is it mixed herbs?"

"It's a roll up, it's not exactly smoking."

How can you argue with someone who has a blatant death wish? Bad idea of Olly's showing her how to make homemade wine, candles would have been a safer bet, if she hadn't burnt her hand while making them, pissed, that is.

"Another funeral to look forward to." Hollow-legged Joe strode past, carrying a plate piled high with a loaf's worth of jam sandwiches.

"Joe, dinner's in half an hour."

"It's a Scooby-snack, Mum."

"Joe, if you're eating in the lounge..."

"I know." He mimicked a nagging voice, "roll the rug back, rah, rah, rah."

The hardest thing, harder than your own pain, is knowing

your children are suffering and not being able to fix it. My heart bled for my innocent babies, even though they were adults. My natural motherly instinct wanted to protect them, not inadvertently cause them to suffer grief as a result of the family I had been born into. If I wasn't in the mood for Ramtha I'd cry myself to sleep. The heartache was intense at times. Everything and everyone was pulling me down. Although there was *some* light in my wretched existence – Ella, who put a smile on my face every day, especially when she came out with this little gem: "You don't let people walk on Sally's rug because you love her. I love her too, Nana."

"And she loves you, sweetheart."

"I know she does, she told me."

"Did she?" I asked, somewhat discombobulated. "What else did she say?"

"I'm such a pretty bubba."

Whoa! The exact words Sally had said the last time she had held Ella in her arms.

"Anything else?"

"Sorry she didn't buy me an Easter egg."

On the subject of eggs, a simple conversation about whether penguins lay them turned into a full-blown argument between me and Olly. He was right, of course, which made me even more miserable that I couldn't get anything right, including cheese on toast. Olly tried to help and show me a handy tip to avoid burning it, but I was still fuming over the penguin eggs.

"I don't need advice from you, thanks!" I shouted.

"Clearly you do!" he shouted, equally angry.

That was the final straw. The straw before was me biting his head off for suggesting we watch *Mamma Mia*. Why would I want to watch Sally's last film, pray tell? I threw the burnt-cheese-covered spatula at him and stormed off.

I brave-faced my way through aerobics feeling guilty the whole time about Olly-Flower. Arguing over penguin eggs and grilled cheese; how silly. I couldn't wait for it to finish so I could tell him how sorry I was. I got home a couple of hours later than usual bogged down with wine and gifts after an emotional night of goodbyes. I was knackered, but relieved to have survived my last-ever class. Something to celebrate.

"Hello?" I called, cheerfully.

No response. I wandered around; no sign of him, but the bedroom dust sheet had been replaced with a shiny new door. Ah, the alpha-male way of saying sorry. Maybe he was in his man-cave, putting away tools? Nope. Perhaps he was in the studio staring wistfully at his dusty keyboard as he often did. He wasn't there. Weird. I went into the bathroom. His toothbrush had gone…

Next step; boxer shorts and socks drawer. It was empty. Shit.

I didn't know how or when things had started affecting our relationship, it must have been chipping away the whole time. After the initial shock had worn off, I felt relieved. I didn't want to be in a relationship. I had nothing to give. My emotional fuel tank was on empty.

"Where the fuck has he gone?" asked Lel.

"Don't know, don't care." And I meant it. I could do stubborn too.

"Can't say I blame him, Lovey."

"Thanks."

"Sian, I wouldn't want to be around us. I don't even want to be around myself. I'm seriously considering fucking off to Australia, meeting new people and saying, "Hi, I'm Lesley, I'm an only child.""

I knew what she meant. Looking at Olly's face was like looking in the mirror of pain, reflected back 24/7. It can't have been easy, being my rock whilst carrying the burden of my family's deaths which had turned me into a fun sponge. I'd been walking around with a churning hole for a stomach and a face like a smacked arse for so long (bar the brief tickety-boo interlude) that it felt normal. How could I give myself to anyone when my heart was an empty penguin egg? On top of which his beloved music career was over. There weren't any media jobs out there for in-house composers. Olly not doing what he was born to do, music – bear with a sore head. I understood why he left. I felt sorry for him, but that didn't stop me sending abusive messages. I hated him. The stubborn phone-ignoring bastard, leaving me over penguin eggs and grilled cheese.

Armed with an empty glass, I searched the loft for his demijohn stash of Olly-Flower wine so I could drink it all and piss him off. Ha, found it. I also found Dave and Sara's wedding album, what a kick in the teeth. I sat myself on the floor, cross-legged, me and the cobwebs, with a ten pack of Marlboro, and flicked through the photos. In my mind's eye I saw a black cross on each of their happy faces. I tossed it aside in disgust. It wasn't about penguin eggs and grilled cheese, it was about Di, and Sally, and Mum, and now Steve. I missed them all so much. Steve had been gone three months and it seemed like yesterday. I longed to see those gappy teeth and hear that contagious cackle, and the way he rolled his head back and his shoulders shook up and down. I yearned for our deep meaningful conversations, his drunken phone calls, home-made jokes, Cockney rhyming slang and the silly expression we used to pull at each other in the advert break of Star Trek. I smoked and drank and laughed and cried myself into a self-piteous stupor, reminiscing...

"Damn, I forgot milk," I said. "Keep an eye on Dean while I nip to the shop."

"What do I have to do?" asked Steve.

"Nothing." I laughed. "Leave him in his bouncer."

"What if he cries?"

"He won't cry, Steve, don't fret, I'll be fifteen minutes."

I came back to find hot under the collar Steve rocking a battered Dean in his arms. He had a bruise on his forehead and his lips were navy blue. "What have you done to my baby?" I snatched Dean off him.

"He cried as soon as you left, so I gave him a pen to play with."

I was so stressed I couldn't speak properly. "Steve, you can't give a one-year-old to a pen!"

"You can't give a pen to a one-year-old either, coz they put it in their mouth and suck it. I rang 999, they said if it wasn't a fountain pen he'll be fine."

"You rang the emergency services?"

"Sian, I thought he had ink poisoning! I put him in the chair while I was on the phone, that's why he's got a bruise on his head, before you ask."

"You can't put a one-year-old in a chair, Steve!"

"I know that now don't I, coz he fell out of it! He was so upset I gave him a bit of Turkish delight to keep him quiet."

"You can't give Turkish delight to a one-year-old, Steve!"

"Tell me about it. He started bloody choking on it."

"If he's upset all you need to do is give him Barbara." I glanced around the room. "Where's Barbara?"

My worn-out brother pointed at the window. I looked out. There was Dean's special teddy lying in the pouring rain, covered in mud.

"I took him over to the window to show him the birds. I thought it might stop him crying but he threw it out," he whined, exasperated...

The home video I made of frustrated Steve unable to contain his laughter, saying repeatedly "It's a wily woodpecker," and five-year-old Joe arguing repeatedly; "It's a Willy woodpecker." And the one of Steve dancing around with Joe's pants over his face crooning "nana, nana, nana, nana, pant-man!" to the tune of Batman. I felt a glow realising I had captured those treasured moments. Almost half a century spent making fond memories like that. Sad as I was to lose my best buddy, an underlying acceptance came with it. Deep vein thrombosis and cheap cider from nine in the morning to nine the following morning, until he collapsed into a drink coma – deadly combo. Steve was a ticking time bomb. No wonder he exploded. No wonder Mum had a battered little red tin with his name on it.

I woke up with the mother of hangovers and an email I didn't want to open from Dylan. I traipsed into the kitchen and gazed through the rainy window of my half-built Lego conservatory at my half-built patio and the huge pile of rubble at the bottom of the garden; it summed up my half-life nicely. I'd had a splitting headache ever since *he* left, and I hardly saw my little buddy Joe anymore, ever since Dylan had taken him under his film industry wing as a video assistant. I had no motivation to do anything. I was so down in the mouth I'd forgotten how to smile. Somewhere along the way I'd got lost and ended up going down *that* road. I didn't blame Olly for leaving, who would want to be with me, a cursed freak of a Grim Reaper? I would leave me if I could.

"Hmm, headaches." The doctor scanned my notes. "My word, you've experienced a terrible amount of tragedy. I see there's a history of manic depression and suicide here. Tends to run in families, this sort of thing."

"Lifestyle doesn't, nor does personal choice," I counter-offered.

Dr Death ogled me with concern. "Are you feeling depressed at all?"

"Yes, because I've had a headache for two weeks."

His face clouded over. "Hmm, mother suffered an aneurysm, sister suffered an aneurysm, both brothers suffered an aneurysm – right, see how you get on with these." He scribbled me a prescription. "Hopefully it's post-traumatic stress disorder, but if the headaches don't go, it's imperative you come back in seven days."

Nothing like instilling the fear of God in you, is there? What was I supposed to think? My brain was about to explode? Mum suffered an aneurysm because she was old. Di suffered an aneurysm because she was a stressed-out smoker. Steve suffered an aneurysm because he was a full-time pisshead and Dave survived his, so that didn't count. As for 'manic depression' 'suicide' and 'post-traumatic stress disorder,' Go away with your freaky labels.

I went to the chemist and grabbed my prescription, a lavender wheat bag and a box of Clairol Root Touch-Up. I got home and opened my pot of pills. They were red and white. Uh-oh. Not a good sign. I'd avoided antidepressants all my life (apart from the time I swallowed hundreds) and I wasn't about to swallow one now. There was only one place those red and white pills were going – down the toilet.

Dylan's email informed him that the hospital had admitted liability for Sally's death and offered him a paltry sum. Too little too late, but he accepted it. He could have got thousands more but it wasn't about the money, he needed the distress to end, so he could move on. I understood that. Dirty bits of paper weren't going to bring her back.

"It's an insult, that's what it is, four grand in exchange for a life – ouch!" said the long-suffering but indestructible DB, back up and firing on eleven of his twelve cylinders.

"You all right, Dave?"

"Yeah, bit painful at times."

"I can't believe Dr Frankenstein agreed to operate."

"I made it easy for him, Liz. I said, 'Doc, open me up and if you feel good do it, and if you don't, don't.' I knew once he was in there he'd get stuck in." he laughed.

"Not funny, Dave, you could have died."

"Kiddo, I don't do sick, and I don't do death either." There was a moment of 'Steve' silence between us. "I figured I've got a few guardian angels watching over me now, eh, little one? Anyway, enough about me, I got a disturbing message from Olly today telling me something I didn't want to hear."

"Lucky you, he ignores my text messages."

"Liz, don't be stupid, text is shit, stop being a ratbag and talk to him."

"I would, if I thought he would answer my call."

"You haven't tried, have you?"

I laughed. Brothers and sisters, how well they know their fellow siblings.

"Come on, kid, life is too short, we know the score more than anyone, you two are joined at the hip, stop messing about, and stop taking your pain out on each other. Ring him!"

I snuggled into bed, placed the heated wheat sack on my head and imagined myself shrouded in Sally's golden light. I drifted off to sleep praying to all my family members on the other side to sprinkle some of their magic healing power on me.

When I woke up in the morning, my headache had gone.

CHAPTER NINETEEN

What a hoot

Grief, hell bent on destroying my happiness, had crept in there, taken the very thing I held dear and trashed it – Olly. Beneath my misery I understood it wouldn't be normal if I didn't feel this rotten. I didn't need antidepressants, I needed time, to process everything, to heal. If only Sally had thought twice before she'd swallowed that first tablet...

By September 2011, after three months of living my glass half-empty single life, I'd had enough. I wandered into the bathroom and stared at my face in the ugly mirror. Who was this woman? An old face with wishy-washy bloodshot eyes peered back at me, my hair was a frizzy mess interspersed with grey stragglers. I stood there, staring, until a familiar Cockney voice in my head said, "Have you done your hair?"

Taking antidepressants seemed possibly less scary than the prospect of talking to Olly, that's how scared I was, but

I didn't fancy polluting our already fragile relationship with delusional thoughts. I wiped the dust off my Clairol Root Touch-Up, dyed my hair, dug beyond the doldrums, plucked up the courage and pressed the 'phone-ignoring bastard' button on my mobile. I was shaking like a leaf inside but I had to do it. Hell would freeze over before he called me.

"We need to talk, Olly."

"How are you, Liz?"

He ignored my statement so I ignored his question. "Do you want to come to the house?"

"I can't."

I wanted to scream, but I knew if I did he would hang up and block me and I'd never see him again. I trod carefully, small talk; much safer. "Where have you been, anywhere nice?"

"Hell and back, Liz."

I ignored the guilt trip. "Dave told me you were in Swanage, how are they?"

"The usual, Dad wants to go on a cruise, guess what Mum said?"

"What a hoot?"

"No, surprisingly." He continued, adopting his best mum's voice, *"Why would I want to go on a cruise, Ross, it's like being in a floating prison with a high risk of drowning."*

We both laughed at that.

"Your dad's probably trying to get away from you," I joked.

"I'm not there anymore, Liz."

"You're not there?"

"Liz, I do want to meet you."

He was holding back, I could tell. I counted to an angry ten in my head. "Where are you, Olly, tell me please?"

"Maidenhead."

"You're at Sonia's?"

"Not exactly…"

He was in Maidenhead but not at his sister's, he couldn't come to the house but he wanted to 'meet' me. The plot thickened. I knew it; I'd pushed him into the arms of someone else. What a fool. Words were needed with my number one confidante to stop me falling apart inside.

"What are you going to do, Mum?" Teri was concerned.

"I'm going to drive to Maidenhead."

"And do what?"

"I honestly don't know, but I will when I get there."

I hated driving in the rain and dark but needs must. As I turned into Sonia's cul-de-sac, a familiar silhouette stepped out of a motorhome. HOLY CRAP.

"He's bought a house Teri – on wheels!" I wailed.

"What? When? Where's he going?"

"Scotland?"

"Why Scotland?"

Who knew? All I knew was I didn't want my Flower to go anywhere. It was the wake-up call I needed to shake me out of my victim mindset.

'Unknown' rang my phone. Probably some pilchard from

the office wanting to have a go about what colour pen I was using, or maybe it was that stranger I once knew called Olly with a new identity, or worse, his new girlfriend. As a rule I didn't answer unknown numbers.

"Hello Sian," said a distinctive deep female voice.

"Di – oh my, you've got a phone!"

We spoke for three-quarters of an hour. I reminded her of the time she bought me a horse picture for my thirteenth birthday. I was never into horses – she was. She also bought me an abdominal cruncher I didn't need, I did PE four times a week. "I thought we could share them," she had pouted in response to my ungrateful sulk. "I knew it, you're so selfish!" I shouted, flashing my angry eyes and storming out of the house.

Di snorted with laughter at that memory. It triggered her to tell me about the horses outside her window. She also told me Mum had appeared in the shape of a robin who perched on her windowsill, in her disjointed wordy-missy way. "Never thought – see that?" She sounded chirpy. She told me John-boy and Steve were outside her window chatting and laughing like nothing had happened and there was no bad blood between them. I couldn't wait to speak to the girls.

"I didn't think you were going to tell your mum Steve died, Lu?"

"I didn't," admitted Lucy. "Not after Sally and Nana, it's too much, Sian."

I rang Amy, she said the same. She and Lucy had made a pact not to tell her.

"Is she communicating with them, or is it all in her damaged mind, Ame?"

"I hope it's all in her damaged mind Sian – she told me today Nana and Sally were getting a place ready for her."

I didn't want to hear that. "It's great she's got a phone, isn't it?"

"She rings me all the time." Amy giggled. "She called earlier and shouted, 'Amy, get the horse in.' I told her to stop panicking, Sonny was already in and she said, 'Horseshit. I can see him out of my window in the field'."

I laughed. "She must get the Oompa Loompas to press the buttons."

"Yep, she's a real diva now."

"Has Lel been to visit her lately?"

"What do you think?"

"She'd rather sit around with her cronies drinking."

"It's not that. I had a go at her about it and she fell apart, Sian, she's lost so much confidence since… well, everything, and don't forget, Mum's her other half, she can't hack seeing her suffering anymore, I felt bad afterwards."

I hadn't given the Tweedle twin thing a second thought. Di, the Dee to Lel's Dum. Now I felt bad too.

I drove into the golf course car park and there it was, the ominous bachelor mobile and Olly standing beside it. The independent boy who'd installed his own BT line and put a doorbell on his bedroom door at the age of fourteen was bound to do something unusual. My stomach flipped at the sight of him but was instantly quashed by a melange of anger and jealousy when a blonde baseball cap-wearing female stepped out of the passenger side. Hell hath no fury, I wheel span out of the car park like a neurotic woman scorned.

Five seconds later my phone rang.

"Liz, why did you speed off?" the stranger asked.

"Go away, Olly!" Crying, I cut him off. It rang again. "You could have told me you'd met someone else, you didn't have to rub my nose in it!" I shouted.

"What?"

"I saw her, Olly, step out of the truck, I'm not fucking blind."

"Oh, Liz!" He burst into a laughing fit. "It was Sonia, you silly thing."

"But – that woman had blonde hair, Sonia's got…"

"Highlights, Liz, but she doesn't like it so she's dying it back to brown, her hairdresser mate lives on Penn Road so I dropped her off."

I didn't feel like a stupid idiotic birdbrain at all… much. Not as much as I was swamped with enormous gratitude for being wrong. I drove back into the golf course and parked next to Olly's converted shit-heap of a rusty horsebox.

If you can't say anything nice don't say anything, said Sally. With 'nice' firmly planted in the forefront of my mind I got out of the car and casually walked over to him feigning surprise. "That looks, um, nice."

I wanted to fling my arms around him, but I didn't, but I

did. Some things needed to be ironed out, like what the hell are you playing at, Olly, have you lost your goddamn mind?

"Aren't you going to invite me in for a tea?" I asked, waving the metaphoric white flag.

It turned out he had lost his mind. He felt dreadful putting his problems on his retired parents, and Sonia could only offer him a floor and a cushion. Not everyone had a family as accommodating as mine.

"Olly, why didn't you tell me?"

"I thought you hated me, Liz."

"Oh, Olly, what made you think that?"

He scrolled through his phone and read aloud. *I hate you. When you came into my life everything went wrong. It's your fault my family are dead. I never want to see you again. Fuck off to Scotland.*

Duly noted. He looked up from his phone, and seeing those sad green eyes fill with water dissolved my anger faster than Alka Seltzer. I reached out to him and we hugged. It felt exactly the same as it did when we hugged for the first time and got stuck, only this time he didn't laugh. His body crumpled in my arms and he sobbed his heart out and cried. I felt nothing but compassion for him. The bullshit was stripped, nothing else was left, just raw love.

We remained in the truck and cuddled and cried and talked and cried non-stop for eight hours, breaking every so often to nip to the loo.

"Shall we go and get some food?" Olly eventually suggested.

We filled our faces with junk food. I had a vegetarian triple cheese pizza, Di would approve of that. Olly, my yin to my yang, had triple pepperoni.

It was getting late, so I gingerly broached the subject. "What will you do now?"

"Stay here, we could meet tomorrow and talk some more, if it's all right with you?"

I pointed to the 'two hours max parking' sign outside.

"Great." He sighed. "I'll park at the rec."

We drove in convoy to the rec, and I pointed at the 'no overnight parking' sign. In my rear-view mirror I saw him banging his head on the steering wheel in despair. I wound my window down. "I know somewhere you can park," I said, laughing my conkers off.

What's that saying? Ah yes, every silver lining has a cloud, that's the one. Amy told me Di had contracted a severe respiratory infection, so I rang Lel and talked her into coming by agreeing to meet me there. When I arrived Di was sleeping peacefully, but her chest was rattling. The next blow, Lel walked in. I was unpleasantly surprised at how skinny she was.

"Oh my God, how much do you weigh?" I asked.

"Hello, Lovey," she smiled, ignoring my bluntness and giving me a cuddle.

"You were eight and a half the last time I saw you."

"Oh, I don't know, Lovey, eight."

"Pointless lie?"

"All right, seven and three quarters."

"Why are you not eating?"

"I am, it's the emphysema, Sian."

That shut me up. I felt rotten. "Like your new teeth." I tried not to grin, imagining her launching them at my head.

Straight-faced, she replied, "I look like fucking Shergar."

Di opened her big blue eyes and wonky-smiled. She looked happy, bless her beautiful heart. "How – you – Sian?" she asked me.

"All the better for seeing you." I kissed her on the head.

Out of the corner of my eye I caught Lel sneak a massive baguette out of her bag and stuff her face with it. Ellen told us Di had the brain equivalent of a four to six-year-old, but it didn't mean she didn't have eyes in her head. Selfless Di didn't care, I did.

"How could you, Lesley?"

She spun around, spooked, and stopped chewing. "Sorry, Di, I was testing my new teeth," she muttered, barely moving her lips. A dismal attempt at disguising her mouthful of food.

"How – you – Lel?" Di asked.

"I've got such a headache, Di," she replied, quickly chewing away the evidence and shoving the rest in her bag.

"I wish," said Di.

A headache versus brain damage. No competition.

"That's why I needed to eat, Di," Lel explained, making matters worse for herself.

"I wish," Di repeated.

Poor Lel, she looked gutted when Di said that, and in all fairness, she was ill too. Torn between two Tweedles, I softened and tried to help.

"She needs to put weight on, Di, it's her emphysema."

"I wish," said Di again.

Poor Di, how awful must life be, to wish you had a headache, to wish you could eat, and worst of all, to wish you had emphysema.

The Relate counsellor was so empathetic I had to hand her back the tissue box. She couldn't believe what we had been through and survived as a couple. Olly told her we had become two norths of a magnet. She deduced that if we were two norths of a magnet we must have once been a dynamic duo. It was painful, but we discovered a lot about each other's feelings. I admitted I'd cried myself to sleep for the last three months. Olly spilt the beans; he'd cried every morning for three months. She said it was a blessing. We needed to de-grief, and breaking up was the best way to make that happen.

I felt really happy as my feet sank into the soft hot sand, not just normal but happy, for the first time in three years, since Di's crash. I hadn't thought I would ever feel normal again, let alone happy. Here we were, swimming in a turquoise sea, basking in the sun, drinking extra-large cocktails and loving the lazy beats played by the resort's resident DJ. Our first holiday together as a couple.

It was a last minute.com deal, a dismal broom-cupboard apartment in Corsica. It was all we could afford, but that was the single best piece of advice from our Relate lady. I felt a bit lost and tearful at times, especially when Olly spotted a Steve-alike walking along the beach and we had to do a double take. I almost ran over and touched a total stranger. I had to keep checking in with home too.

"Any dramas today, Joe?"

"No, everything's cool, I'm going to Dad's for the weekend, Dean's going to stay with the dog, relax, enjoy your holiday, Mum."

"Everything okay back at the ranch?" Olly asked.

I smiled and nodded, gazing at the hazy sun setting over the mountains. "It's magical here."

"It's inspiring." Olly beamed. "I've got so many riffs floating around in my head I might write a chill-out track when we get home."

"Blow the dust off your keyboard and write some music. So what if you don't work for a media company, do it for you."

"If we get home – in one piece."

"Why did you call it an elastic band plane?"

"It's a propeller, not a jet engine, they remind me of the balsa wood elastic band models I used to make as a kid." He laughed.

"And the cable cars you made out of Lego and string – for your hamsters."

We both laughed.

"I want us to do this again, Olly."

On the last night on the balcony of our surprisingly unexpected luxury penthouse apartment we booked another holiday, three months from then, in Fuerteventura.

ONE WEEK EARLIER

We got as far as one junction before Gatwick and hit standstill traffic.

"Don't worry," Olly reassured me, confidently, "we've got two hours until check in and we're only ten minutes away…"

I jumped out of the car and grabbed both suitcases as Olly sped off like Stirling Moss. Puffing, panting, I ran through the North Terminal. In the distance I saw them closing the check-in point. "Wait, please!" I shouted, dragging the suitcases as fast as I could. "Sorry, my part – um, husband's on his way, he's parking the car, he'll be here any second."

The security woman glanced at her watch. She shook her head. "Sorry, you're too late, the gate closed ten minutes ago."

"Can't you open it? We've got half an hour before take-off."

Olly appeared, sweating and puffing so bad he had to bend over and put his hands on his knees.

"She's not letting us on the plane, Olly." I was close to tears.

"The plane's here, what's the problem?" Olly quizzed her, gasping for air.

"I'm sorry," she said, awkward but firm. "I can't let you on the flight."

I sensed a panic attack coming on. This was not happening.

Olly shook his head. "I had to park three miles away. I have high-jumped three barriers, climbed an eight-foot metal - for all I know - fucking electrified fence, we are getting on that plane."

"I'll see what I can do."

Red-faced, she darted off, talking into her radio mic, and returned with a male security guard (safety in numbers). "I'm sorry, the pilot said no," he explained, impervious to our plight.

Olly put his arms around me. "Please, don't do this, my part – um wife's been through so much, if you knew."

"There's one flight a day to Corsica and that was it, I'm afraid."

I buried my head into Olly's torso and cried. Why was I so cursed?

"There must be something you can do?" Olly begged him.

"There's one going to Nice." He scanned his iPad.

"Tsk," I mumbled into Olly's chest, "fat lot of good."

"There might be a connection to Corsica – ooh, you're in luck."

That piqued my interest. I lifted my head. "Will there be extra to pay?"

"Fifteen hundred pounds."

"Pay twice!" I complained. "We can't afford to do that."

"Liz, we have two choices, either waste fifteen hundred by not going, or stick fifteen hundred on the credit card and actually have a holiday, if we don't, it'll be Canada all over again."

"You have to hurry," he informed us, "it leaves in ten minutes."

A twinge of adventure stirred in my belly. "Stuff it, let's do it, Olly."

"Ah, unfortunately we have a problem," said he, ogling his iPad. "It's the South Terminal."

Olly glanced at his watch. "We'll never make it."

"Worth a try?" smiled Mr optimistic. "What have you got to lose?" Only fifteen hundred pounds.

"I can do tickets on the monorail, but we'll have to run – like now."

What a hoot! We ran. Following the Terminator T1000 security man, through cordoned-off zones we weren't meant to, dragging our suitcases, being stared at by people. With seconds to spare, we jumped on board the elastic band plane to Nice and got a connecting elastic band plane direct to Corsica.

"Don't worry, everyone who speaks French speaks English, Flower," I stated confidently.

Except when in Corsica. The bus driver hadn't heard of the place we couldn't pronounce somewhere in Porto Vecchio. Reluctantly we had to let the bus go and try the next one. Same-same. Come bus number three we were saved by an expat who told him we were going somewhere completely undecipherable.

We arrived in the wee small hours, tired and tattered, to discover the hotel had rebooked our dismal broom cupboard because we weren't on the transfer coach seven hours earlier, so we spent the night on the uncomfortable reception couch. Next morning the rep was tripping over himself. There was one apartment left in a neighbouring resort. Begrudgingly we accepted his offer of redemption. A luxury penthouse suite…

Home, relaxed, re-energised, fifteen hundred pounds poorer but feeling like a million dollars, I plonked my suitcase on the floor. The first thing my bionic eyeballs detected was a faint stain on my precious rug, so faint Olly said it wasn't a stain, it was the light. I took one look at Dean's reddening face. It wasn't the light.

"Mum I don't know what to say, I'm so sorry."

I scrutinised the rug and sniffed it. "Smells like red wine."

"It was, I scrubbed and scrubbed it. I even hired an industrial cleaner, sorry, I'll buy you a new one, exactly the same."

"You did well to get a red wine stain out." I grinned.

"Mum, why are you smiling? I thought you were going to lay an egg. I haven't slept for two nights; I've been sick to my stomach about telling you. I wanted to ring you while you were away but Teri said not to ruin your holiday. I've had such bad anxiety."

"Ruin my holiday!" I laughed. "Oh Dean, you know Sally would find this hysterical. Material things don't mean a fig to me, whereas you mean the world to me."

His downturned smile upturned, the pair of us crying over a red wine stain on a rug. Chrysanthemums sprang to mind, a refreshing reason to be upset. Dean was off the hook and couldn't wait to escape.

"He doesn't like red wine," said Olly, closing the door behind him.

"That bimbo he's been seeing does." I laughed.

I was too happy to care. Counselling taught us you can't split up when you're joined at the hip. The relate lady explained trauma doesn't have to define you, and death is a profound experience, it can refine you. She said sometimes we have to know darkness before we can appreciate the light and gave me a book to read called *Soul Mates*. The first line read: "If you think being with your soul mate means you're in for an easy ride, think again."

And the ride wasn't over, by a long shot.

CHAPTER TWENTY

Walking with the trees

———◇◇◇———

I couldn't wait to visit Di. Being in a foreign country had not only made me feel far away but guilty for enjoying it. Di was in her special wheelchair when Olly and I got there, gazing out of her window at the horses.

"You had sex?" she asked us.

A typical question from her. I wasn't exaggerating when I said Di was stripped of the constraints of society.

"That's a bit personal." Ellen walked in laughing. "Di, this is Chris, he's our latest newbie."

Di winked at me and pointed at the embarrassed young male carer. "Dish."

I laughed. The tart who loved to flaunt herself was still in there. Some things never change.

Ellen chuckled. "I'll bring him back later, Di, when Sian and Olly have gone, yeah?"

Olly showed Di his new iPhone. It had a piano app which she could plonk with her fingers. I watched them having a whale of a time, enjoying their shared love of piano. I felt a pang of sadness. It didn't seem long ago Di was desperate to learn *Midnight Sonata* because Olly could play it and she couldn't. How hard she practised, day and night until her fingers were sore, then she played it down the phone to Olly on loudspeaker note perfect. When she finished we gave her a rapturous round of applause...

Tired but happy, time for us to leave Di in peace. I kissed her on the head and off we went hopefully in time to have a bit of an evening.

iPhone piano plonking had left Olly inspired.

"I've done it, Liz!"

"What's it called?"

"Output 1-2."

"How romantic, Olly."

"My software labelled it," he admitted, "you know me and words, Liz, I'm good at music."

"What were you thinking about when you composed it?"

"Corsica, and what a soulful place it is for lovers."

"And there's your name, right there, *Soul Lovers.*"

Several more relate sessions and another holiday later Olly and I were back to being a dynamic duo, on a higher level of understanding than before.

"How was your holiday, kid?" DB asked me.

"Great, if you like a good old force nine gale and being hit on the head by coconuts."

"I figured you must have, Fuerteventura means 'strong winds'."

Note to self; ask worldly-wise brother's advice before booking holiday in future.

We knuckled down and finished all the jobs which needed finishing, garden landscaping, butterfly removal, painting the exterior jasmine white instead of Angel Delight pink. Being the can-I-have-a-go sort, Olly had learned not only how to lay bricks but also plastering and plumbing on the building site with Dan, plus we had Dean for the electrics and Joe for general labouring. Come April 2012, a year after Steve's passing, one break-up, and two holidays later, we had cracked it and were ready to sell. Our renovations increased the house's value from two hundred and seventy-five to three hundred and sixty grand, and we did it all on a shoestring with the three boys' help, Olly's favourite – YouTube videos and Di's favourite – eBay. We discovered how phenomenally brilliant it was when Olly sold the rusty horsebox and more than got his money back. Happy days.

Having been busy with the house, I hadn't seen Di as often as I would have liked; we were well overdue a visit. Olly and I wandered around M&S trying to find a pair of purple silk pyjamas for her. She'd lost a bit of weight recently and her current ones were a bit sack-like.

"Look at this, Olly." I held up a striped nightshirt. "My

mum used to buy me nighties like this." A twinge of sorrow came over me.

"Why don't you buy it for yourself, from your mum?"

Drifting off to sleep I felt snuggly, like a baby in the womb, as if Mum had bought it for me.

Di, eternally grateful for visits and gifts, thanked us about ten times for her pair of silly purple pyjamas. As we were leaving she beckoned me close and whispered, "look after my girls."

"I will, Di." I kissed her on the head and thought nothing of it. I was accustomed to her saying random things. "Love you," I said, as always.

"Love you more," she said, as always.

The housing market remained dead. It took us eighteen months to find a buyer. Finally, in October 2013 the 'sold' board went up and a strange thing happened. Our unapproachable, milk-bottle-glasses wearing, bandy-legged odd-bod of a neighbour knocked on the door. I'd spoken to him twice in the three years we were there, once informing him a neighbour was reporting his untaxed van, second to tell him his dog had pooed outside my gate.

"Now you've sold I'm putting my house on the market," he announced. "Do you want to come and see it?"

"No thanks, it's out of our price range," I replied.

"It wouldn't hurt to look." Olly grinned, repeating my famous sentence.

I didn't take much convincing, me being the nosey sort.

A Pandora's Box of delights it was. In need of work, yes, but at least it wasn't pink. Five double bedrooms, twice the size of the Angel Delight house and full of character. I fell in love with Brian's house. Sadly, as I explained to our new friendly neighbour (who had a name, and didn't kill his wife and kids and bury them under the patio, she left him), it was beyond our grasp with a value somewhere around four hundred and fifty thousand.

During the course of the last twelve months Di's health had been up and down, but overall it was gradually deteriorating. She was out for the count when we got to Hafod-y-Green. I watched my sister sleeping; it didn't give me the same sense of comfort it usually did. Her skin was deathly pale, her breathing was laboured. Amy and back-to-platinum-blonde Lucy were sitting in silence, either side of the bed, holding her hands.

"Mum's got an infection, Sian, she's been back and forth to A&E all week," Amy informed me.

"She's forever getting infections, antibiotics will clear it, won't they?"

"It's because of all the drugs she's so ill, Sian, she can't have any more," said Lucy.

It turned out Lucy was right about the Avon unit. They'd put Di on Temazepam and Diazepam the whole time to keep her quiet and although Ellen did a sterling job of getting her off them, coupled with six years of antibiotics and God knows what harsh drugs she needed for her condition, the damage had been done. Di couldn't have any more medication, and medication was the only thing keeping her alive.

"Her liver's packing up, Sian," said Amy, in the same kind of tone you might use if you'd just found out you'd run out of milk.

She was putting on a brave front, but those doleful blue eyes gave the game away. I knew that look. It had remained etched on my heart ever since the godawful day I'd found her rummaging in the boot of Di's car.

"There must be something they can do." I was trying to sound positive.

"All they can do is put her on Pathway," added Lucy.

"What is that? What does it mean?" Olly quizzed them both.

"A mixture of morphine and steroids," replied Lucy.

"It means we've signed Mum's death warrant, Olly," Amy sighed.

Those girls. I couldn't look at them without feeling overwhelming sadness. They were about to become orphans, like me, the difference being they were far too young. They had no surrogate-Sally. No father. No hierarchy back-up plan. No nothing. Just one busy uncle and two useless aunts, one who lived miles away and one who had emphysema.

"Aw, guys." Lucy smiled through teary eyes. "She broke my heart earlier, she said to me, you have no idea how much I struggle to stay on the level for my family."

Poor Lulu. I worried about her, she didn't have the same feistiness as Amy, she was such a kind, sweet little thing, like her mum in that way. What would become of her? Would she dye her hair bright blue in contrast to Amy's vivid red? To complement her multiple piercings and growing collection of tattoos?

"She manages to stay on the level because she's a superbrain," said Olly, breaking and entering my random thoughts.

I agreed. "And constantly putting others before herself. How hard must it be for her to control her brain and stop it wandering off into cuckoo land?"

"It is, Sian," Amy explained. "Ellen told me Mum's a unique case. She showed me thermal images of her DAI, you can see one side of her brain has sheared off. It should have killed her, or at best, left her in a vegetative state. Ellen can't get over how strong her mind is."

Deep down we had all known this day would come, but it didn't make it any easier. I gazed at my sleeping sister and swallowed hard the huge lump which had risen in my throat.

I cried all the way home.

We hadn't long been back from visiting Di when the doorbell rang. I stared at my watch; it was ten o'clock. "Who could that be?" I gawped at Olly.

"Whoever it is will get a piece of my mind." He stomped off.

Ten seconds later he walked in with our newfound friend Brian. He appeared to have something on his mind, so I unusually offered him a cup of tea, which I'm pleased to say he declined. I sideways-glanced at Olly, he was thinking the same – why are you here, Brian? He leaned against the fireplace, took off his milk bottle glasses, rubbed the bridge of his nose and came out with it.

"Go on, you can have it for three sixty."

I'll never forget that moment. Olly and I gawped at each other in shock.

"If you do it quick, I can't be doing with estate agents and people, can you do it quick?"

Needless to say, no conferring, no umming or arring, we bit his arm off.

Next morning, I wasn't sure if I'd dreamt Brian coming over. Olly was in the kitchen making a cup of tea.

"Olly, did that happen last night?"

"I can't believe it either," he said, with a glint in his eye, "it's like winning the lottery."

"It's like a fairy tale, things like this don't happen in real life."

"Sally told Linda, we should carry on with the plan, she said she would continue to help us, didn't she?"

I couldn't deny it. Sally told me the smiling lady was our buyer, and she would give us the full asking price, and that came true. It felt like some kind of divine intervention was happening and bandy Brian was an unlikely angel from heaven.

There was one snag.

"I can't do it, Olly, it's almost a hundred grand under

value. I feel like we're taking advantage, perhaps he's crazy or something."

Trust me to pee on the moment. Olly let out a big reality crashing sigh. "You're right, Liz, I feared the same to be honest, things that appear too good to be true usually are. It's bound to go wrong somewhere down the line. He must be off his nut, we ought to go round there and say thanks but no thanks."

Brian was adamant. He didn't give a fig about money. We discovered he was an ex-rugby pro and something of a recluse. He didn't care for people, all he wanted was out, as quickly as possible. It was a classic case of being in the right place at the right time. Luckily our solicitor was an old friend, who was more shocked than we were. Jo told us she would pull strings and push it through fast.

Fearing each one would be the last, Olly and I increased our visits to Di, as did Dave and Sara, as did Lel. Sometimes she was full of life, sometimes she was slipping away before our eyes. Being on Pathway, Di was supposed to drift away gradually, but instead she sprang back to life, so they took her off it. As soon as they took her off it she deteriorated again, so they put her back on it. It was a horrible emotional rollercoaster of a time.

Arriving home from the most recent 'perky' visit, Amy called. Di had gone downhill since we left. She was see-sawing between life and death.

"It's doing my head in, Sian, and Luce isn't sleeping."

Amy was flipping out. "They've done this four times in a row."

"Why do they keep taking her off Pathway?"

"Ellen said they can't kill someone so alive, so I said keep it off, and she said she can't, otherwise Mum will die a painful death."

"They need to leave it on then. All this taking it off, leaving it on. God knows what Di must be going through. This is so stressful."

"That's what I said, Sian! I got really cross and shouted, 'Ellen, fucking leave it on. My family and I cannot keep going through this she's going to die, she's not going to die crap'."

Feisty red-head Amy, at it again, fighting her feisty mum's battles for her.

"Do you think I should come and see her?"

"When are you moving?"

"Tuesday, if it happens. We keep going back and forth to the solicitor signing pointless crap because Brian's ex-wife is making everyone's life difficult. She keeps threatening to pull the plug, it could collapse any moment and we're so close, it's making me a nervous wreck."

"Aw, Sian, you can't afford to lose the house, it's a right bargain, it's a few days, don't worry, Mum's a bloody die-hard she keeps bouncing back to life, this'll go on for another six years probably."

February 2014. Despite four months of wobbles we pulled

it off, and it was a dream come true, the stuff of fairy tales. Did Sally make it happen? We'd notched up three death-free years since Steve, and sad as it was leaving behind another family member, the excitement of getting Brian's house matched it in equal measure. I was thrilled we were moving from number six to number seven. Easy, in theory. There was no need to hire a van, it was directly opposite. It got to the point where I didn't bother with a box. Why pack the cutlery tray when Teri could nip across the road and put it straight in the kitchen drawer for me?

"What is this, Mum?" Teri grilled me, dangling a lock of dark brown curly hair between her finger and thumb with a disgusted expression on her face.

"Oh that, I haven't decided what to do with it yet."

"Are you kidding me? Uncle Dee-Dar's hair, in with the knives and forks?"

After a moment's uncomfortable silence I heard my nutty-goon of a brother cackling in my head. I grinned at Teri, game over, we both disintegrated into fits of laughter. The highlight of a thoroughly exhausting day. No removal van meant we went back and forth across the road a zillion times.

The first week proved eventful. Day one of new house, Olly decided it would be fun to check if the upstairs Jacuzzi bath was working. It wasn't. The taps got stuck on and turned the downstairs master bedroom's mirrored wardrobe into a cascading waterfall. I cried helplessly, watching my bed turn into a paddling pool while Olly struggled to turn off the seized stopcock. It was the start of many 'not workings'.

Day two of new house, Izzy escaped through the garden fence, ran into the road and got run over. A close shave, but she survived with minor injuries and a hefty vet's bill. I thanked heaven. Though it was falling apart, it wasn't a house with the red-cross of the Black Death on the door – yet.

Day three of new house, we found out the car's MOT had expired – a week ago.

Day four of new house Dylan rang. He was driving around aimlessly, trying to find local storage for Sal's stuff and getting nowhere. It was only a 'few bits' he told us, so we offered to help. He turned up in a Luton van with a double garage's worth of antique furniture. Instantaneous pain gripped me. Sally's nemesis 'stuff' had come back to haunt me. I blotted it out. Time to go into automaton mode. It was like a Benny Hill scene, re-emptying our newly filled garage to make space, but we did it with not an inch to spare and breathe out. Olly closed the shutter, out of sight, out of mind. Tomorrow I was definitely going to see Di.

Day five of new house, also Valentine's Day, two months before her sixtieth birthday, Amy rang and told me Di had passed away peacefully in her sleep...

It sounds stupid to say I wasn't expecting to hear that, but I wasn't. Di was invincible. Even in her fragile state she had survived Sally, and Mum, and Steve. Amy cried buckets relaying the news to me and I felt nothing, only emptiness.

Lel the same; she said it was because we lost the real Di when she had the accident and we'd been grieving ever since. True, but in some ways it was a double loss. I had grown to love my new beautifully different sister, and it seemed wrong, I couldn't cry. I'd never had a problem laughing at her all my life. I rolled around the grass in hysterics when she sat on a red ants' nest at the school fete and had to pull her jeans down in front of the parents. I split my sides when she posed in front of John-boy showing off her glittery blue eyeshadow and he said she looked like Coco the clown. Infuriated, she threw a lit match in his cup of tea. John retaliated by slapping his slice of bread and butter in her face. I'll never forget the demented look in her eyes as it slid down her gold hexagon glasses. I smiled recalling the time we drank a vat of La Mancha before stumbling into bed. Luckily, fifty pence fell out of my jeans pocket, reminding me to sneak it under Lucy's pillow in exchange for her tooth. In the middle of the night she'd toddled into the bedroom desperately needing a wee.

"Use the potty, Lula," Di groaned, half asleep.

"I can't Mummy, the tooth fairy filled it up," she wailed.

Poor Lulu. Di and I had filled it to the brim because we couldn't be bothered to go downstairs and use the bathroom. The silly list goes on...

Out of nowhere *On White Horses* came into my head; Di's favourite programme, especially the theme tune. The perfect send off for her, right there. If I could find it? It was very old.

"YouTube," said Olly.

I found it, and as soon as I heard it, it gave me goose bumps. I pictured Princess Di prancing around the lounge with a hairbrush microphone, singing it with that dreamy expression on her face. I played it about ten times; that did it, I crumbled.

I felt compelled to go walking with the trees in the days following Di. It was healing, soothing ointment for the soul, and a bonus for Izzy to chase squirrels. Wherever she was, Di was now whole, flying high on a white horse, free from the shackles of her long-suffering damaged brain and paralysed body. My superbrain sister wasn't hallucinating. Di *was* communicating with them, they *were* getting a place ready for her, the seventh family member to be reunited with the heaven gang. Princess Di, the selfless one, who showed us the true meaning of *love is all there is*. How spectacularly appropriate for her to leave this earth plane on Valentine's Day.

Sick to death of funeral talk (funny, but not) I'm going to share one thing – what the undertaker said to my twenty-one-year-old son: "Don't feel you have to do this. It's a bit daunting for a young lad like you to carry a coffin."

"Nah, that's cool," replied Joe. "This will be my fourth, I'm quite the expert now."

CHAPTER TWENTY-ONE

Planet Martin

A lot happened in the months following Di's death. Dylan met and married the love of his life, Sarah, on a beach in Croatia. It made my broken heart sing to see him happy again. Dean hooked up with a normal girl called Lindsay and her cute five-year-old son Harrison. Fingers crossed, end of the bimbo era. Joe quit the film game to join the army, but failed his final entry exam. Naturally, he was devastated, after John-boy's experience, I can't say I was. Dylan came to the rescue, like mother like son, and got him on board *The Monuments Men*. Destiny at work, it would seem.

And, one after the other, like dominoes, Olly lost his remaining grandparents. They were like something out of the film *Cocoon*, all in their late nineties and Grandma had reached a hundred. An achievement, nonetheless sad, for

Olly, who was close to his higher-hierarchy. All three of them in the space of nine months.

Talking of nine months, Teri made an announcement.

"I'm pregnant," she said, then burst into tears.

"Teri don't cry, you, Dan and Ella, you're a family now it's okay."

"They think it might be twins."

"Oh my God, cry!"

Feeling the weight of responsibility for the whole twins-miss-a-generation thing I rang Dave immediately. I couldn't wait to share the frighteningly exciting news.

"Congratulations, kiddo, have you told Lelly-Bertus?"

"Not yet, I'm on the way there as we speak."

"Good, we need to step up the effort, now it's just the three of us," said my only brother.

"Fantastic news, Lovey. Maybe people will stop dying on us now," said my only sister.

Unlikely, with her COPD death wish and her new mid-week hobby with her not nice friend, Sharon. Thank God today was Thursday. "So, what did the two of you do this Vodka Wednesday? Anything else apart from drink vodka?" I asked, blatantly sarcastic.

"We watched football, *actually*," she replied, in her defence.

"Did we win?" I quizzed her, not having the slightest interest in football.

"Humph, England can't win *It's a Knockout*, even when they're playing the joker." She went on. "Lovey, I met her husband this time."

"What's he like?" I asked, making an effort to care and not judge, and accept that my sister was allowed to be friends with whomever she chose.

"He's fucking tiny," she laughed. "I said to Sharon, you could have warned me your old man was a midget."

"How to win friends and influence people," I chuckled.

"I know, she got the hump and said, 'He's not officially a dwarf, he's an inch taller.' That cracked me up even more, and then she introduced me, Oh Sian, it was so embarrassing."

"Oh no, what did you do?" I dared to enquire.

"I didn't know whether to shake his hand or what, so I just patted him on the head." We both collapsed into a fit of giggles. My sister was the funniest woman on earth, when she wasn't getting on my nerves. "Lovey, I've got Old Mother Hubbard's cupboard, Dot's coming to take me shopping, I'll cook us something nice for tea, ring me when you're halfway."

"What's she cooking?" Olly asked as we sped along the M40, keeping a healthy distance from foreign lorry drivers.

"She won't cook or go shopping, she's given up giving a shit. Give it half an hour and she'll ring back and say let's get a takeaway."

Half an hour later my mobile rang. "Lovey, how do you fancy a kebab?"

"Kebabs are something people have when they can't be bothered to cook."

"Really? It's a treat for me."

"Well I hate them."

Olly and Lel tucked into their chicken doners, chatting and laughing, while I gazed out of Mums lounge window feeling sorry for myself.

"Are you sure I can't get you something to eat?" my sister kindly offered.

"Like a tub of past-its-sell-by-date margarine, or an ice cube?" I complained.

"I've got cheese," she suggested.

"I'm not a mouse."

"I can see. How much weight have you put on since I last saw you, and when was the last time I saw you?" she asked, shovelling her face with food.

"Di's funeral," said Olly.

"I've been eating for comfort ever since," I added, still facing the window.

"Lovey, your legs, I've never seen them so big, they're tree trunks, like Dad's," she laughed.

"Pish-tosh," I grumbled. Dad's favourite conversation-killing phrase.

"And you didn't want a kebab." She laughed all the more. "Fatso."

She was trying to cheer me up, but it wasn't working. It wasn't the same being in Mum's house ever since the jam tarts and lemon slices had been replaced with vodka and kebabs. I stared at the rolling fields and snow-covered mountains beyond.

"Why don't we go up Snowdon tomorrow?" I said.

The scenic ride through the snow-covered mountains was

breathtaking. It was a bit cosy on the train, knees touching knees type thing, but worth it to get to the summit.

"This is awesome." Olly inhaled a deep breath. "The air is so different. I can't believe you've never brought me here before."

"It's a lot better when you can see." I was trying to focus in zero visibility. "Where's Lel?"

"Three guesses." Olly pointed through the mist toward the visitor centre.

It was cringeworthy, everyone back in their seats with their paper cups of tea, and the train guard fretting we were going to be late. "I can only give her another minute," he said apologetically.

"Don't bother, just go, leave her up here to rot in the snow," I replied, in front of all the passengers.

Olly laughed. "Except she won't rot, the snow will preserve her. Wait here, Liz, I'll go and find her."

Five minutes later they returned. Lel was the only person with a plastic glass of red wine, which she spilt on the knee of the man sitting next to her when we went over a bump. God knows how many she'd necked at the bar, but we went up the mountain with Lel and came down with Mr Hyde. She was constantly jabbing Olly in the ribs, making snide comments about me, generally behaving badly and making the passengers squirm. I stared at her in sheer disgust for the whole journey, antagonistic troublemaker Lel at her worst. It was all I could do to stop myself throwing her wine in her face.

"You're so out of order, Lesley!" I hissed, as we got in the car.

"You thought it was funny when Steve was tipsy," she whinged.

"Steve *was* funny, you're aggressive." In my passenger wing mirror I caught her poking her tongue out behind my back then take a roll up out of her bag. "Put that away, you're not smoking in this car."

"Whatever." She was sulking like a child.

"You've got a death wish, you have."

"So what if I have?"

We drove in silence all the way back to Mum's.

"I'm never ever going up there again," I moaned to Olly on the way home, "ever."

We pressed on with DIY. For Olly it was building site by day, busman's holiday by night. Not wanting to sound ungrateful, but there comes a time when the fairy tale ends and reality kicks in. There was a lot to tackle: damp, faulty electrics, dodgy plumbing, a whole host of problems came with Brian's money sponge of a rough diamond. Every spare penny we had went into it, but we wanted it done. I couldn't bear the prospect of living on a building site, not with two babies on the way. They weren't my babies, but it didn't stop my nesting instinct, a grandmother thing I figured.

Teri's second scan revealed one baby.

"Mum, it's a girl," she exclaimed, "and I'm going to call her Rena." It was a dart straight to the heart. Our tears were instantaneous.

Never a dull baby moment. Shortly after that, Dean, Lindsay and Harrison announced they were expecting Penelope. I went from being the grandmother of one to potentially four, like overnight. And pink-haired Lucy told me she was having another little boy and calling him George. Ah, Princess Di would have loved that. But bad news followed the good. Olly's beloved mum Pam was struck down with cancer for the second time. It was a battle she had bravely fought and won ten years ago, but this time it wasn't to be.

In June 2015, Teri gave birth to Rena, the complete opposite of Ella with a thick mop of black hair and dark shiny eyes. I held her in my arms and kissed her forehead and Rena the Second scrunched her little face at me.

A month after Rena was born, we returned from Swanage drained by the devastation of saying goodbye to Olly's lovely mum. The talented Pamela Martin had made a name for herself since retiring there and had become a highly regarded member of the community. She'd taught music to children, played piano and violin at events, sang with the Belvedere Singers; music was her life, she had so much to offer, but it was cruelly taken away. Pam was seventy, the same as my dad and, like him, a gentle soul, bless her. The fourth 'Martin' funeral. Olly had fast-tracked and caught up with me.

"Thanks for having Izzy." I winked at Teri, noticing the red wine stain on my rug which had reappeared, had semi-disappeared again.

"I tried to scrub it out but it's stubborn, Mum. So I rang a company, they can clean it professionally, my treat," she offered.

"Let's play I spy, Nana!" Ella squealed, oblivious to the boringness of being a grown-up. "I spy with my little eye something beginning with – house!"

She did make me laugh. She also made me think. This house was meant to be a new beginning; a year and a half later, so many births and deaths I'd lost count, but it wasn't too late. The rug, the cause of much grief, was off to its new life – at the tip.

"By the way, Mum, it's Ell's sports day next week; will you two be able to come?"

"So long as I don't have to participate." I scrunched my face like Mum.

"Oh, I've put you down for the grandparents' sack race."

"Are you kidding me?"

I was so incensed it took a while for me to clock Teri biting her bottom lip hard.

My rock had turned into a marshmallow and there was nothing I could do to ease his pain, other than understand how difficult it is to help someone suffering from intense grief. He loved his mum dearly. Gifted musician Pam had been the driving force behind Olly learning piano and violin from the age of four, and drums from the age of ten. When he was twelve he got a placement in the East Berks Orchestra, making his mum proud. Music was in his blood, which made it all the harder watching him struggle with back-breaking DIY. I was beginning to doubt that Sal's great plan of renovating properties was such a good idea after all, but he threw himself into it with dark shadows under his eyes, ignoring his tired body and soul.

Then came the worst news ever. My better half announced that he was selling his prized possession, his mum's treasured piano.

"Flower, don't be silly."

"I don't think I can write music any more."

"Yeah you can, you're buried in DIY, and you're upset."

"I can't believe I'm never going to hear her say it ever again."

"You mean, what a hoot? Aw, Olly, it will take time to get used to using your mum's piano, you can't get rid of it."

"What's the point? Nothing's ever going to come of it."

Once upon a time getting signed by a record label was the only way to make a success in music. Nowadays streaming services such as Spotify and Apple Music have created a whole new era, opening the industry's closed doors to indie artists. Olly had put *Soul Lovers* on Spotify as an experiment. It cost five dollars a month and was bringing in five dollars a month.

"I might as well take it off," said Olly.

"You might as well keep it on," said me.

Communication between me and Lel had dwindled to necessary calls only, but it didn't stop her being there for Olly. She rang him often and he poured his heart out to her, for which I was glad. She loved his music, especially *Soul Lovers*, consequently, he'd found himself writing more chill-out tunes for his number one fan because it helped her relax. When he confessed he was quitting music, she lost the plot. He relayed their conversation,

"Stop fucking about knocking walls down, Oliver Martin, you're a musical genius. Honestly, what planet are you on?"

"Planet Martin." Olly laughed.

"Planet Martin, that's a funky name, call yourself that Olly Boll, and I'm not mucking about, I'm serious, your mum's piano is special, you promised me a new CD so pull your finger out."

"I didn't promise, Lel."

"Oh, shut up. I'm going to pester you, Planet Martin, and make sure my CD is happening."

"Okay, Lel, three bags full, Lel," he laughed.

"Now we've got the nonsense out of the way, I've been meaning to ask you, I made some wine, it tastes foul, have I done something wrong?"

"Did you follow the instructions?"

"Yeah, apart from I put the finishings in first."

"Why?"

"I thought it might speed things up a bit."

"Lel, you're supposed to put them in last, the clue's in the name, that's why they're called finishings."

"Oh fuck off, Olly Boll."

"Oh you do make me laugh Lel."

"Oh we do make us laugh, quitting music…"

Cold January came around, and our dazzling, brown-haired, brown-eyed granddaughter Penelope was born, or as Lel renamed her 'Penelo-Dean'.

"Lovey, it's like looking at Deano in a flipping dress," she coughed.

Not the best time of year for Lel, she was starting to get bronchitis – a lot.

By June 2016, the internal renovations, the passing of time, and a massive market boom meant bandy-legged angel Brian's money sponge of a rough diamond was revalued at six hundred thousand. The house was stunning, but Olly was beat. Time to take a breather and go window shopping for our next project.

For the fun of it we viewed a house in need of updating. It also had, as Olly put it, an 'interesting' dome in the garden. I wasn't impressed.

"Yuck, it's hideous, like something out of Wyevale Garden Centre."

"Yeah but it's a swimming pool." Olly had a familiar twinkle in his eye.

"And out of our league. Six hundred and fifty grand, why are we even here?" I moaned.

"Because you said it wouldn't hurt to look."

Déjà vu…

We'd shot up the property ladder, but not high enough for the pool house. We moved on from our pie in the sky to a house where you could see the sky – in places. We'd found our next project. It needed a proper roof instead of a broken flat one, a bigger, scarier challenge than before, but this was what Sal wanted – *que sera*. We put in an offer and they accepted, so all we needed now was a buyer. It should be relatively easy, the estate agent confirmed, the market was buoyant. Exciting times lay ahead, time to move on. We were ready to sell in time for Brexit to come along and kill it. So far, we had lost Di, all of Olly's grandparents, his beloved mum, and now Brexit. Could things get any worse?

Always. I got a call from Dot saying Lel had been rushed to hospital with a cracked rib and punctured lung. She had been celebrating her sixtieth Steve's way, and fell into Sal's glass coffee table. Her lungs were in a poor state, and there was no way she would pull through.

As soon as I set eyes on my painfully thin sister lying there breathing with an oxygen mask, the bullshit was stripped. Nothing else was left, just raw love. I couldn't be bothered to hate her anymore. I, more than anybody, understood why she had a death wish. Living with COPD she had no quality of life, no mum to look after, no Steve to wind up, no Sal telling her off, and no Tweedle twin to bicker with. She'd lost all her reasons to care.

Yet Lel, the underdog but no less indestructible other half of Di, made a full recovery and was sent home after a few days. Dave tried to get her to stay with him in Cardiff and I tried to get her to come back with me, but she wanted to stay at home. At least the Sharon ship had sailed off to Lilliput and she had her nice friends Dot and Jan there to help her. I rang her every day to make sure she was okay, and she was; it lasted five days.

"I'm having a nice cup of hot chocolate," she slurred.

"Good for you, Lel."

"Guess what Lovey, I'm on the Facebook."

"You mean Facebook."

"That's what I said, the Facebook, anyway, Dot's at the door with me shopping, got to go, love you, Lovey."

"Love you too, Lovey."

I gave up trying to change her and decided to just love her for still being here. We spoke frequently, via Skype or phone, I didn't answer sometimes, particularly early evening when she was suffering from vodka-driven phoney-itis, but she always left a message and I always rang back, usually before lunch when I was walking the dog and I knew it was safe o'clock.

We knuckle-dragged our way through the boring Brexit induced housing market crash, and eight months later, in February 2017, we had our buyer. As luck would have it the dilapidated flat-roof house was still available.

"Sian, how much do you trust me?" asked Lel.

"As far as I could throw you."

"Oh come on, you and me, we have a special bond, don't we?"

"I'm messing, course we do, Lovey."

"Ever since you were knee high to a grasshopper you said I was special."

"You are – special needs."

"Sian, you can't buy the flat-roof house." She sounded authoritative like Dad.

"Why?"

"It's too much work for Olly Boll."

I laughed. Since when had she become a property expert?

"It's not a laughing matter, Sian. I had a dream of Sal, she said I had to stop you."

"A pointless lie if ever I heard one."

"It's the God's honest truth!"

"Were you Mimi or Fifi?" I asked, diverting off topic.

"Mimi. Get the house with the pool, you love swimming, live for the moment, Lovey."

"Why are you hell bent on me getting the pool house? Stop going on about it. Ella keeps pestering me as well, it's too expensive, it's not going to happen, and it still needs work."

"Not as much as the flat-roof house."

"Too late, we've put in an offer and they've accepted."

"Don't buy it, Sian, it's a mistake you'll live to regret, I'm telling you," she coughed.

"Lel, are you okay, that's a hacking cough you've got."

"I've got bronchitis, same old, the doc's given me steroids, I'll be all right tomorrow," she wheezed. "Lovey, why have you got a plant on your head?"

I laughed. "Put your glasses on, Lel, it's on the shelf behind me."

"It's not me," she scrutinised the screen, "it's the Skype." The Skype. The Facebook. I turned my laptop round to face the mirror. "Ugh, what the fuck is that?"

"Sal's ugly man."

"Oh nice, didn't put up the collage I made of all your kids, took me bloody days it did."

"I have, I'll show you." I traipsed up the stairs to prove it.

"Aw, you did, all this time I thought you'd thrown it away." She sounded happy. I dismissed the fleeting thought, *why am I showing you this?*

"Sian, I dug out some old photos to pass the time away, remember when Deano was thirteen and I changed his name."

"Dean-ager." I laughed. "I still call him it sometimes."

"How is he getting on with Lindsay, Harrison Ford and Penelo-Dean?"

"Yeah they're good."

"And how's Parker, he still working with Didge?"

"He's okay, still with Dylan, Lovey, why *do* you call Joe Parker?"

"Cos he's a bloody nosey parker," she coughed. "I spoke to Tezzle-pops earlier, I love that kid to death."

"I know you do, Lel." I dismissed another fleeting thought: *why are we having this conversation?*

"She's more my daughter than yours. Remember when

you were pregnant and you said I could have her?" She coughed again.

"I do – then I changed my mind, didn't I, Mimi."

"Yeah, you fucking bitch."

Oh we did make us laugh – and cough.

CHAPTER TWENTY-TWO

A twinkling star

———⬧———

Time for a sort out, the upside of constantly moving home. I opened my car boot, and noticed a small brown box was nestling in the corner. I opened it and inhaled the dust which flew into my face. Steve's ashes! I'd forgotten I had them. My nutty-goon of a brother had travelled more in the three years he'd been in my boot than he had during his whole lifetime.

Olly and I stood at the top of Yat Rock, Steve's favourite place, watching the peregrine falcons circling below, patiently waiting for everyone to leave the viewing point until we had the spot to ourselves.

"Do it, quick!" I urged.

Olly snuck the box from under his coat and launched Steve's ashes over the edge with all his might. I peeked over the edge. They had fallen onto a ledge below and landed in a huge clump.

"That wasn't how I imagined this moment."

"It's too still, Liz, I did say, didn't I? We should have waited for a windy day..."

He hadn't finished talking when a huge gust appeared and blew a massive plume of the ashes into the air. They danced around for a bit, then the wind disappeared as quickly as it came. We peered down at the ledge. The clump was gone.

"What just happened, Olly?"

I woke with a burning urge to share yesterday's uplifting experience with Lel, but she didn't rise until at least half ten these days so I waited until after breakfast. Nine thirty was as far as my patience would stretch; I rang the house phone. Sad as it was seeing 'Duffer HQ' on the screen, I couldn't bring myself to change it. No answer, I knew there wouldn't be, but I didn't care, I rang her mobile instead, that would get her out of lazy bed. Lel's friend Jan answered;

"Oh Sian, I was about to call you, it's Lel, she's struggling to breathe, the ambulance is on its way."

The four-hour journey took forever, thanks to the sod's law of multiple roadworks. If only I could wiggle my nose and be there, like Samantha in *Bewitched*. The whole time I was on tenterhooks praying to my guardian angel twin, John, Dad, Sal, Mum, Steve and Di, for help.

"It'll be a repeat of last year, she's probably overdone it." Olly squeezed my leg. "She'll pull through, Liz."

We zoomed past the all too familiar chapel of rest, slung the car into a space and ran into the hospital. God, I hated this place. I won the Most Cowardly Family Member trophy for refusing to visit Dad when he was rushed into Ysbyty Gwynedd. I couldn't look him in the eye knowing he had begged me the day they took him away from the comfort of his bed; *'Please don't let them take me, I don't want to die in hospital, Sian.'* It was Lel who forced me to visit him under the guise of keeping her company when it was her turn to be on 'Dad watch'; I'll never forget it. The pungent smell of death hung in the air as we passed beds of groaning invalids and entered Dad's side room. As soon as I set eyes on him, I wanted to run. He had deteriorated to the point where he looked like Skeletor from *He-Man*, poles apart from my man of steel. I started backing away like a wimp.

"Think of Dad, Sian, and how happy he'll be to see you," my brave sister had smiled, placing an arm around my shoulder, forcibly guiding me over to his bedside. "He's on morphine, and in and out of consciousness, it might take him a while to figure out who you are."

She was wrong. I grabbed Dad's bony fingers, and he opened his eyes and smiled at me. He proudly told me that he'd given up smoking and then whispered, "Sian, I'm so glad you came," as he squeezed my hand.

And they were the last words he ever said.

Olly and I raced into the hospital. The receptionist informed us Lel was in Gogarth. I dismissed the worrying connection:

why was she in the same ward as Dad? We raced along to the ward and were met by the head nurse, who explained they were pumping oxygen into my sister in a desperate attempt to reduce her carbon monoxide levels. The familiar smell of death again hung in the air as we passed beds of groaning invalids and entered Lel's side room.

As soon as I set eyes on her, the pit of my stomach churned. She was connected to an oxygen machine and didn't look too clever at all. I watched her torso expand and contract, and it dawned on me that she wasn't breathing by herself, the machine was doing it for her. I rushed over to my poorly sister. Her eyes were rolling around her head and her chest was rattling loudly.

I grabbed hold of her hand. "I'm here, Lovey," I comforted her.

Her eyes stopped rolling, slowly came into focus and she smiled at me. "Sian, I'm so glad you came, Dad's here," she whispered into her oxygen mask. Then she squeezed my hand, released one long breath and gently closed her eyes.

"Lel?" I waited for her to say something, but she didn't. "Wake up, Lovey," I said, shaking her hand. She didn't respond. I turned to Olly, behind me – why was he crying? I turned to the nurse. "Why isn't she breathing?"

The sombre-looking nurse shook her head. "I'm so sorry, my love." She put a comforting hand on my shoulder. "I'll leave you in peace." And she left the room. Just like that.

I glanced at the big clock on the wall, at Lel, at the big clock on the wall, my insides collapsing with every tick and willing the hands to go backwards. That's when the enormity of the situation hit me. The ticking clock went fuzzy, someone let go of my puppet strings and I collapsed onto the floor. Olly picked me up and held me tight, and I sobbed, and I sobbed.

The end of my world.

The doctor came in, confirmed the worst and told us we could stay with Lel as long as we needed. Bad idea. I stood there holding her lifeless hand, crying and staring at her like a jerk, replaying her five hundred voice messages on loudspeaker. The cheeky tomboy, so full of life, now so un-full of it. She looked frail like Mum, and she squeezed my hand as Dad had, and she breathed one long last breath as Dad had. Difference being, I was prepared for that, I wasn't prepared for this. I wasn't finished with her. The day before yesterday we were having a normal sisterly conversation. Her last words to me were "You fucking bitch". I smiled through my tears telling Olly that.

Why didn't I see this coming? And why did I feel like taking a photo? A peculiar thought interrupted by a call from Dean. He'd been working nights and just woken up. He freakily told me he'd dreamt I showed him a Polaroid picture of Lel, dead, while I was staring at her, dead. In my usual Blurty-McBlurt style I told him she was.

One down, rest of the family to go. How was I supposed to break the news to Dave? And his brood, Jo-Jo, Fraser, David Jnr and Freddie? Then there was Joe, Dylan, Amy,

Lucy and Teri. Oh God, Teri! She and Dan were off for a spa weekend today, their first break since having Rena. I couldn't do it. I couldn't tell her that her favourite auntie/ godmother had gone. *Yeah you can, Lovey, we're veterans at this now* I heard Lel say, and it made me feel better. She always cheered people up, even in their darkest moments. She nursed Dad when he was dying. She cared for Mum to the end. She tried her hardest to help Sal, and she was on the hospital's case making sure they did right by Di.

I don't know how long I stood there transfixed, holding her hand, minutes, hours, possibly? Long enough to sense Olly's hand squeeze my shoulder. I looked at the big clock on the wall, at Lel, at the big clock on the wall. The hands were going in one direction, forward. Time to say goodbye.

I waited for Teri and Dan to arrive at their destination so she was away from the children. This was a spa break she would likely not forget for the rest of her life. Fingers shaking, I called her. She didn't say, "Hello, Mum." Her first words were, "How's Lelly, is she okay?" All I got to say was, "Teri, sit down," before she responded by shouting, hysterical, "don't say it, Mum, please don't say it!" over and over, so I didn't. I didn't have to, I just cried with her.

Lel's cause of death was recorded as frailty and exacerbation of emphysema. Considering she'd been living with this for nine years it came and took her spectacularly suddenly. The visions I had of my sister breathing with an oxygen tank and me somehow trying to blow cigarette smoke into it for her were not to be. I was glad she didn't have to suffer that.

As you would expect, Lel's funeral was a crazy alcohol fest for all. Without her by my side I didn't have the courage to read my eulogy; my brave boom-boom mini-me niece, Jo-Jo, read it out for me.

I cried on and off most of the way home. This grief journey had started with Lel's COPD and finished with Lel's COPD. Trust her to put the finishings in first. She outlived everyone.

Olly, the Clyde to my Bonnie, my partner in crime, my better half, tried to make me see the bright side. I dried my eyes with my jumper sleeve as we pulled into the petrol station. Olly squeezed my leg.

"Come on, my love, Lel wouldn't want you to be upset, she's with the rest of them now."

I gazed out of the window at the Sally-bow seemingly following us and the strangest thought popped into my head. "She's going to put the mockers on the flat-roof house, Flower."

"She'd better not, I've already built the pitched roof." He pointed at his head. "Up here."

"I've already decorated – in fact, I've bought the wallpaper for the lounge," I sheepishly confessed.

We arrived home to a message from the estate agent telling us he was sorry but our buyers had pulled out, so the flat-roof house was back on the market. You couldn't write it.

"Don't worry, Liz, Alex is certain we'll get another buyer long before the flat-roof house does and we can pick up where we left off."

"The race is on."

"The race *is* on, but we're the favourites." He winked.

Back to Groundhog Day and crying in coffee shops with Teri. I missed Lel more than anyone I'd ever missed, ever. I didn't expect it to hit me so hard, but it was glaringly obvious now. She'd been flying a flag for others while she was still here and now she had gone, leaving me completely sisterless. The loss of my special needs sister, my one remaining sister, was more than my heart could stand.

Over the course of the next few weeks, being the executor of Lel's will, I sorted out her affairs and closed her bank accounts. I was humbled to learn my chain-smoking, farting, swearing, caring angel of a sister had monthly direct debits for Age Concern, PDSA, NSPCC, Cancer Research and Headway. I was saddened to learn after reading her medical notes that at the age of sixty-one, the emphysema gave her the equivalent lung age of a ninety-year-old. She never told me that.

No prizes for guessing, the favourites lost the race and the 'long shot' won. Someone else bought the dilapidated flat-roof house. No, you really couldn't write it. Death perspective kicked in. Whatever. I was past caring. I needed a break from the blood, sweat and tears of constant renovating during this brutal time.

September 2017, six months after Lel's passing, Amy gave birth to Jack, the image of her, and a handsome little brother for Megan. The child Di miscarried when John died she was going to call Jack, strangely. Dean and Lindsay had another baby too, a little boy. I had missed sharing that announcement with Lel by a couple of days, sad times and happy times. Grandson Leo; a proper chocolate box baby with blond hair and blue eyes, 'beautifully different' from his sister Penelope. Dean, just like his uncle John, said he was the milkman's, ridiculously funny, seeing as he was a ringer for Lindsay and Harrison.

Fast forward; nine months of false buyer pains later, we hung our brains up on selling and spent our solicitor's fees on a birthday treat holiday to Sardinia instead. We tempted fate and it worked – a couple of days later Alex rang to say we had another buyer. Big wow. It was bound to fall through again, plus we'd lost the flat-roof house which I'd wanted so badly. Why did Lel do this to me? Was it a pointless lie or was she in cahoots with Sal? My off-the-wall doom-n-gloom thoughts were doing overtime.

"What you thinking, Beak?"

"Why did they put the mockers on the flat-roof house when there's nothing else out there?"

"Apart from the pie in the sky house," said Olly, full of excitement.

"It's out of our price range." I sighed, disappointed.

"I've just been speaking to Alex, and the seller said seeing as we've already viewed it and to save putting it on the market, if we still want it, he'll reduce the price by fifty thousand."

"Fifty thousand? That means…"

"We can afford the house with the pool! Imagine Liz, how great it would be for all the kids."

"But – that was nearly two years ago, why do we keep being offered houses that aren't on the market and way under value?"

Olly winked. "Why do you think?" He pointed at the sky.

"It's like the plan's mapped out for us," I mused. "I don't feel like we have any say in this."

"It's apparent we don't," he laughed. "It's what Lel wanted, and quite obviously, Sal."

"Can't share the news with them though, can I?" I pulled a solemn face.

"You can, when we get to the party."

"What party?"

"We're all on the same bus going to the same party, Liz. It's just some of us get off the bus before others. Don't we owe it those we have loved and lost to try and enjoy our time on the bus instead of feeling sad?"

It was September 2018, ten years since Di's accident, and we'd journeyed through hell and made it to paradise. Moving-in day was fun. A confusing whirlwind of stressful excitement, unpacking on Olly's birthday then re-packing the following day on my birthday to go on our badly timed holiday, as you do. We discovered there wasn't a lot to do in Sardinia apart from trek to the complex piscine two miles away. Hot, bothered and bewildered, and feeling strangely homeless, we stopped and gazed through the locked metal fence at the stinking stagnant green water.

"We've got a crystal clear blue swimming pool at home," Olly sighed.

"Why can't we ever have a normal holiday, like normal people?" I sighed.

After seven days of triple cheese pizza, Limoncello and befriending stray cats we returned to the news that we had been made redundant. Both of us. Oh we do make us laugh, and cry. Dan was gutted he didn't have any more work for Olly and chocolate headquarters waited until I was on holiday to send a cowardly letter saying they no longer had a position for me. We may have made it to paradise but we didn't have a pot to pee in. We had no choice other than to sell as quickly as possible. The dream was over.

I sat myself at the edge of my pool and stayed there until twilight, desperately trying, and failing, to recapture the holiday vibe. My feet dangled in the cool blue water, Olly-Flower wine in one hand, Lel's electronic cigarette in the other, replaying her five hundred voice messages, as miserable as sin. Eighteen months later, I still missed her so much it hurt.

Out of nowhere Lel's all-time favourite song came into my head: *Heaven Must Be Missing an Angel*. Not any more. My caring, angel of a sister had finally been reunited with the rest of them. Grief; was it not the ultimate act of selfishness?

Why would I want her to be suffering down here, when she was with John, Dad, Sal, Mum, Steve, my twin, and Di, her Tweedle twin who she struggled to live without? Lel wasn't afraid of dying. She believed there was a better place, and I believe that was the reason she had a death wish.

A twinkling star popped into the sky. Aw, Princess Di loved the stars. She even had a constellation book which mapped out where they all were, the superbrain. When Di passed Lel had said to me, "I looked up at the darkening sky and thought, if you're there, Di, prove it – and this twinkling star popped into the sky out of nowhere."

I looked up at the darkening sky and thought, if you're there, Lel, *you* prove it, and a very odd thing happened before my eyes. Two aeroplanes streaked across the sky in opposite directions and formed a vapour trail kiss. My heavy heart lightened as I marvelled at it. I was fed up with feeling fed up. So what if it was nothing more than a fleeting mirage in the desert? So what if we were destitute?

"I wish," I heard Di say. Absolutely, you have to be alive to be destitute.

"Everything's temporary, Sian," I heard Steve say.

"Live for the moment, Lovey," I heard Lel say.

"All shall be well, Heart," I heard Sally say.

"You always come up smelling of roses, Lizbeth," I heard Mum say.

"Beak!" Olly came running out of the house shouting, spilling wine everywhere. "I've discovered something amazing."

"Me too," I pointed at the kiss in the sky. "That's from Lel."

"You better believe it. Remember when I put *Soul Lovers* on Spotify, and it wasn't making any money, but you told me to keep it on there?"

"Yes, you ignored me and cancelled it."

"I cancelled the direct debit, but I forgot to cancel Spotify, they've been taking the monthly payment out of my royalty account for the last three years."

"Royalty account?"

"I didn't know I had one either. I stumbled across it, after discovering a 'Spotify for Artists' page I didn't know I had – Liz, it had two grand in it!"

"How come?"

"*Soul Lovers* is making us fifty dollars a month!"

"I thought it was making five dollars?"

Olly had spoken to the editorial team at Spotify. They had explained that music streaming had taken time to flourish, but now it had gone through the roof. Additional songs he submitted now would hit the ground running, because of the success of *Soul Lovers*.

"Imagine Liz, if I put all my tunes on Spotify."

"You've written loads, Flower, ever since Lel nagged you to."

"And I can write loads more."

"On your mum's special piano, and maybe we could afford to stay here?"

"Who knows? One thing I do know, thanks to your sister, Planet Martin is a thing!"

"What a hoot!"

"And guess what else. Alex rang, the people who bought the flat-roof house were refused planning permission. We dodged a bullet there, Liz, Lel was right."

"It wasn't a pointless lie!"

"Nope, I reckon she really did dream about Sal telling her to stop us, and that's why she put the mockers on it, bless her."

We laughed and cried and hugged and gazed at the fading vapour trail. Sal and Lel had wanted us to buy the pool house, and here we were.

"Thank you, Lovey." I blew a kiss into the sky.

"Oh we do make us laugh, quitting music." Olly raised his glass toward the heavens. "Cheers, Lel, see you at the party."

Epilogue

We're all on the same bus and we're all going to the same party, that's all death is. Some countries celebrate it by burning their dead children, as Sally found out. Where there is deep grief there is great love, and it needs to be channelled – not on those who have got off the bus, but those who are still travelling. Especially the next generation who have just got on, like Nirvana, Ella and Rena, Harrison, Penelope and Leo. And Megan, who is starting to look so much like her Nana Di, little Jack, Dylan Jnr and George. At the time of writing, Dylan and his wife Sarah have brought Rudy onto the bus, Sally's first grandson. These are the 'little ones' now, and I am the hierarchy, the circle of life. It keeps on going regardless.

I spent a long time believing I was cursed, but the more life tried to take me down *that* road the more I walked the other way. I believe we have two choices; that was my choice. Taking the alternative route, or you could say, a spiritual path, allowed me to develop faith. I have faith that there is more to life than we realise, and wherever my family are, they are all okay.

The loneliness has been unbearable, the silence has been deafening, the loss irreplaceable. I've lived through those dark times, and I've learned to befriend anxiety. Grief and I are like old mates, I embrace it with open arms when it comes for an uninvited visit and happily wave goodbye when it leaves. Acceptance is a war I am slowly winning, to be at peace with the silence, to exist without the chaos of my crazy, funny, dearly loved family.

Somewhere along the way I discovered who I am. A little bit of all of them, all mashed into one 'me', and there's something rather magical about that. My heart-breaking bus journey taught me that I am as blessed as I am cursed; we all are, for having the gift of life. I am grateful for that, more than I ever was. The sky seems bluer, the grass greener, I appreciate beauty in trees and flowers in a way I hadn't done before, and the sea is soothing ointment on my soul. Sometimes we have to know the darkness before we can appreciate the light.

Trauma doesn't have to define you; death is a profound experience and it can refine you. The other side is not as far away as you think, it's behind the door, or above the ceiling. We just have to open our eyes to seeing them differently. Once a year or so when I drive past the colossal weeping willow, I see John. Boxing Day will always be Father's Day. Sally's a rainbow. Mum's a robin. Steve's a wily woodpecker,

I hear him in the woods occasionally, if I'm thinking about him and feeling sad. Pam has proved herself to be a white feather, often spotted on Olly's piano. Di is a twinkling star and Lel is a kiss in the sky, I don't see that all the time, usually when I'm floating on a Lilo gazing into the blue abyss....

There were two in the bed and the big one said...

"Do you have any idea how important this makes you?"

The big one, the VIP who has been on this journey with me, who almost got off the bus but didn't. My boom-boom brother, David "I don't do death" Ball.

THE END

One more thing…

What is it about lofts and memories? Olly dug out his antiquated Apple Mac, de-cobwebbed it, fired it up and discovered some old dance and some classical songs he wanted to put on Spotify. He also discovered something else, something far more important…

When Sal was in hospital she was worried about her virtual 'stuff' and asked Olly if he would back up her computer, so he did, and forgot all about it. A decade had passed since she uttered those life-changing words to me "Sian, I've got some bad news. I need you to understand, it's bad, but it's not the worst, okay?"

We found everything, and more. Diaries I never knew she'd kept, about Di, and Mike, and John and Dad's death, and how she smelt cigarette smoke whenever Dad was around. And we found her memoir! All those captivating stories and oodles of notes throughout her working life. It was like finding gold. We also stumbled across this:

IMDB.PRO. Sally Jones

Trivia; Member of the Guild of British Camera Technicians (GBCT). Filmography

Prisoners of the Sun (script supervisor) (post-production) 2010

The Big I Am (script supervisor) 2008

Harry Brown (script supervisor) 2009

Mamma Mia! (script supervisor) 2008

Adventures of Young Indiana Jones: Winds of Change (script sup) 2008

Adventures of Young Indiana Jones: The Perils of Cupid (script sup) 2007

The Contractor (script supervisor) 2007

Big Nothing (script supervisor) 2006

Flyboys (script supervisor) 2006

Ask the Dust (script supervisor) 2005

Heidi (script supervisor) 2004

The Phantom of the Opera (script supervisor) 2004

Sky Captain and the World of Tomorrow (script supervisor) 2004

Vanity Fair (script supervisor) 2004

To Kill a King (script supervisor) 2004

The I Inside (script supervisor) 2003

Plots with a View (script supervisor) 2002

Alone (script supervisor) 2002

Black Hawk Down (script supervisor) 2000

Proof of Life (script supervisor) 2000

Great Performances (TV) (script supervisor - 1 episode)

Jesus Christ Superstar (2000)

Quills (script supervisor) 2000

House! (script supervisor) 2000

Angela's Ashes (script supervisor) 1999

Adventures of Young Indiana Jones: Daredevils of Desert (s. sup) 1999

You're Dead... (script supervisor) 1999

The Last Seduction II (script supervisor) 1999

The Adventures of Young Indiana Jones: Tales of Innocence (s. sp) 1999

The Adventures of Young Indiana Jones: Masks of Evil (script sup) 1999

The Man in the Iron Mask (script supervisor) 1998

The Man Who Knew Too Little (script supervisor) 1997

Snow White: A Tale of Terror (TV movie) (script supervisor) 1996

Evita (script supervisor) 1996

The Haunting of Helen Walker (TV movie) (script supervisor) 1995

Braveheart (script supervisor) 1995

The Three Musketeers (script supervisor) 1994

The Young Indiana Jones Chronicles (script sup - 6 episodes) 1993

Death Train (TV movie) (continuity) 1993

Patriot Games (script supervisor) 1992

The Power of One (script supervisor) 1992

ELIZABETH COFFEY

Shining Through (script supervisor) 1992

One Man's War (TV movie) (script supervisor) 1991

Bullseye! (script supervisor) 1990

Treasure Island (TV movie) (script supervisor) 1990

Great Balls of Fire! (script supervisor: UK) 1989

How to Get Ahead in Advertising (script supervisor) 1988

Willow (script supervisor) 1997

Withnail & I (script supervisor)

Club Paradise (script supervisor) 1986

Return to Oz (continuity) 1985

The Razor's Edge (continuity) 1984

Blame It on Rio (script supervisor) 1983

The Sender (script supervisor) 1982

Lion of the Desert (continuity) 1981

Savage Harvest (script supervisor) 1981

Heaven's Gate (script supervisor) 1980

George and Mildred (continuity) 1980

Hanover Street (script supervisor) 1979

A Man Called Intrepid (TV mini-series) (script supervisor) 1979

Return of the Saint (TV series) (continuity - 5 episodes) 1978-197

The Deep (continuity) 1977

327

The Eagle Has Landed (continuity) 1976

Find the Lady (continuity) 1976

To the Devil a Daughter (continuity) 1975

The Little Prince (script supervisor) 1974

Man at the Top (script supervisor) 1972

Dr Jekyll & Sister Hyde (script supervisor) 1971

Whoa, forty years of film and TV. My great plan to buy all of those DVDs might take a while…

Mamma Mia, Sally's last film and also the last time she was proper happy. *Harry Brown,* not so. That's when things started going downhill. She walked out halfway through, only the second time out of almost 70 jobs, the first being when she suffered a miscarriage on-set, working on *The Deep* in Jamaica. Reading her CV brought a smile to my face and tears to my eyes. We'd often sit and watch a movie that she'd worked on together and talk and laugh about how she was standing right there, around about where my rock salt lamp was positioned, to the left of the TV. Tonight, I made an executive decision. I was going to watch *Mamma Mia,* knowing Sally was there, around about where my rock salt lamp was – behind the door, above the ceiling – what difference.

I was so proud of her. She visited practically every country on the planet. We joked her passport was like reading a novel it had that many stamps and scribbles. She'd lived a lifetime already, maybe that's why her time was cut short.

My big sister achieved a lot and helped so many people sitting on her golden pedestal waving her magic wand, she really was one very special human *bean*. It kind of made sense for her to leave this earth plane in a spectacularly shocking fashion...

My idol, my second mum, my Sally Sunshine, the lovely lady who taught us "All shall be well because love is all there is".

Mañana, Sal. x

Printed in Great Britain
by Amazon